Existential Openness in Law

Berner Reihe philosophischer Studien

Herausgegeben von

PD Dr. Andreas Bächli und PD Dr. Martin Bondeli, Universität Bern
Prof. Dr. Guido Löhrer, Universität Erfurt

Band 52

Diese Reihe versammelt Arbeiten, die im Umfeld des Instituts für Philosophie der Universität Bern entstanden und sich entsprechend der hier weiten Ausrichtung mit sehr unterschiedlichen Thematiken und Denkern verschiedener Observanz auseinandersetzen. Dabei orientieren sich die Autorinnen und Autoren an den Standards von Klarheit und Kohärenz und stellen ihre Beiträge in den Dienst der Sache.

Diego Pérez-Lasserre

Existential Openness in Law

A hermeneutical approach to Carl Schmitt's early legal thought

PETER LANG
Lausanne · Berlin · Bruxelles · Chennai · New York · Oxford

Bibliografische Information der Deutschen Nationalbibliothek
Die Deutsche Nationalbibliothek verzeichnet diese Publikation in der Deutschen Nationalbibliografie; detaillierte bibliografische Daten sind im Internet über http://dnb.d-nb.de abrufbar.

Library of Congress Cataloging-in-Publication Data
A CIP catalog record for this book has been applied for at the Library of Congress.

ISSN 1421-4903 br.
ISBN 9783034347792 br.
ISBN 9783034348058 ePub
DOI 10.3726/b21427
ISSN 2235-5847 eBook
ISBN 9783034348041 ePDF

Published by:
Peter Lang Group AG, Lausanne, Switzerland

info@peterlang.com - www.peterlang.com

This publication has been peer reviewed.

"All fear is illusion. Walk straight ahead no matter what"[1]

David R. Hawkins

1 David R. Hawkins, *The Map of Consciousness Explained*, (California: Hay House, 2020), 273.

To Rosario Olivares, Joaquín Pérez and Mateo Pérez

Acknowledgments

The journey to creating this manuscript has been enriched by the guidance, support, and encouragement of many individuals. While a few paragraphs may not suffice to recognize everyone's contributions, I want to extend my heartfelt gratitude to several key individuals.

My warm thanks go to Fernando Pérez, Jacqueline Lasserre, Enrique Olivares, and Mónica Abrego for their unyielding support at the family level. Rosario Olivares and Francisca Pérez deserve special recognition for their backing during the most challenging moments when the finish line seemed distant.

Professionally, the advice from Hugo Herrera, Thomas Sören Hoffmann, Bernardo Ainbinder, and Eduardo Sabrovsky significantly enhanced the text's content. I also appreciate the insightful conversations with Pablo Manterola and Mateo Belgrano that fueled my motivation and resolve to keep writing. Equally significant were Margaret Cabaniss and the *de Nicola Center for Ethics and Culture* of the University of Notre Dame. Their generous provision of time, space, and resources was invaluable in the creation of this book.

Immense gratitude goes to Dr. Carlos Vio and "Vicerrectoría de Investigación y Doctorados de la Universidad San Sebastián". Their guidance, support, and assistance in securing the necessary funding for this publication have been critical to the fruition of this project. Their commitment to fostering research and scholarship is truly commendable.

Last, but certainly not least, I want to express my deep respect and gratitude to Joaquín García-Huidobro, the man who fostered my belief that a life dedicated to philosophy was within my reach.

Abstract: The purpose of this work is to justify that in the early legal writings of Carl Schmitt (1912–1922), one can identify a theory of human understanding with hermeneutical characteristics. In particular, we will illustrate how, through the examination of the legal phenomenon, the German jurist identifies and explores human finitude and historicality, both in their personal and epochal dimensions. We will also see how this exploration prompts Schmitt to question the roles of metaphysics, language, and decisions in the interpretation and configuration of the world. In other words, we will argue, drawing upon interpretations such as those offered by Ojakangas and Herrera, that Schmitt's examination of legal and political phenomena leads him to thematize how human understanding operates in general.

Keywords: Schmitt, hermeneutics, human understanding, historicality, finitude, language

Table of contents

Introduction

The purpose of this work is to argue that there are hermeneutical traits in Carl Schmitt's early legal thought. The fundamental premise on which we will base our hypothesis is that Schmitt recognizes with astounding clarity that legal statutes need a human being for them to emerge on practical reality. More specifically, we will see that Schmitt identifies that in the process of interpreting and applying legal texts something quite marvelous occurs: the positive legal texts emerge with human characteristics. This realization leads him to undertake an arduous task: to elucidate the nature and characteristics of human understanding. That is to say, the consideration of the human being as an active agent who shapes the abstract meaning of normative texts leads him to try to elucidate the particular existential characteristics that this agent (the human being) inevitably projects to written law in this process. At the same time, we will see that the recognition of the intervention of human subjectivity in the emergence of legal statutes brings to Schmitt's awareness the dangers of relativism in the legal phenomena. That is why, from the beginning of his academic production, he focuses his attention on the formulation of a criterion which ensures, within the limits of what is humanly possible, that legal decisions are correct (and not arbitrary).

Throughout this text we conceptualize the "adherence" or "acquisition" of human characteristics by legal statutes as *humanization of law*[2]. The logic behind the idea of the "humanization of law" is that the

2 The rationale for this decision will be elucidated during the revision of the text *The Value of the State and the Significance of the Individual*. Carl Schmitt, "The Value of the State and the Significance of the Individual," in *Carl Schmitt's Early Legal-Theoretical Writings: Statute and Judgment and the Value of the State and the Significance of the Individual*, trans. Lars Vinx and Samuel Garrett Zeitlin (New York: Cambridge University Press, 2021), 159–243.

entity that interprets and applies law (a concrete human being) brings himself and all of his existential characteristics to said process of "coming to life" of legal statutes. Our argument is that Schmitt's early legal thought can be considered as hermeneutic because he argues, as do existential hermeneutics, that human understanding is of interpretative and projective nature. Even though we will deepen into this matter later, we find it prudent to mention at this point that the core ideas behind existential hermeneutics can be summarized as follows: when a human being approaches reality, it does not do it as an "empty vessel" that is ready to receive that which is presented to its senses in an "unpolluted" manner. We already possess a series of concepts and structures that allow us to elucidate what is presented to our intuition so that those same concepts set a horizon (a paradigm) from which understanding operates. As Wrathall explains, "to understand is to be in the world in such way that everything is projected upon, that is, makes sense in terms of particular possibilities"[3]. Differently put, with the concepts that we already possess in our mind (and that have been acquired and transmitted by humanity throughout history) we interpret the world and its phenomena. Therefore, understanding the world is at the same time receptive (we need something to present itself to our intuition) and productive (we *give* meaning to the world from a set of concepts that we already possess)[4]. The purpose of the first chapter of this text, which is devoted to Heidegger's and Gadamer's thought, is to clarify the "conceptual measuring stick" to be used later to verify whether Schmitt's legal thought can be considered as existentially hermeneutical or not.

---

3 Mark. A Wrathall, "Heidegger on Human Understanding," in *The Cambridge Companion to Heidegger's "Being and Time,"* ed. Mark A. Wrathall, Cambridge Companions to Philosophy (Cambridge: Cambridge University Press, 2013), 181–82.

4 Cf. Steven Galt Crowell, *Normativity and Phenomenology in Husserl and Heidegger* (New York: Cambridge University Press, 2013). This, however, does not exclude the possibility of attaining new knowledge. We will delve into this when we revise Gadamer's thought.

Why should we consider Schmitt's legal philosophy as hermeneutical? Mainly because the recognition of the intervention of human existential characteristics in the emergence of legal statutes leads Schmitt to demand from legal theory the recognition of a certain *openness* towards the concrete aspects of existence. This core aspect of Schmitt's early legal philosophy allows us to include him in the hermeneutical lineage because

> the defining trait of hermeneutics is precisely not any kind of relativism, historicism, subjectivism or idealism, but rather an incompleteness theorem. The conditions of possibility of making sense of our experience (in whatever rigorous vocabulary) are simply such that we cannot achieve a total overview. Reality cannot be an object of even the best theoretical articulation of how it appears to us. Rather, different scientific theories provide us with fallible glimpses of their specific domain of objects, which can be transferred into more comprehensive theories without ever leading to a final theory[5].

As we will thoroughly justify throughout this book, this openness (or incompleteness) is a defining trait of Schmitt's concept of law.

The legitimacy of our hypothesis, that Schmitt's early legal thought can be considered as hermeneutical, is reinforced by the fact that a contemporary hermeneutic philosopher, Hans-Georg Gadamer, argues something quite similar when analyzing the complexities of the application of legal statutes. The path that Gadamer clears in the forest of the mysteries of human nature is more or less the following: he argues that human understanding, which is temporally determined, is characterized by a constant tension between principles, concepts, and prejudices that are bestowed upon us by tradition (and thus come from what we commonly call "the past") and a new situation that demands bringing those same principles, concepts, and prejudices to light. The tension is generated because the process of human understanding does not consist in a mere subsumption of the categories inherited by tradition to the

5 Markus Gabriel, "The Ontology of the Work of Art and the Universality of Hermeneutics Reconsidered: Gadamer and New Realism," in *The Gadamerian Mind*, eds. Theodore D George and Gert-Jan van der Heiden (New York & London: Routledge, 2021), 541.

new and exceptional cases that everyday life puts before us. It is rather characterized by reciprocal feedback between the new and old. Differently put, human understanding is somewhat creative. That which in a certain sense is "given" to us by tradition acquires a new meaning and perspective in light of the new and exceptional situations to which it is confronted.

For Gadamer, then, the task of administering justice entrusted to judges does not consist of a mechanical process, one characterized by the uniform application of legal norms and principles to concrete cases. If it were that easy, we could entrust it to computers with artificial intelligence (which, no doubt, are much more efficient and accurate than humans in the task of matching rules to cases). On the contrary, the task of trying to bring justice into practical reality is far more complex. First, the judge is typically confronted with two poles: one normative, which corresponds to written statutes, and the other concrete – the specific cases that demand a legal solution. Also, written laws rarely arise at the same time that the particular cases to which they are to be applied. They are usually preterit texts which, though they find their immediate origin in a process of normative production regulated by the state since modern times, are traceable to classical legal institutions (such as those of Roman law). Judges, then, find themselves in the need to mediate two poles: a normative one that comes "loaded" with tradition, and another concrete one that places before the judge a new and exceptional case that requires justice. Law, then, like human understanding, Gadamer tells us, is characterized by a tension between two poles that requires a synthesis for a "solution" to emerge.

In this work we will argue that Schmitt follows a similar path to that of Gadamer. We shall present, following authors such as Herrero, Herrera, Rash, and Ojakangas, a reading of the early legal works of the German jurist (1912–1922) that allows us to identify in his juridical and political thematization of law a portrayal of human understanding as hermeneutic. The particular manner through which we intend to justify this assertion is the following:

a. Schmitt begins his academic career criticizing the scientistic "horizon of meaning"[6] from which law has been interpreted from modernity. That is, he sets out on his journey by questioning the theoretical and practical basis on which the way of understanding that is usually called "Legal Positivism" is constructed.
b. After elucidating the theoretical and practical limitations of the scientistic approach to understanding law, Schmitt undertakes an even more challenging task: to propose a new perspective, a more suitable horizon of meaning, from which to comprehend this phenomenon.
c. This titanic task leads Schmitt down a winding and unexpected path: towards the elucidation of human understanding. This is due to the following reasons: Schmitt realizes that legal positivism, in its eagerness for objectivity and purity, eliminates from the equation a fundamental element for law: the human being. Schmitt tells us that this is naive, as legal statutes cannot be generated, interpreted, or applied without the intervention of a concrete human being. In other words, the presence of an agent of legal praxis (a human being who interprets and applies the law) is a requisite, a condition of possibility, for the existence of law. Such a proposal inevitably prompts Schmitt to question the nature and characteristics of the agent who connects legal statutes with the specific and contingent cases that require a just solution. Put differently, Schmitt introduces the human being into the "juridical equation". This, rather than simplifying matters, further complicates the issue, as it now becomes crucial to elucidate the manner under which the understanding of what we call "humanity" operates.
d. Therefore, almost as a syllogistic conclusion, we can state that the thematization of law leads Schmitt first to elucidate human nature and subsequently to propose a theory of human understanding with general implications.

---

6 This concept will be thoroughly explained in the first chapter.

Having already clarified the central theme of this manuscript (our hypothesis), as well as the specification of the conditions under which it can be considered plausible, it is appropriate to present the road map that we will follow to go from where we are, the mere enunciation of a proposition in an assertive manner, to our destination, which is none other than the speculative legitimization of said assertion. In the remainder of this brief introduction, we will explain the *raison d'être* of each of the chapters that make up the body of this work. This is not only because it is something that is usually done in academic presentations endowed with a certain seriousness but also because the treatment of such diverse and complex topics and authors (Heidegger, Gadamer and Schmitt) makes a previous explanation essential to clarify that this work is not a haphazard compilation akin to a dish made from assorted leftovers found in a refrigerator at month's end (something that, unfortunately, is not uncommon in academic literature), but rather an exotic and varied, but consciously articulated, menu.

§ 1. From human understanding to law: Heidegger and Gadamer

The objective of the first chapter is to elucidate the interpretative framework (horizon of meaning) underpinning our reading of Schmitt's work. Throughout this study you will encounter a range of concepts not originally present in Carl Schmitt's thought. Therefore, it is both natural and legitimate to question their origin and meaning. This initial aims to preemptively address such inquiries, providing answers before the questions are explicitly raised.

However, the reader should be aware that the authorial biases presented and explained in the first part of this manuscript are not without justification. As illustrated by the works of Ojakangas and Herrera, there appears to be a thematic link connecting the ideas of Heidegger, Gadamer, and Schmitt. These thinkers collectively seem to explore a 'magic formula' that reconciles the abstract nature of concepts with the tangible aspects of reality, and the unique attributes of the subject tasked with resolving this dichotomy: the human being. In this context, as argued in another work dedicated exclusively to this topic[7], interpreting these authors through a lens mutually enriched by their ideas does not obscure their philosophies. Instead, it sheds light on them, revealing illuminating insights.

In short, the path from human understanding to law, as explored in the first section of this work, serves a twofold purpose: to demonstrate that a thorough examination of the nature and characteristics of human understanding can lead to acknowledge that legal understanding is paradigmatic with respect to the manner in which practical reason operates (1), as well as to explicitly outline the interpretive framework (horizon of meaning) from which we propose a hermeneutic reading of Schmitt's early legal texts (2).

§ 2. From law to human understanding: Carl Schmitt's approach

The second chapter forms the epicenter of this work, delving into Carl Schmitt's legal thought as expressed in his early works (1912–1922). As previously mentioned, our reading of these texts posits that Schmitt's focus on the juridical phenomenon drives his exploration into the nature and characteristics of human understanding. Specifically, we argue that Schmitt undertakes two primary tasks: first, he identifies the shortcomings of the prevailing understanding of law at the turn of the twentieth century, namely, legal positivism. Following this, he exposes the theoretical and practical limitations of this perspective. Subsequently,

7 Pérez-Lasserre, Diego. "Humanidad y derecho: una lectura de la obra temprana de Schmitt" Díkaion 31, no. 2 (20): e3123.

Schmitt endeavors to establish a more suitable approach to law. This effort leads him, as we will detail, to reintegrate a previously overlooked element in the "juridical puzzle": the human being.

Schmitt's task can be understood as twofold, involving both a destructive and a constructive aspect. In the second and third chapters, we will address both of these dimensions accordingly. Firstly, we will present how Schmitt, from the onset of his academic career, is committed to exposing the theoretical and practical weaknesses underpinning legal positivism. While references to other works by the Plettenberg jurist will be made, this chapter primarily focuses on a thorough analysis of Schmitt's first two legal writings: *Statute and Judgment* and *The Value of the State and the Significance of the Individual.* This focus is justified by the fact that in these works, Schmitt primarily "attacks" legal positivism in strictly juridical terms. Unlike his later works like *Political Theology* and *Dictatorship*, which address the shortcomings of a mechanistic law understanding from a broader philosophical perspective, his 1912 and 1914 works are more confined to the legal domain. In *Statute and Judgment*, Schmitt discusses the inability of legal positivism to provide a criterion ensuring correct legal decisions. Meanwhile, in *The Value of the State and the Significance of the Individual*, he critiques the lack of solid theoretical justification for the modern state and law, analyzing the weaknesses of legal positivism from a political law perspective. Additionally, considering the limited secondary literature on these early works, we find it pertinent to conduct a detailed analysis of them, contributing to the ever-expanding corpus of literature on the German philosopher and jurist.

The third chapter is devoted to Schmitt's constructive contributions to the understanding of law and statute. After effectively challenging the scientistic positivist approach to law through rational and practical arguments, Schmitt gradually develops a more fitting horizon of meaning for addressing the juridical phenomenon. This section will argue that Schmitt's conceptualization of law includes the human being as a formative agent (to a certain degree) in the creation of law. This perspective necessitates an in-depth exploration into the nature and characteristics of human understanding. In other words, recognizing the human being as an active participant who shapes the abstract meanings of normative texts compels Schmitt to elucidate the unique existential attributes that this agent—the human being—inevitably imprints on written law during this process of interpretation. The manner through which we will justify our assertion is the following:

a. We will begin with Schmitt's incursion into law, particularly focusing on the conditions that determine the correctness of a legal decision. This topic, we will argue, leads Schmitt to delve into the problem of normativity, a central concern in practical philosophy.
b. This exploration then brings Schmitt to juridically thematize not just the tension between normative and factual elements, but also to question the specific characteristics of the agent who must navigate these two realms: the human being.
c. This line of thought leads Schmitt to attempt to elucidate the ontological-existential characteristics inherent in human understanding. We will argue that in his early legal works (1912–1921) the thinker from Plettenberg identifies key ontological structures in human understanding, namely: finitude, historicality, language as a world-shaping force, and metaphysics as an inevitable aspect of the human condition.

Simply put, the second and third chapters of this book illustrate how Schmitt's transition from law to human understanding transforms him into a "soldier-artist". He acts as a demolitionist who then utilizes the cleared space to create a beautiful yet ominous work of art.

§ 3. The problem with "Humanized law". How do we know if a legal decision is correct?

Finally, the fourth chapter aims to address, within Schmittian thought, a fundamental question that that remains indispensable in the field of philosophy of law: how can we determine the correctness of a legal decision? To sufficiently clarify the scope of this chapter, it is necessary to provide some context: Schmitt's demand of an existential openness in law does not entail an absolute freedom for the judge and the sovereign in the context of decision-making (unlike the *Freirechtsschule*). On the contrary, acknowledging the legal decision as a synthesis between two dichotomous poles leads Schmitt to identify two existential positions that are perilously extreme and must be avoided at all costs: the romantic and the technical. These positionalities, while similar in context, differ in content. This implies that in both cases, existence is reduced to just one aspect of reality, yet they diverge in the specific pole each selects to define truth in an all-encompassing manner. The way these existential positionalities manifest in legal is as follows: the technical takes the form of normative legal positivism, a line of thought which asserts that written rules exhaust the object of study of the legal phenomenon; any alien element, be it ethical or factual, must be eliminated from the legal discussion. The romantic, on the other hand, manifests in law as capricious decisionism. Here, the judge uses the decision as an instance for deploying his subjectivity without restrictions, thus transforming himself into a quasi-divine legal entity where the roles of legislator and judge are united in one person.

To prevent these positionalities from manifesting, Schmitt demands rationality in legal decisions. It is in this context that he demands the human element to be included in the juridical equation, so that it engages in a reflective exercise (the hypothetical procedure he presents in *Statute and judgment*), which we argue can be understood as an instance of "reflective endorsement". As we will see with Heidegger, understanding is an openness towards existence as *Being-possible*. To understand oneself from a possibility is to be able to *be* that possibility, to project oneself existentially as that possibility. For Schmitt, legal understanding seems to be an instance of appropriation of a possibility. That is, positive legal statutes present the judge with a range of possible interpretations. The judge must then decide which of these hermeneutic possibilities he will "bring to life" through his decision. In this chapter we will argue that the hypothetical exercise he demands judges to perform, that is, to understand that "a judicial decision is correct, today, if it is to be assumed that another judge would have decided in the same way"[8], is to be considered as mechanism for ensuring that this appropriation of a legal possibility is done in a rational manner.

Finally, we warn the reader that Schmitt is an author whose thought is difficult to locate from the political, legal, and even existential point of view. As Herrero points out, he oscillates freely and frequently from one position to another, so it is natural to be puzzled by the shift of paradigm in his proposals[9]. In juridical matters the German jurist oscillates between legal openness and legal certainty. Schmitt, then, can be read as a "legal mystic": he demands jurists to define law as an aperture towards the concrete. At the same time, however, he is pragmatic: he does not wish the legal phenomenon to turn into a tool for the dogmatic deployment of particular subjective positionalities. We will argue that this characteristic is precisely a product of the hermeneutic nature of Schmitt's intellectual proposal. In this book, we aim to offer a hermeneutic context that facilitates an understanding of this "intellectual fluctuation".

---

8 Carl Schmitt, "Statute and Judgment: An Investigation into the Problem of Legal Praxis," in *Carl Schmitt's Early Legal-Theoretical Writings: Statute and Judgment and the Value of the State and the Significance of the Individual*, trans. Lars Vinx and Samuel Garrett Zeitlin (New York: Cambridge University Press, 2021), 103.

9 See: Montserrat Herrero, "Estudio preliminar," in *Posiciones ante el derecho*, by Carl Schmitt (Madrid: Editorial Tecnos, 2012).

1 Hermeneutics and law: Heidegger and Gadamer

§ 1. Knowledge and understanding

The branch of philosophy primarily concerned with the operation of human knowledge is known as epistemology. The central question this area of philosophy addresses is how our minds (those of *subjects*) can acquire knowledge of something external to our subjectivity; how we are capable of knowing something about an object that belongs to the "real world". In Aristotle, for example, we human beings play a passive role in the act of knowledge. The substance of the object is composed of matter and form (both are already *in* the object), and when we are confronted with them, we *receive* the form from the object[10]. Kant, on the other hand, argues that we play an active role in the act of knowledge. As Aristotle, he claims that we, human beings, are inevitably doomed to acquire knowledge of reality through our senses. We need something external, that is part of the "objective reality", to present itself to our senses in order to procure a representation of a phenomenon (through a process that he calls "schematism"). Our perception of the world is not productive (by merely thinking something it becomes real), but sensitive (things are imposed on us). However, unlike Aristotle, Kant posits that the "form'" of the object is not derived from reality, but rather is imposed by the subject. Sensibility only furnishes us with raw data, which must then be organized by the intellect (an activity governed by categories and pure intuitions). Differently put, to comprehend the world, sensibility must supply us with intuitions, or "data" derived from experience. Once this occurs, our understanding assimilates this data,

10 Aristotle, "Metaphysics," in *Complete Works of Aristotle*, ed. Jonathan Barnes, vol. 2, 2 vols., The Revised Oxford Translation (Oxford: Princeton University Press, 1991).

"processes" it, and generates a concept[11]. If our senses receive no input, knowledge acquisition is impossible; conversely, if our understanding fails to process the sensory data, the world appears as an amorphous chaos. In Kant's words, "thoughts without content are empty, intuitions without concepts are blind"[12].

This brief explanation of how knowledge operates, according to Aristotle and Kant, offers a perspective on how understanding is analyzed epistemologically. The focus is on how the subject manages to acquire or articulate a concept from something that exists beyond itself. However, when we refer to a "theory of understanding", we are addressing something distinct. An approach from the perspective of understanding does not focus on how reality is constituted through the subject-object relationship, but rather on the meaning that reality acquires for the subject apprehending it. In simpler terms, epistemology concentrates on how the world manifests in/for the human mind. Its primary concern, we might say, is the legitimacy and objectivity of what presents itself to us as reality. In this context, human reason, perceived as a processing machine, takes center stage. This is attributable, as Hawkins explains, to its

> capacity to synthesize and utilize linear abstractions and symbols of great complexity [. . .]. Intelligence comprehends hierarchical fields of organizational rank and discerns value as to reliability, implied worth, or significance. It stratifies via sequence to classification systems that are analogous to paradigm, domain, category, class, species, subspecies, genus, and then finally, a specific example. This complex function is analogous to a rapid sorting system that is simultaneously capable of integration and selection[13].

---

11 Kant, *Critique of Pure Reason* (hereafter CPR) B59–B73. We used the following translation to English: Immanuel Kant, *Critique of Pure Reason*, trans. Paul Guyer and Allen W. Wood, The Cambridge Edition of the Works of Immanuel Kant (Cambridge: Cambridge University Press, 2009).

12 CPR, A51/B75

13 David R. Hawkins, *Transcending the Levels of Consciousness* (California: Hay House, 2015), 224–25.

A theory of understanding, on the other hand, is concerned with the meaning that it all (reality) has. That is, it is also concerned, as epistemology, with the "emergence of the world", but it argues that reality already unfolds with a meaning that can be grasped by the human mind. As Hawkins explains it, "while all the foregoing [mind as a machine that processes the data provided by the senses] represents an impressive mass of information, the basic question remains the same as it has throughout all of history: What does it all 'mean' (i.e., hermeneutics)?"[14]. A theory of understanding directly addresses the question concerning "the meaning" of that which is presented to our senses.

An example will be helpful in clarifying this matter: two researchers, one with an epistemological approach and the other with an interest in understanding, analyze a person contemplating a painting. The first researcher focuses his enquiry on how the painting, which is located on a pole beyond the subject, is able to enter the mind of the individual who contemplates it; in how the subject is able to represent in his intellect what is located outside of it (the frame, the drawings, the colors, etc.). The second researcher, on the other hand, focuses on something completely different: meaning. That is, his enquiry will focus on what the painting *means* to the subject that contemplates it (if he finds it beautiful, ugly, offensive, inspiring, boring, etc.) and why it acquires that particular meaning. Therefore, if he examines the conditions for the possibility of human knowledge, it will not be with the purpose of elucidating its operation, but rather to determine how human knowledge attributes meaning to the world and to identify the fundamental structures within human knowledge that enable the emergence of such meaning.

Good examples of theories of understanding are Heidegger's and Gadamer's philosophies. This is mainly because they are not concerned with how something from the real world "enters" the mind of the subject (Aristotle), or how concepts already present in the human mind "emerge" from it to organize the raw data presented to intuition (Kant).

---

14 Hawkins, 225.

These philosophies presuppose that reality is a given, and posit that the role of philosophers is to clarify how and why reality attains meaning. They also seek to identify the part humans play in the "emergence" of the world. The next section will briefly review Heidegger's and Gadamer's theories of understanding, not only because their thought is exemplary in this regard but also because their names will frequently appear in this work.

§ 2. Two theories of understanding: Heidegger and Gadamer

Being is always the Being of an entity
– Martin Heidegger[15]

A theory of understanding is a distinct philosophical approach to the operation of the world and our knowledge of it. Its uniqueness lies in its focus not only on the concrete pole, often referred to as 'reality,' and the ideal pole, encompassing the conceptual articulations of the mind that enable us to comprehend that same reality, but also on the specific characteristics of the agent who comprehends the world. In other words, a theory of understanding assumes that the knowledge acquired *from* the world is to some extent conditioned by the way in which the cognitive subject *can* attain such knowledge.

Allow us to illustrate the aforementioned with an example: if a godlike entity were able to penetrate the essence of objects and acquire absolute knowledge of reality, then its knowledge of it would be "tainted" by that same absoluteness (and said entity would, in fact, be the cause

15 Martin Heidegger, *Being and Time*, trans. John Macquarrie and Edward Robinson (HarperPerennial, 2008), 29. In the German edition it reads: „Sein ist jeweils das Sein eines Seienden". Martin Heidegger, *Sein Und Zeit* (Tübingen: Max Niemeyer Verlag, 1967), 9.

of that object). On the other hand, if an entity is condemned to perceive only some aspects of the world, that is, is limited by its own ontological characteristics, then its knowledge of the world would also be to some point determined by those same characteristics. If we were located above time and history, then our knowledge would be supratemporal and ahistorical. If we are inevitably thrown to time and history, as Heidegger and Gadamer argue, then our knowledge of the world can only be relative, that is, determined by that same temporality and historicality. This, however, does not entail any kind of relativism. Quite the contrary, it is just a recognition that, even though there may be an absolute aspect of reality, we can only perceive it in relative terms[16].

The above allows us to consider that in order for a philosophical approach to be regarded as a "theory of understanding", its examination must focus on at least the following:

i. The real pole of existence, that which provides our intuition with sensations for our understanding to "process".
ii. The ideal pole, which processes that which is given to our intuitions in order to obtain a concept.
iii. The particular characteristics of the agent that mediates both realms.
iv. The interplay between these three elements—reality, ideality, and the ontological characteristics of the subject—and how they are interconnected or relate to each other.

As we already mentioned, we believe that Heidegger's and Gadamer's philosophies meet these requirements in an exemplary manner (and through explaining their thoughts, it will become clearer what we mean by this concept). Therefore, we will briefly revise them in order to clarify in what specific sense they are able to perform this task.

16 We will come back to this topic when reviewing Gadamer's thought.

a. Subject and object are one: Martin Heidegger

Before delving into Heidegger's thought, it's essential to address a fundamental distinction that concerns the intellectual followers of these authors: the differentiation between the first and second Heidegger[17]. This distinction is crucial because in this section, we will explore some of Heidegger's works from his initial period, primarily *Being and Time*, and others from his later philosophical development, including *The Essence of Human Freedom* and *The Fundamental Concepts of Metaphysics.*

The first Heidegger, the secondary literature argues, ends in 1929 with the publication of *What Is Metaphysics?*[18] The main difference between his first and the second intellectual epoch is the following: while before 1929 the primary focus was on *Dasein* as an entity capable of projecting possibilities from a particular factual context, the second Heidegger shifts his attention to *Dasein* as a being thrown into existence and the endeavor necessary to claim or appropiate [*ereignen*] the meaning that emerges in existence[19]. For some, such a Richardson[20], there is an abandonment by the second Heidegger of the analytic of *Dasein*

---

17 William J Richardson, *Heidegger: Through Phenomenology to Thought.* (Dordrecht: Springer Netherlands, 2013). In the same sense: Herman Philipse, *Heidegger's Philosophy of Being a Critical Interpretation* (Princeton: Princeton University Press, 1999). Cristina Lafont, *Lenguaje y Apertura Del Mundo: El Giro Lingüístico de La Hermenéutica de Heidegger* (Madrid: Alianza, 1997).

18 Cf. Richardson, *Heidegger: Through Phenomenology to Thought.* Herrmann argues that the most important work of the second Heidegger is *Ereignis.* Friedrich-Wilhelm von Herrmann, "Die 'Beiträge Zur Philosophie' Als Hermeneutische Schlüssel Zum Spätwerk Heideggers," in *Heidegger Neu Gelesen*, ed. Markus Happel (Würzburg: Königshausen und Neumann, 1997).

19 Cf. Mateo Belgrano, "'El Origen de La Obra de Arte': ¿un 'Oasis' En El Pensamiento Heideggeriano?," *Areté* 32, no. 1 (2020): 12.

20 Emad criticizes Richardson and says that the "Heideggerian turn" must be understood as a step back and forth between transcendental-horizontal thinking (Heidegger I) and onto-historical thinking (Heidegger II). Parvis Emad, *On the Way to Heidegger's Contributions to Philosophy* (Madison University of Wisconsin Press, 2007), 205.

as a fundamental ontology[21]. For others, as is the case of Gadamer, there is a continuity, since Heidegger's thought must be understood as a progress that is characterized by a return to the beginning: the question concerning *being*[22]. For the purposes of this work, however, we will consider that the continuity of themes (or perspectives) discussed by Heidegger I and II—such as historicality, finitude, existential hermeneutics, among others—allows us to treat them as forming a unified framework. This approach gains even greater legitimacy when we consider that the references to Heidegger's thought here serve a propaedeutic purpose, contributing to the perspective from which we will interpret Schmitt's work.

Continuing our exploration of Heidegger's philosophy, it's important to note that already at the beginning of *Being and Time*, one of his greatest works, we see that the philosopher from Freiburg sees knowledge of the world not as a relationship where the subject is merely a vessel that receives what is *out there*. Understanding the world is to make sense of it, to give it meaning, and human beings

---

21 Richardson, *Heidegger: Through Phenomenology to Thought.* Kisiel even understands *Being and Time* as a failed project. Theodore J Kisiel, *The Genesis of Heidegger's Being and Time* (Berkeley, Calif.; London: University of California Press, 2003). In the same sense: Carl Friedrich Gethmann, "Philosophie Als Vollzug Und Als Begriff Heideggers Identitätsphilosophie Des Lebens in Der Vorlesung Vom Wintersemester 1921/22 Und Ihr Verhältnis Zu Sein Und Zeit," *Dilthey-Jahrbuch Für Philosophie Und Geschichte Der Geisteswissenschaften* 4 (1986): 27–53. Alejandro G Vigo, *Arqueología y aleteiología: estudios heideggerianos* (Berlin: Logos Verlag, 2014). Ramón Rodríguez García, *Heidegger y La Crisis de La Época Moderna* (Madrid: Ediciones Pedagógicas, 1994). Günter Figal, *Der Sinn Des Verstehens: Beiträge Zur Hermeneutischen Philosophie* (Stuttgart: P. Reclam, 1996).

22 Hans Georg Gadamer, *Heideggers Wege: Studien zum Spätwerk* (Tübingen: Mohr, 1983). Other authors that defend a similar idea are as follows: Richardson, *Heidegger: Through Phenomenology to Thought.*, 12–13. Daniel O Dahlstrom, *Interpreting Heidegger: New Essays* (New York: Cambridge University Press, 2011). Frederick A Olafson, "The Unity of Heidegger's Thought," in *The Cambridge Companion to Heidegger*, ed. Charles Guignon (New York: Cambridge University Press, 1993), 97–121. Richard Polt, *The Emergency of Being. On Heidegger's Contributions to Philosophy* (London: Cornell University Press, 2006).

(the *Dasein* as he calls it) participate actively in this process[23]. In Heidegger's words:

> Basic concepts determine the way in which we get an understanding beforehand of the area of subject-matter underlaying all the objects a science takes as its theme, and all positive investigation is guided by this understanding. Only after the area itself has been explored beforehand in a corresponding manner do these concepts become genuinely demonstrated and "grounded". But since every such area is itself obtained from the domain of entities themselves, this preliminary research, from which the concepts are drawn, signifies nothing else than an interpretation of those entities with regard to their basic state of Being. [. . .] Laying the foundations, as we have described it, is rather a productive logic[24].

In other words, when the *Dasein* approaches reality, it does not do it as an "empty vessel" that is ready to receive that which is presented to the senses in an "unpolluted" manner. We already possess a series of concepts that allow us to elucidate what is presented to our senses so that those same concepts set the limits from which the comprehensive act operates. As Wrathall explains, "to understand is to be in the world in such way that everything is projected upon, that is, makes sense in terms of particular possibilities"[25]. That is, with the concepts that we already possess in our mind (and that have been acquired and transmitted by humanity throughout history, as we will see with Gadamer), we interpret the world and its phenomena. Therefore, understanding the world is at the same time receptive (we need something to present itself

---

23 Cf, Sacha Golob, *Heidegger on Concepts, Freedom and Normativity* (Cambridge: Cambridge University Press, 2014), 211.

24 Heidegger, *Being and Time*, 30. In the original German it reads: „Grundbegriffe sind die Bestimmungen, in denen das allen thematischen Gegenständen einer Wissenschaft zugrundeliegende Sachgebiet zum vorgängigen und alle positive Untersuchung führenden Verständnis kommt. Ihre echte Ausweisung und »Begrün-dung« erhalten diese Begriffe demnach nur in einer entsprechend vorgängigen Durchforschung des Sachgebietes selbst. Sofern aber jedes dieser Gebiete aus dem Bezirk des Seienden selbst gewonnen wird, bedeutet solche vorgängige und Grundbegriffe schöpfende Forschung nichts anderes als Auslegung dieses Seienden auf die Grundverfassung seines Seins". Heidegger, *Sein Und Zeit*, 10.

25 Wrathall, "Heidegger on Human Understanding," 181-182.

to our intuition) and productive (we *give* meaning to the world from a set of concepts that we already possess)[26].

The peculiarity of the *Dasein*, however, is even more fundamental. As Heidegger explains, "Dasein is an entity which does not just occur among other entities. Rather it is ontically distinguished by the fact that, in its very Being, that Being is an *issue* for it"[27]. That is, unlike rocks or animals[28], we engage with Being. We are the only type of beings we know (so far) that have a relationship with our own being. Our own being is not predetermined. We are not condemned to respond to certain stimuli in ways *preset* by our nature (as occurs, for example, with animals and food, mating, etc.). On the contrary, we are able "to determine one's own action purely through *oneself*, to give oneself the law for one's action"[29]. In the words of Wrathall, for Heidegger I, as a *Dasein*, "understand my own thrown disposedness by projecting myself out into the world, thereby discovering what kind of possibilities shows up for such a being as me"[30]. That is, we are able to *choose ourselves* in each moment (which also implies that we are fully responsible for ourselves).

Allow us to illustrate the aforementioned with and example: imagine you have an important report to deliver at work that is due the following day. It is already 6 pm, and you still have not managed to finish it. This situation presents different *possibilities* from which to choose. You can stay late until the report is finished because you want to be an

---

26 Cf. Crowell, *Normativity and Phenomenology in Husserl and Heidegger*. This, however, does not exclude the possibility of attaining new knowledge. We will explore this in greater depth when we revisit Gadamer's philosophy.

27 Heidegger, *Being and Time*, 32. In the original German it reads „Das Dasein ist ein Seiendes, das nicht nur unter anderem Seien-den vorkommt. Es ist vielmehr dadurch ontisch ausgezeichnet, daß es diesem Seienden in seinem Sein um dieses Sein selbst geht". Heidegger, *Sein Und Zeit*, 12.

28 Martin Heidegger, *The Fundamental Concepts of Metaphysics: World, Finitude, Solitude* (Bloomington, Ind: Indiana University Press, 2012).

29 Martin Heidegger, *The Essence of Human Freedom: An Introduction to Philosophy*, trans. Ted Sadler (London & New York: Continuum, 2002), 15. This is what Heidegger calls *positive freedom*.

30 Wrathall, "Heidegger on Human Understanding," 191.

exemplary worker. You can do it quickly and deliver it as it is because you are not willing to sacrifice your family time for a job. You can use that moment to reflect on the choices you have made on your life and seek a new career path, or you can talk to your boss to see if it is possible to reschedule the report delivery (among many other options). The decision you make will determine the way in which you understand yourself (as a good worker, a good father or mother, a conciliatory person, etc.). You have the freedom to choose among many *possibilities* who you are in each case (and if you choose not to decide, to let yourself be carried away by the tide of life, you are also choosing *not* to decide). That is, in broad terms, what Heidegger means when he claims that "Dasein always understands itself in terms of its existence—in terms of a possibility of itself"[31]. In that sense, this "appropriation of one's own possibilities" is not something that occurs to a few enlightened beings, but is an everyday occurrence. As Blattner explains, "conscience discloses me as 'my own self', as the target of norms, as the one who is called forth to understand who I am. This 'own self' is not something other than the everyday self. It is a transcendental aspect of the everyday self"[32].

Therefore, according to Heidegger, we, as human beings, are a unique type of entity. We have a distinctive way of relating to ourselves. This uniqueness doesn't only apply to our self-relationship but also extends to how we interact with the world. In his words,

> if we tell what it is for [des Wozu], we are not simply designating something; but that which is designated is understood *as* that *as* which we are to take the thing in question. That which is disclosed in understanding—that which is

31 Heidegger, *Being and Time*, 33. In the original German it reads: „Das Dasein versteht sich selbst immer aus seiner Existenz, einer Möglichkeit seiner selbst, es selbst oder nicht es selbst zu sein". Heidegger, *Sein Und Zeit*, 12.

32 William Blattner, "Authenticity and Resolutness," in *The Cambridge Companion to Heidegger's "Being and Time,"* ed. Mark A. Wrathall, Cambridge Companions to Philosophy (Cambridge: Cambridge University Press, 2013), 328.

understood—is already accessible in such a way that its "as which" can be made to stand out explicitly[33].

That is, when we perceive an object, we are not passive recipients of information from the object. Instead, we actively participate in shaping its significance within a network of meanings that exist in the world. According to Heidegger, then, an object's understanding isn't confined to a single interpretation. Rather, every object presents a range of possibilities from which it can be understood. Hence, the way a phenomenon is revealed depends, to some extent, on the mode in which the perceiving subject unveils it.

The exemplary path is once again useful to us in clarifying the meaning of what we wish to convey: Imagine you are presented with an apple. You can perceive this apple as an entity you can use for food, as an inspiring object that leads you to create a work of art with or from it, or as an entity that can cause harm to another person when thrown at them (among many other possibilities). In each case, the apple remains the same. What changes is the way you understand it, the manner in which you interpret (give/unveil meaning to) the apple. This variability in interpretation is a fundamental aspect of human experience, a point eloquently captured by Heidegger, who argues that "when something is understood but is still veiled, it becomes unveiled by an act of appropriation, and this is always done under the guidance of a point of view, which fixes that with regard to which what is understood is to be interpreted. In every case interpretation is grounded in *something we see in advance*—in a *fore-sight*"[34]. That is, we are all inevitably equipped

33 Heidegger, *Being and Time*, 189. In the German original it reads: „Die Angabe des Wozu ist nicht einfach die Nennung von etwas, sondern das Genannte ist verstanden als das, als welches das in Frage stehende zu nehmen ist. Das im Verstehen Erschlossene, das Verstandene ist immer schon so zugänglich, daß an ihm sein »als was« ausdrücklich abgehoben werden kann". Heidegger, *Sein Und Zeit*, 149.

34 Heidegger, *Being and Time*, 191. In the German editions it reads: „Die Zueignung des Verstandenen, aber noch Eingehüllten vollzieht die Enthüllung immer unter der Führung einer Hinsicht, die das fixiert, im Hinblick worauf das Verstandene ausgelegt werden soll. Die Auslegung gründet jeweils in einer Vorsicht, die das

with a series of pregiven concepts (prejudices) from which we apprehend reality. From such concepts, we interpret what is presented to our senses. Interpretation, then, "takes what is projected in the understanding, and acts on the basis of the possibilities it has in view. In doing this, it makes the understanding its own, enriches it, and potentially even alters it"[35]. Consequently, if I were an artist, it is more likely that I would understand reality in an artistic manner and possibly see the apple from the given example as an object from which I can create art (if I am not hungry at the time, of course).

Now, does reality depend exclusively on the subject's interpretation of it? The answer is negative. As Heidegger explains, "in every case Dasein [. . .] has already got itself into definite possibilities"[36]. That is, everything that presents itself to human beings offers a range of possibilities for how it can be understood. Thus, the object itself has limitations in regard to the way in which it can be comprehended. The apple from the example cannot be understood as a means of transportation because it does not offer that possibility (regardless of how much a subject may desire it). To put it simply, the "world" presents a series of possibilities for how it can be understood. The subject unveils and interprets the phenomenon presented to their senses according to one of those possibilities, but cannot exceed said range of possibilities offered by reality.

This whole process is what we call "understanding", which, according to Palmer,

> is not free but a matter of disclosing, or bringing to manifestness, what a thing is; it brings it out of concealment into the light of day. The mind does not project a meaning onto the phenomenon; rather, what appears is an ontological manifestation of the thing itself. Of course, through dogmatism a thing can be forced to

---

in Vorhabe Genommene auf eine bestimmte Auslegbarkeit hin »anschneidet«. Das in der Vor-habe gehaltene und »vorsichtig« anvisierte Verstandene wird durch die Auslegung begreiflich". Heidegger, *Sein Und Zeit*, 150.

35 Wrathall, "Heidegger on Human Understanding," 180.

36 Heidegger, *Being and Time*, 183. In the original German it reads: „Das Dasein ist als wesenhaft befindliches je schon in bestimmte Möglichkeiten hineingeraten". Heidegger, *Sein Und Zeit*, 144.

> be seen only in the desired aspect. But to let a thing appear as what it is becomes a matter of learning to allow it to do so, for it gives itself to be seen. *Logos* (speaking) is not really a power given to language by its user but a power which language gives to him, a means of being seized by what manifest through it[37].

That is, language enables us to unveil the various aspects that the world presents, but this does not imply that we can dominate it through it [language]. As finite beings, we are bound to unveil the world in ways defined by existence itself, rather than according to our own whimsical desires.

Now, as far as understanding is concerned, it's important to clarify that although we have distinguished the subject and object as two dichotomous poles in confrontation throughout this explanation, this has been done solely for pedagogical purposes. Heidegger argues that the subject apprehending reality, the "objects" of the world, and the relationship entangling them (that of understanding) should be viewed as a unified whole[38]. In his words, "the compound expression 'Being-in-the-world' indicates in the very way we have coined it, that it stands for a *unitary* phenomenon"[39]. That is, even though our intellect engages in knowledge in a discursive manner (rather than in an intuitively creative way), the configuration of the world requires the involvement of the subject. Heidegger argues that "it is not the case that man 'is' and then has, by way of an extra, a relationship-of-Being towards the 'world'—a world with which he provides himself occasionally"[40]. This

37 Richard E. Palmer, *Hermeneutics: Interpretation Theory in Schleiermacher, Dilthey, Heidegger, and Gadamer*, Studies in Phenomenology & Existential Philosophy (Evanston: Northwestern Univ. Pr, 1972), 128.

38 Cf. Mark. A Wrathall and Max Murphey, "An Overview of Being and Time," in *The Cambridge Companion to Heidegger's "Being and Time,"* ed. Mark A. Wrathall, Cambridge Companions to Philosophy (Cambridge: Cambridge University Press, 2013), 19.

39 Heidegger, *Being and Time*, 78. In the original German it reads: „Der zusammengesetzte Ausdruck »In-der-Welt-sein« zeigt schon in seiner Prägung an, daß mit ihm ein einheitliches Phäno-men gemeint ist". Heidegger, *Sein Und Zeit*, 53.

40 Heidegger, *Being and Time*, 84. In the original German it reads: „Der Mensch »ist« nicht und hat überdies noch ein Seinsverhältnis zur «Welt», die er sich gelegentlich zulegt. Dasein ist nie »zunächst« ein gleichsam in-seins-freies Seiendes, das zu-weilen die Laune hat, eine »Beziehung« zur Welt aufzunehmen.

implies that no human being exists in isolation from the world. Rather, being human inherently involves an active engagement with the world. As Murphey and Wrathall explain it, the world

> presents us with an organized totality of activities on the basis of which particular entities are able to be encountered in their involvements (ordinarily as equipment) [. . .]. Dasein inhabits a world by assigning itself to a way of taking a stand on its being, in terms of which it makes sense of its particular projects and activities. So the world is that wherein Dasein can take up the tasks of interpreting and taking responsibility for its existence[41].

We cannot separate ourselves from the world to ascertain our true nature; being a human entails being and deploying our existence within the world. Therefore, the task of elucidating human nature requires us to immerse ourselves deeper into the world, aiming to clarify the fundamental and inevitable relations that we, as *Dasein*, maintain with it. In essence, our existence is relational, and a significant aspect of Heidegger's philosophy is devoted to identifying and explaining these relationships[42].

Solches Aufnehmen von Beziehungen zur Welt ist nur möglich, weil Dasein als In-der-Welt-sein ist, wie es ist". Heidegger, *Sein Und Zeit*, 57.

41 Wrathall and Murphey, "An Overview of Being and Time," 9.

42 If we consider the ontological structure of reality to be relational, then we must inquire: How has Western philosophy traditionally engaged with the world? The German philosopher posits that this engagement has predominantly been scientific and rational, interpreting the world in a physical-objective manner and asserting this as the sole "truthful" way of relating to it. In essence, Western thought has, either explicitly or implicitly, championed the belief that the correct approach to understanding the world is through science and objectivity. However, as we will analyze in greater detail later when revisiting Schmitt's critique of positivism, the notion of an "objective" world is flawed. Due to the inseparable interweaving of man and world, the structure the world assumes is, to some extent, dependent on how the *Dasein* (being-there) interprets or relates to it. Therefore, even though one might argue that it is essential for an apple to be seen as an entity for human and animal nourishment—an interpretation often perceived as objective and correct—this does not preclude an artist from interpreting it as a source of inspiration. Each perspective offers a different relational understanding of the same object, highlighting the multifaceted nature of interpretation and perception.

Heidegger asserts not only that our being-in-the-world is relational, but also that we, as human beings, are "thrown into a world that is already taken care of"[43]. As Wrathall and Murphey put it,

> [t]here is a significant *passive* aspect to being-in. Dasein finds itself already situated in a particular world that is arranged in a definite, concrete fashion and where particular things have already shown up as mattering. Heidegger refers to this as Dasein's "thrownness" (*Geworfenheit*): we are "thrown" into the world. We also find ourselves with characteristics that shape our engagement with the world. [. . .] These are fact-like constraints but still meaningfully taken up and constituted[44].

Another way to express this is as follows: at birth, we are literally "thrown" into a world that has already been interpreted, where pre-existing relations of understanding towards that world are already in operation (and in this sense, it has already been "taken care of").
Let's further clarify the aforementioned concept with a simple example: if you were born before 2006 (which is my case), you probably learned in school that Pluto was the last planet of the solar system. That is, you were taught that the last massive structure in our solar system was understood as a planet. However, if you were born after that date, you were probably told that Neptune is the last planet in our solar system and that Pluto is merely a dwarf planet. In both cases, we are literally thrown into a pre-existing manner of understanding the world. We don't need to elucidate what Pluto is; its definition has already been taken care of. The same applies to the objects and people we interact with. We already have an understanding or interpretation of them (as illustrated in Heidegger's example of the hammer[45]).

Heidegger's philosophy, which we have characterized as a "theory of understanding", is concerned not with how we understand a specific object, but rather with how any form of human understanding (that of the *Dasein*) is possible. Philosophically, his insights are directed towards the ontological dimensions of human understanding, rather

43 Cf. Heidegger, *Being and Time*, 235. Cf. Heidegger, *Sein Und Zeit*, 191.
44 Wrathall and Murphey, "An Overview of Being and Time," 14.
45 Cf. Heidegger, *Being and Time*, 109.

than the ontic ones. Although this subject warrants a lifetime of dedicated research, our current focus will be on what is pertinent to our work: the fundamental ontological relations to the world that, according to Heidegger, are inescapable and irreducible (what he refers to as *existentiale*).

In *Being and Time* Heidegger articulates two fundamental ideas that are crucial to our analysis, namely, that "in understanding, as an *existentiale*, that which we have such competence over is not a 'what', but Being as existing. The kind of Being which Dasein has, as potentiality-for-Being, lies existentially in understanding"[46] and that "while Being-in-the-world cannot be broken up into contents which may be pieced together, this does not prevent it from having several constitutive items in its structure"[47]. What the philosopher from Freiburg is conveying is as follows: his philosophical quest aims to elucidate what has been overlooked by Western philosophy, namely, *Being*. However, due to our inherent limitations as human beings, we cannot directly access Being itself. Consequently, our analysis (and that of Heidegger) must necessarily focus on an existing being.

Heidegger contends that there is no entity more suitable than human beings (*Dasein*) for elucidating the nature of Being. Why is this the case? Because, as we explained in *supra*, we are the only beings (that we know of) to which our own being is an issue, that can decide in each moment who we are and how we relate to the world. We have a special relationship to Being; its existence and nature are presented to us with a certain degree of transparency (even if minimal), which allows us to grasp some aspects of it.

---

46 Heidegger, 183. In the original German it reads: „Das im Verste-hen als Existenzial Gekonnte ist kein Was, sondern das Sein als Existieren. Im Verstehen liegt existenzial die Seinsart des Daseins als Sein-können". Heidegger, *Sein Und Zeit*, 143.

47 Heidegger, *Being and Time*, 78. In the German original it reads: „Die Unauflösbarkeit in zusammenstückbare Bestände schließt nicht eine Mehrfältigkeit konstitutiver Strukturmomente dieser Verfassung aus". Heidegger, *Sein Und Zeit*, 53.

The aforementioned transparency of human existence should not be misconstrued to mean that Heidegger is interested in the particular characteristics of a concrete person's life (not even his own). Rather, his interest lies in the structures that make human existence possible (and here is where the concept of *existentiale* comes into play). Given that Heidegger's inquiry into the nature of being starts with the *Dasein*, he recognizes the necessity to identify and describe the structure of its existence. This is precisely the role of *existentiale*: they indicate or delineate the form of (human) existence. Through them, Heidegger aims to identify and indicate these structures, but without compromising on their content[48]. Consequently, *existentiale*, serving as formal indications, succeed in characterizing human existence in its entirety.

One key quality of these ontological characteristics is their co-originality. This means that there is no hierarchy among them; each is equally essential for human understanding. Put differently, if any of these fundamental world relations were absent, the entity before you would not be a human being. This is because being human entails being constrained to exist in the ways indicated by these *existentiale*; thus, none is more significant than the others. Before delving into Gadamer's thought, let's briefly review three of the *existentiale* identified by Heidegger in *Being and Time*, which are crucial for our forthcoming analysis of Schmitt's ideas. These are understanding, historicality, and language.

Typically, to "understand something" implies that we, as passive recipients of information, can grasp knowledge from the external world. When I apprehend something external in the form of an idea (or concept), it means I understood it. For Heidegger, however, the concept "understanding" is entirely different from this conventional description. The philosopher from Freiburg affirms that "if we interpret understanding as a fundamental *existentiale*, this indicates that this

48 Cf. Wrathall and Murphey, "An Overview of Being and Time," 21. Wrathall explains that Heidegger understands formal indications "as ways of directing our attention in an ontologically noncommittal way to the phenomenon in question" Wrathall and Murphey, 10.

phenomenon is conceived as a basic mode of Dasein's *Being*"[49]. This means that for Heidegger, understanding is not the ability to capture an external phenomenon and develop a concept from it. Instead, "understanding" refers to the structure that constitutes human existence. As Wrathall puts it, "to understand is to *be* in a certain way, to embody a particular way of existing in the world, rather than to think or believe or know that such and such is the case"[50].

Do you understand English? Do you understand differential equations? These questions about understanding are essentially inquiries about one's "know how". When we ask "do you understand English?", we are enquiring whether the person possesses the ability to speak, read or write in English. Similarly, the second question seeks to determine if the person has the knowledge of how to solve differential equations. This reveals that, in essence, understanding is openness of existence as *Being-possible*. To understand something means that you are able (that it is possible for you) to be a version of yourself who is able to perform a task. Differently put, to understand oneself from a possibility is to capable of *being* that possibility, to project oneself existentially as that possibility. Therefore, "*understanding is the existential Being of Dasein's own potentiality-for-Being; and it is in such a way that this Being discloses in itself what its Being is capable of*"[51].

Through understanding we disclose (unveil) a possibility of the world or ourselves. Therefore, understanding is itself a structure that allows the being-in-the-world, the *Dasein*, to exist. If we were unable to understand, then our existence would be impossible. We would not be able to relate with the world, with others or even ourselves. It

---

49 Heidegger, *Being and Time*, 182. In the original German it reads: "Wenn wir dieses als fundamentales Existenzial interpretieren, dann zeigt sich damit an, daß dieses Phänomen als Grundmodus des Seins des Daseins begriffen wird". Heidegger, *Sein Und Zeit*, 143.

50 Wrathall, "Heidegger on Human Understanding," 108.

51 Heidegger, *Being and Time*, 184. In the original German it reads: „*Verstehen ist das existenziale Sein des eigenen Seinkönnens des Daseins selbst, so zwar, daß dieses Sein an ihm selbst das Woran des mit ihm selbst Seins erschließt*". Heidegger, *Sein Und Zeit*, 144.

is understanding which allows these relationships to exist (and we must remember that our existence *is* inevitably relational). In Wrathall's words,

> the function of understanding, then, is (a) to disclose "in advance"—that is, before we engage in any particular concrete activities—the relations that constitute entities as the entities that they are and (b) to place us "within" contexts of relationships "with familiarity"—that is, to enable us to know our way around the world, to find it intelligible or understandable. The structure that allows understanding to perform this function, Heidegger claims, is "projecting onto possibilities"[52].

Before moving on to the next *existentiale*, we will review one final aspect of understanding, namely, its interpretative character (even though we will deepen on this subject when revising Gadamer's thought). Heidegger's reflections concerning understanding showed us that existing in human form entails projecting oneself into possibilities of existential execution. We are always projecting ourselves as a "Being-possible" with respect to people, things and ourselves. When we understand, the existential possibilities available to us become explicit, they come into presence. The entity to which one is projecting comes to presence "as something". Therefore, to understand

> is to be in the world in such a way that everything is projected upon, that is, makes sense in terms of, particular possibilities. Projecting is not necessarily a cognitive act but a stance or orientation to things around us (which may, of course, involve cognition). In order to inhabit this understanding, however, I must develop it and appropriate it by acting on the basis of it. Interpretation is the appropriation of the understanding, and it is a pervasive, ongoing activity[53].

That is, when we understand and entity, we interpret (*auslegen*) it, we bring it into presence, "as something". This means that we highlight an existential possibility of it, making it explicit, putting it out and exposing it. For example, a pen opens multiple possibilities for being brought into presence. It can be interpreted as an object with which I can write

52 Wrathall, "Heidegger on Human Understanding," 189.
53 Wrathall, 182.

or draw, as a toy for relieving anxiety, as a tool for performing an improvised tracheotomy (if I have learned this medical skill sufficiently) or even as an object that is useful for performing a basic illusion (moving it up and down so it looks like it bends). The manner the pen will come to surface depends on how I, the *Dasein* which is relating to it through understanding, interpret it. However, and as we already explained in *supra*, not everything is possible[54]. The same pen, for example, cannot be understood as an entity with which a human being can be fed, because the pen itself does not allow that possibility to be brought into presence. I can bring into presence only the possibilities that the intermundane entity, in this case the pen, present to me.

In sum, understanding as an *existentiale*, which has an interpreting character, implies that we human beings have an active role in the configuration of entities (at least to some extent). When we understand an object, another *Dasein* or me *as something*, we project ourselves and bring into presence (actualize) a possibility which that phenomenon opens (provides).

The *Dasein*, according to Heidegger's argument, is also historical. Historicality is inherent to the *Dasein* to such an extent that it cannot be removed or suppressed, not even in a purely theoretical sense, without erasing the essence of the *Dasein* itself. In other words, historicality, as

---

54 Thomson explains it in the following manner: "We then have to project ourselves into this ontological phenomenon in order to be able to understand (in the 'fulfilling enactment') how it actually conditions the ontic phenomenon. By providing a bridge from the ontic to the ontological in this way, formal indication allows Heidegger to present an ontological interpretation that is not simply arbitrary or idiosyncratic. On the contrary, Heidegger's ontological interpretations may be judged compelling only insofar as we too can experience and so recognize and personally attest that the more basic but previously unnoticed ontological phenomenon Heidegger describes does indeed condition our own experience of the everyday ontic phenomenon with which we are all familiar and from which the formal features of the more fundamental ontological phenomenon are first drawn". Iain Thomson, "Death and Demise in Being and Time," in *The Cambridge Companion to Heidegger's "Being and Time,"* ed. Mark A. Wrathall, Cambridge Companions to Philosophy (Cambridge: Cambridge University Press, 2013), 276.

an aspect of temporality, is also considered an *existentiale*. To comprehend this ontological characteristic of the *Dasein*, we must delve into two concepts we've previously mentioned: temporality and historicality. We will being with temporality.

According to Heidegger, temporality (*Zeitlichkeit*) is also an *existentiale*. By this concept, he doesn't just mean that human beings are affected by time, but that we *are time*. As Crowell puts it, "Dasein is radically temporal—not merely in time, as are all things, but rather 'temporalizing' already in a world but always ahead of itself, pressing into possibilities"[55]. Differently put, being a *Dasein* is inherently linked to the nature of time. We don't exist within time; rather, we exist as time itself. We tend to overlook this fact and conceptualize time differently. We often mentally construct time as something separate from ourselves, as something objective and linear. However, according to Heidegger, this is a misconception because

> neither the way time is conceived in our ordinary experience of it, nor the problematic which arises from this experience, can function without examination as a criterion for the appropriateness of an interpretation of time. Rather, we must, in our investigation, make ourselves familiar *beforehand* with the primordial phenomenon of temporality, so that *in terms of this* we may cast light on the necessity, the source, and the reason for the dominion of the way it is ordinarily understood[56].

---

55 Steven Galt Crowell, *Husserl, Heidegger, and the Space of Meaning: Paths toward Transcendental Phenomenology*, Northwestern University Studies in Phenomenology and Existential Philosophy (Evanston: Northwestern University Press, 2001), 211.

56 Heidegger, *Being and Time*, 352. In the original German it reads: „Der Zeitbegriff der vulgären Zeiterfahrung und die ihr entwachsende Problematik können deshalb nicht unbesehen als Kriterien der Angemessenheit einer Zeitinterpretation fungieren. Vielmehr muß die Untersuchung sich vorgängig mit dem ursprünglichen Phänomen der Zeitlichkeit vertraut machen, um erst aus ihm die Notwendigkeit und die Art des Ursprungs des vulgären Zeitverständnisses und ebenso den Grund seiner Herrschaft aufzuhellen". Heidegger, *Sein Und Zeit*, 304.

That is, Heidegger argues that neither the mental elaborations that we have made of time nor the information that we can gather from our experience of it allows us to unveil the nature or characteristics of this phenomenon. Through his analysis, the philosopher from Freiburg aims to specify, as much as humanly possible, what time is without relying solely on the experiences of it that we human beings have. Now, this topic—that of temporality—is one that is profoundly discussed by Heideggerians, and understandably so, as it is one of the most complicated themes this philosopher analyzes. In our review of the topic, however, we will not delve deeply into the Heideggerian elaboration of this phenomenon, given the instrumental nature of this chapter. Instead, we will focus on highlighting some main points that the German philosopher clarifies in *Being and Time*.

When we think of time, we often conceive it as flowing from the past to the present and into the future, extending infinitely in a linear fashion. Yet, Heidegger argues that our actual experience of time is intimately connected to the concept of *care*. When we project ourselves in time, we do it while thinking that we want to *do* something or *become* someone. The concept of care, therefore,

> refers to the way in which we are always oriented toward concrete future possibilities; we understand both ourselves and the things we encounter in terms of possibilities. This is not an explicit, cognitive accomplishment, a matter of "comporting oneself towards a plan that has been thought out", but something that is implicated even in routine and unthinking encounters[57].

That is, we experience time as possibilities that we hope will be actualized in our lives. For example, while I am writing this book, I am at the same time thinking of its possible failure in sales, or maybe of the many successes that will come after it is published, or even of what I am going to have for lunch after a productive morning of writing. We live ahead of ourselves, and it is time that allows this to happen.

57 Matthew Ratcliffe, "Why Mood Matters," in *The Cambridge Companion to Heidegger's "Being and Time,"* ed. Mark A. Wrathall, Cambridge Companions to Philosophy (Cambridge: Cambridge University Press, 2013), 161.

Therefore, we, as human beings, think of the past, present and future at once. They are all jumbled up in human experience. We project possibilities to the future that may never come or ruminate over what might have been if we had done things differently in the past in a non-successive manner. Time, then, is essentially subjective (in the sense that *we are time*) and does not operate the way we usually think it does. Moreover, the possibilities we project to the future exist prior to linear time. This means that we experience the possibilities we project to the future or past in our mind as present and real (and that is what we mean when we say it is subjective).

Another way of explaining it is as follows: we usually have, in our pre-scientific or natural perception of reality, the idea that time has a lineal structure. That is, we think that the past comes before the present and the future after the latter. Heidegger, argues, however, that this is an illusion (at least to some extent). That which exists is only the present[58]. The past is a tool through which I define myself and the world in the present. It is "that aspect of the unified non-self-coincidence that grounds my being poised to deal with every situation I encounter and to project into possibilities"[59]. From the past we get an image (concept) of ourselves and the world which allows us to anticipate the possibilities that may unfold in the future and project the actions that we should take for one of those possibilities to actually manifest itself. The future, then,

> is not a "now" which has not yet become "actual" and which sometime will be for the first time. Instead, the future is the impulse or movement of coming (*Kunft*), of self-realization, for a being that does not simply and purely coincide with itself. Anticipation is the authentically futural being of Dasein, for in anticipation we have recognized our ownmost ability to be, and we project ourselves upon it[60].

---

58 We do not ordinarily are conscious of this. We feel that the past is a "now that is gone", and the future is something like a "now to come". That is why "it is important not to think of this temporality in the way we ordinarily think of time — namely, as a procession of now moment". Wrathall and Murphey, "An Overview of Being and Time," 33.

59 Wrathall and Murphey, 34.

60 Wrathall and Murphey, 33.

Yet, all this process, the synthesis of past-future so to speak, takes place in the present. As Heidegger points out, "[t]emporalizing does not signify that ecstases come in a 'succession'. The future is *not later* than having been, and having been is *not earlier* than the Present. Temporality temporalizes itself as a future which makes present in a process of having been"[61]. That is, human mind does not experience time as a succession of "nows" but rather moves chaotically from past (through remembering) to future (planning or anxiously projecting possible events). Even if I am remembering something that transpired 10 years ago, I experience it in my mind as a present event (and the same goes for the future). Time, then, and temporality (*Zeitlichkeit*) as an *existentiale* is responsible for the unity of *Dasein*. Temporality "assures the unity of the world [. . .] because it pre-structures the different temporal ectases in such a way that they depend on each other"[62]. It is time, considered as a phenomenon through which we project possibilities, that makes human experience cohesive. Human experience is encapsulated in time. Therefore, time is a fundamental and originary structure that allows human experience to transpire.

Heidegger's thematization of time brings up the question concerning historicality. In his words: "*[I]n analyzing the historicality of Dasein we shall try to show that this entity is not 'temporal' because it 'stands in history', but that, on the contrary, it exists historically and can so exist only because it is temporal in the very basis of its Being*"[63]. In other words, the fact that the *Dasein* is temporal entails that it is also historical. By this he does not mean that its existence (that of the

61 Heidegger, *Being and Time*, 401. In the original German it reads: „Die Zeitigung bedeutet kein «Nacheinander» der Ekstasen. Die Zukunft ist nicht später als die Gewesenheit und diese nicht früher als die Gegenwart. Zeitlichkeit zeitigt sich als gewesendegegenwärtigende Zukunft". Heidegger, *Sein Und Zeit*, 350.

62 Wrathall and Murphey, "An Overview of Being and Time," 43.

63 Heidegger, *Being and Time*, 428. In the original German it reads: „*Die Analyse der Geschichtlichkeit des Daseins versucht zu zeigen, daß dieses Seiende nicht »zeitlich« ist, weil es »in der Geschichte steht«, sondern daß es umgekehrt geschichtlich nur existiert und existieren kann, weil es im Grunde seines Seins zeitlich ist*". Heidegger, *Sein Und Zeit*, 376.

Dasein) takes place in a particular moment in history, but that *Dasein* embodies history on an ontological dimension. Differently put, "Heidegger argues that the historical unity of the Dasein is not a mere sum of actual experiences, nor even a framework that contains various experiences. Rather, Dasein at each moment carries it past (thrownness) and future (death)"[64]. To avoid confusion, Heidegger distinguishes between "history" (*Gesichte*) and *historie.* By the first, he means historicality as an ontological structure of the *Dasein*, and with *historie* he aims at history as the study of a succession of events that unfolded in the past. *Historie*, argues Heidegger, supposes historicality.

Historicality, argues Heidegger, is an ontological characteristic of the *Dasein* through which history, and therefore tradition, actualize themselves in the present moment. We usually consider that history is preoccupied with events that transpired in the past and, therefore, that there is nothing actual and present about that field of study (other than maybe some descendant or material object that was preserved from that past time). Heidegger argues, however, that the description just given is reductionist. History lives through us (human beings) in every act, thought, and interpretation we engage in. For example, when I wake up and go to my kitchen to make coffee for myself and my wife, history comes to life through this mundane interaction. Concepts such as coffee, cup, kitchen, and marriage unconsciously guide my actions. But where did I get these concepts? They originated at some point in history when coffee became consumable for humans, when the use of cups for drinking was established, and when marriage was institutionalized. These ideas and concepts have been transmitted through generations until they reached me. Historians can pinpoint the time and place of their emergence, but they also come to life, even if we are not consciously aware of it, in our everyday lives. This phenomenon, the "coming to life" of history, is what Heidegger refers to as "historicality"[65].

---

64 Wrathall and Murphey, "An Overview of Being and Time," 44.

65 Another useful example is that of the hammer that Heidegger uses in *Being and Time*. Wrathall explains it in the following manner: "The field of possibilities for being a hammer has developed through history by human agents engaging in the practice of carpentry. If one picks up a hammer to discover that it is made

Another *existentiale* which is fundamental for the structure of human understanding is language. According to Heidegger, the thematization and examination of language has been insufficient because most inquiries into this phenomenon have remained at the ontic level and have not explored its ontological character. In his words,

> [a]ttempts to grasp the "essence" of language have always taken their orientation from one or another of these [ontical] items; and the clues to their conceptions of language have been the ideas of "expression", of "symbolic form", of communication as "assertion", of the "making known" of experiences of the "patterning" of life. Even if one were to put these various fragmentary definitions together in syncretistic fashion, nothing would be achieved in the way of a fully adequate definition of "language". We would still have to do what is decisive here to work out in advance the ontologico-existential whole of the structure of discourse on the basis of the analytic of Dasein[66].

Simply put, the attempts to conceptualize the linguistic phenomenon have been unsuccessful, because they have considered its function in an almost mechanical manner (leaving aside its ontological character).

---

of butter, one has been taken in. It is a gimmick, or maybe a work of art. The «hammer» is I outing the functional standards that make hammers what they are, and so could not be a real hammer. Those who understand carpentry, and so make sense of hammers as hammers, appreciate this fake hammer for what it is, and would insist on its unreality if challenged. To be a real or actual hammer, after all, is to accord with certain ontological, in this case, functional, standards". Joseph K. Schear, "Historical Finitude," in *The Cambridge Companion to Heidegger's "Being and Time,"* ed. Mark A. Wrathall, Cambridge Companions to Philosophy (Cambridge: Cambridge University Press, 2013), 362.

66 Heidegger, *Being and Time*, 206. In the original German it reads: „Die Versuche, das »Wesen der Sprache« zu fassen, haben denn immer auch die Orientierung an einem einzelnen dieser Momente genommen und die Sprache begriffen am Leitfaden der Idee des »Ausdrucks«, der »symbolischen Form«, der Mitteilung als »Aussage«, der »Kundgabe« von Erlebnissen oder der »Gestaltung« des Lebens. Für eine voll zureichende Definition der Sprache wäre aber auch nichts gewonnen, wollte man diese verschiedenen Bestimmungsstücke synkretistisch zusammenschieben. Das Entscheidende bleibt, zuvor das ontologisch-existenziale Ganze der Struktur der Rede auf dem Grunde der Analytik des Daseins herauszuarbeiten". Heidegger, *Sein Und Zeit*, 163.

Language is often characterized as an input-output process. In this view, the sender introduces a series of symbols into the world, and the receiver "picks them up" and understands them precisely as the sender intended (assuming, of course, that the sender used the symbols correctly). For Heidegger this kind of description is reductionist since it disregards the fact that when I communicate with others, I am with other Dasein's (*mit Dasein*), I share a *world* (significations) with them. In the context of Greek philosophy, Heidegger explains, language is conceptualized as *logos,* indicating that the foundation of language is discourse. Originally, in Greek, *logos* simply meant "to talk". For Heidegger, language understood as *logos* is something like a vessel through which discourse manifests itself (and it is nothing else than a totality of words). In the words of Ratcliffe, "discourse, for Heidegger, is not spoken language but a condition of possibility for spoken language, the coalescing of a world into structured patterns that are amenable to linguistic expression"[67]. In other words, language is the existential manner through which our discourse comes into being. Therefore, the concept of language is founded on the idea of our engagement with others in conversation. Language would be pointless if it were not used to involve (and disclose) oneself with others and the world.

Building upon this understanding of language as an existential tool for engagement, we can further explore its implications. Language enables us to articulate that which is understandable (intelligible), to appropriate or bring intro presence the network of interwoven significations that constitute the world. This idea gains clarity if we reflect on the following thought from Heidegger:

> It requires a very artificial and complicated frame of mind to "hear" a "pure noise". The fact that motor-cycles and wagons are what we proximally hear is the phenomenal evidence that in every case Dasein, as Being-in-the-world, already dwells *alongside* what is ready-to-hand within-the-world; it certainly does not dwell proximally alongside "sensations"; nor would it first have to give shape to the swirl of sensations to provide the springboard from which the subject leaps

67 Ratcliffe, "Why Mood Matters," 162.

> off and finally arrives at a "world". Dasein, as essentially understanding, is proximally alongside what is understood[68].

Differently put, we do not hear raw sound; instead, we hear significations of beings that are with us in the world. That means that we do not merely receive the impression that something has affected our senses, and then ascribe a meaning to it after subsuming it in under a pre-existing concept stored in our mind. We hear things that are familiar to us. We listen to things that have meaning, not just *pure sound.* For Heidegger listening is a way of making ourselves available to the meaning of the sounds, of unveiling the world.

Discourse, therefore, enables us to disclose or unveil the various possibilities (meanings) presented by the world. This suggests that the ontological character of language emerges *with* others, in our relation *to* the world (and it is in this context that the first Heidegger posits the world as an interwoven network of shared significations). Furthermore,

> understanding has already received a thorough-going conceptual-linguistic articulation that we inherit by being raised in an historical linguistic community that has been engaged in an ongoing process of interpretation. Our every encounter with the world is thus mediated by an interpretation that takes the form of either conversation or textual transmission of the historical tradition[69].

Again, this implies that our existence—that of the *Dasein*—is not one of isolation, but rather a relational one. This means that when we are understanding an intermundane entity *as something*, we are disclosing it in a specific manner. We are interpreting it and, thus, bringing one

---

68 Heidegger, *Being and Time*, 207. In the original German it reads: "Es bedarf schon einer sehr künstlichen und komplizierten Einstellung, um ein »reines Geräusch« zu »hören«. Daß wir aber zunächst Motorräder und Wagen hören, ist der phänomenale Beleg dafür, daß das Dasein als In-der-Welt-sein je schon beim innerweltlich Zuhandenen sich aufhält und zunächst gar nicht bei »Empfindungen«, deren Gewühl zuerst geformt werden müßte, um das Sprungbrett abzugeben, von dem das Subjekt abspringt, um schließlich zu einer »Welt« zu gelangen. Das Dasein ist als wesenhaft verstehendes zunächst beim Verstandenen". Heidegger, *Sein Und Zeit*, 207.

69 Wrathall, "Heidegger on Human Understanding," 183.

of its possibilities into presence. In this context, language serves not merely as a tool for description or communication of ideas and feelings but as a means through which I relate to and ascribe meaning to the world. Language, considered as the vessel through which discourse is manifested, enables us to engage in these relations through the disclosure of intermundane entities, ourselves and other *Dasein's as* something. It allows us to unveil the possibilities presented by the world, and this unveiling *is* the means through which we relate to otherness[70].

Finally, Heidegger also argues that discourse (which manifests in the form of language) is equiprimordial with understanding. This indicates that there is no hierarchical relationship between these two existential structures; they are equally integral to *Dasein's* existence. That is why in *Being and Time* Heidegger states that "only where talking and hearing are existentially possible, can anyone hearken"[71]. While this clearly references the existential equiprimordiality of understanding and discourse, since it emphasizes the fact that understanding presupposes a discourse that is being comprehended, it is impressive that it easily resonates with our everyday experiences. For instance, if someone attends a conference on a topic they know nothing about, comprehending the speaker's words becomes almost impossible. To understand something, one requires a set of pre-existing concepts, a *foresight* of the topic, which enables them to grasp what is being explained. Without this prior understanding, they might hear what the lecturer says but fail to listen to it, to comprehend the meaning of the words.

70 It must be noted, however, that language is not the only manner through which understanding can operate. As the same Heidegger explains in his later works, there are some phenomena, such as beauty in art and prelinguistic experiences, which cannot be fully conceptualized through language, and therefore must be understood in other ways. See: Martin Heidegger, *Nietzsche*, ed. David Farrell, trans. Joan Stambaugh, David Farrell, and Frank A. Capuzzi, vol. III, IV vols. (New York: HarperCollins, 1991).

71 Heidegger, *Being and Time*, 207. In the original German it reads: „Nur wo die existenziale Möglichkeit von Reden und Hören gegeben ist, kann jemand horchen". Heidegger, *Sein Und Zeit*, 164.

In sum, language, considered as the vessel through which discourse manifests itself in the world, equips us with a set of concepts and ideas (acquired through tradition) that enable us to understand—*relate to*— ourselves and the world. It is, therefore, the essential cornerstone that underpins the very possibility of human experience and understanding.

b. *Thematization of the characteristics of the subject of understanding: some conclusions regarding Heidegger's theory of understanding*

We started by suggesting that Heidegger's philosophy could be interpreted as a theory of understanding, excelling in this regard. Now, after a brief analysis, we can understand why. Heidegger focuses on the ideal pole of existence, the real pole, and the subject that articulates an unifies both. That is, although for pedagogical reasons we might distinguish between facticity, ideality, and human beings in Heidegger's thought, he emphatically stresses that these are facets of a singular phenomenon. Their nature is so intrinsically relational that none can exist without the others.

It is worth noticing that, at least in *Being and Time,* Heidegger primarily directs his efforts towards elucidating the fundamental structures inherent in the *Dasein.* In other words, while he frequently references facticity, it is the *Dasein* that takes center stage in his exploration. His focus is not so much on how the existential ontological structures of the *Dasein* manifest concretely (even though his analysis begins with the inescapably ontic nature of *everydayness*). About this particular focus, Heidegger explicitly affirms that his philosophy does not aim to delve deeply into the concrete manifestation of the *Dasein's* existential ontological structures. In his words:

> The question of Being aims therefore at ascertaining the *a priori* conditions not only for the possibility of the science which examines entities as entities of such and such type, and, in so doing, already operate with an understanding of Being, but also for the possibility of those ontologies

themselves which are prior to the ontical science and which provide their foundation[72].

In other words, Heidegger's interest does not lie in specific concrete phenomena, nor in the characteristics of the science that studies these phenomena. Rather, he seeks to clarify and make transparent the conditions that make a science, and its understanding of a phenomenon, possible.

We believe it useful keeping this perspective in mind at this juncture, since in the following section we will see how another philosopher, Hans-Georg Gadamer, also develops a well-articulated theory of understanding, but placing greater emphasis on concrete manifestations through which the ontological characters of the *Dasein* come to light. Gadamer, building on Heideggerian concepts, begins with tangible phenomena like art and the written word, and then moves on to identify ontological characteristics and structures revealed through their analysis. In this context, we will examine how Gadamer's approach, which interprets the ontological through the lens of the ontic and vice versa, positions the legal phenomenon as an ideal subject for exploring human understanding, a theme that will become fundamental when reviewing Schmitt's thought.

c. *Gadamer's ontology of the* Dasein *from the concrete: art, law and language*

As we saw with Heidegger, the world is a plexus of references, and understanding, as interpreting, is an "opening" to the world's references. The projection of possibilities of understanding is the "place"

72 Heidegger, *Being and Time*, 31. In the original German: „Die Seinsfrage zielt daher auf eine apriorische Bedingung der Möglichkeit nicht nur der Wissenschaften, die Seiendes als so und so Seiendes durchforschen und sich dabei je schon in einem Seinsverständnis bewegen, sondern auf die Bedingung der Möglichkeit der vor den ontischen Wissenschaften liegenden und sie fundierenden Ontologien selbst". Heidegger, *Sein Und Zeit*, 31.

from which the references of the world are unveiled. Understanding, as interpreting, opens these possibilities and exposes them, making them present. Like Heidegger, Gadamer argues that the structure of the *Dasein* is that of being-in-the-world. However, Gadamer approaches the problem of the ontological structure of human existence from another angle: through art and the written word. The reason for this is that "he loved poetry, literature, and the arts, disciplines he believed conveyed important truths about the human condition but were sidelined by the reigning scientific method as mere unscientific sources of opinion"[73].

Hans-Georg Gadamer is a philosopher situated within the hermeneutical tradition, a line of thought that places strong emphasis on the art of interpretation. Consequently, it is not surprising that Heidegger's hermeneutical exploration of the *Dasein* piqued Gadamer's interest[74]. As Zimmermann explains, "Heidegger's fundamental move from a self-contained consciousness that encounters a world of objects to learn their meaning, to a consciousness already immersed in a meaningful world for whom understanding is 'a way of being', provides the foundation of Gadamer's hermeneutic philosophy and his works"[75]. Nonetheless, Gadamer takes a different approach than the one pursued by the philosopher from Freiburg. As mentioned earlier, this author begins his explorations by analyzing the aesthetic experience and the written word (i.e. legal and theological texts), and then proceeds to uncover the ontological characteristics that can be discerned through their

73 Jens Zimmermann, "Gadamer's Century: Life, Times and Works," in *The Gadamerian Mind*, ed. Theodore D George and Gert-Jan van der Heiden (New York & London: Routledge, 2021), 13.

74 Concerning Gadamer's intellectual formation, George and van der Heiden comments: "During his university studies, Gadamer had the good fortune to encounter a number of remarkable teachers and mentors. At the University of Marburg, for example, in philosophy Gadamer was influenced by renowned Neo- Kantians, such as Nicola Hartmann and Paul Natorp (Gadamer wrote his dissertation under the latter). No philosopher had a greater influence on Gadamer, though, than Martin Heidegger". Theodore D George and Gert-Jan van der Heiden, "Introduction," in *The Gadamerian Mind*, eds. Theodore D George and Gert-Jan van der Heiden (New York & London: Routledge, 2021), 2.

75 Zimmermann, "Gadamer's Century: Life, Times and Works," 13.

thematization and analysis. Gadamer's unique approach leads him to prioritize dialogue and posit it as *the* fundamental method for unraveling the enigmas of being[76]. Play, literature, the interpretation of sacred texts or the law (statutes), and the contemplation of beauty, Gadamer argues, though merely specific forms of dialogue with *otherness*, enables us to grasp the structure of the relational nature on the *Dasein*. Since our attention will be directed towards Schmitt's discussion of law (statutes) and its interpretation in the following sections of this work, we will now briefly explore Gadamer's insights regarding this particular form of dialogue[77].

First and foremost, it's worth mentioning that Gadamer, like Heidegger, critiques the conventional understanding of language. He asserts that

> It is obvious that instrumentalist theory of signs which sees words and concepts as handy tools has missed the point of the hermeneutical phenomenon [. . .]. The capacity to use familiar words is not based on an act of logical subsumption, through which a particular is placed under a universal concept. Let us remember, rather, that understanding always includes an element of application and thus produces an ongoing process of concept formation[78].

---

76 Zimmermann explains that most of Gadamer's deviation from Heidegger's thought are severely influenced by Plato. In his words, "Gadamer's love for dialogue that he acquired from Plato also accounts for another distinct difference from Heidegger, namely the importance of inter-personal dialogue, that is, the significance of another concrete interlocutor to whom one must listen" Zimmermann, 15.

77 To delve deeper into Hans-Georg Gadamer's thought, the following texts are highly recommended: Dieter Henrich, *Hans Georg Gadamer: Splitter eines Gedenkens* (Warmbronn: U. Keicher, 2008). Jean Grondin, *Hans-Georg Gadamer: A Biography.* (New Haven: Yale University Press, 2011). Jean Grondin, *Introduction to Philosophical Hermeneutics* (New Haven: Yale University Press, 1997). Darren Walhof, *The Democratic Theory of Hans-Georg Gadamer* (Cham: Springer, 2018).

78 Hans-Georg Gadamer, *Truth and Method* (London & New York: Bloomsbury, 2013), 421.

That is, language should not be conceived as a collection of pre-given concepts that align perfectly with reality, leading to understand that the procedure through which we use them is merely one of subsumption (we "fit" particular cases under predefined rules). It would be naïve and overly simplistic to assume that when my intuition perceives something as red, round, sweet that comes from a tree, my cognitive process immediately seeks the concept "apple" from a "cabinet of concepts" and then applies it to that which my intuition is presenting. On the contrary, Gadamer argues that understanding always implies application (that we will see is not the same as subsumption), which entails at least two things: there must be someone who applies these concepts (1), and the process is not merely mechanical, but involves mutual feedback between the rules (concepts) and the particular cases to which they are to be applied (2)[79].

Understanding the written word is paradigmatic in this regard, argues Gadamer, for it needs someone to read and interpret a text for it to come to life. This is especially true in the case of theological and legal texts, as they are intended to have a practical effect on reality, such as bringing justice or salvation. The problem, Gadamer argues, is that we are naïve and commonly believe that when we read something, we are empty vessels merely receiving information. Gadamer presents a different scenario, one which seeks to unravel the mysteries of human understanding through and adequate approach to the understanding of written word.

In *Truth and Method* Gadamer claims that

> The interpreter does not know that he's bringing himself and his own concepts into the interpretation. The verbal formulation is so much part of the interpreter's

79 In this sense, Günter Figal, "The Doing of the Thing Itself: Gadamer's Hermeneutic Ontology of Language," in *The Cambridge Companion to Gadamer*, ed. Robert J Dostal (Cambridge: Cambridge University Press, 2006), 102–25. Whitney Mannies, *Inheriting Gadamer: New Directions in Philosophical Hermeneutics*, ed. Georgia Warnke (Edinburgh: Edinburgh University Press, 2016). Richard Rorty, *Gadamer's Repercussions: Reconsidering Philosophical Hermeneutics*, ed. Bruce Krajewski (Berkeley: University of California Press, 2004).

> mind that he never becomes aware of it as an object. Thus it is understandable that this side of the hermeneutic process has been wholly ignored[80].

In essence, the German philologist highlights that in every act of understanding, the agent of said understanding brings itself, along with all the conscious and unconscious concepts than inhabit its mind, to the very act of understanding. Grondin puts it in the following manner:

> The basic idea is plain: when we understand, a text speaks to us and when we understand it, we also make it speak. A fusion of horizons occurs here because two partners are involved in this encounter, to the point of being fused into one another: the text and the interpreter. Both "speak"—the text speaks and the interpreter makes it speak—yet are fused into one another, since one cannot distinguish here the horizon of the text from that of the one who makes it speak[81].

That means that even though there is something *out there* that is grasped by our intuition (in this case, a text) that has a meaning of its own, that which is apprehended by our mind *from* reality—the mental image that is presented to it— is inevitably "altered" *by* the specific characteristics of the agent who carries out the act of understanding. In other words, the interpreter is a relevant factor to take into account when thematizing and discussing how human understanding operates. The question that arises naturally from what we have just explained is the following: what does Gadamer mean when he says that the interpreter brings himself and his concepts into the interpretation? What does he bring? In order to elucidate this matter as clearly as possible, Gadamer incorporates the concept "horizon of meaning" in his philosophy.

The concept "horizon of meaning" can be explained as follows: in every act of understanding, which is inevitably mediated by language (as we already saw with Heidegger)[82], the subject carries with him what

---

80 Gadamer, *Truth and Method*, 421.

81 Jean Grondin, "The Universality of Hermeneutic Understanding. The Strong, Somewhat Metaphysical Conclusion of Truth and Method," in *The Gadamerian Mind*, ed. Theodore D George and Gert-Jan van der Heiden (New York & London: Routledge, 2022), 27.

82 As Grondin explains, "Gadamer's basic idea here is that understanding occurs, always occurs, through what he likes to call the «medium» of language. To

Gadamer calls his "horizon of meaning". By this, he means that all the ontological structures, which are conditions of possibility of human knowledge (referred to as the *existentiale* by Heidegger), and the cultural, historical, linguistic, and family context in which the particular subject evolves throughout his life, form something like glasses (which cannot be removed) that "distort" everything that is object of said understanding— including the subject himself when he practices self-awareness. It is understandable, then, that a core issue in Gadamerian hermeneutics is the idea that it is not correct to pose the epistemological paradigm in terms of a dialectic between individual subjectivity and the objectivity of what it is intended to be known. To present understanding under this scheme, argues the German philologist, implies that we are starting from the basis of a false antithesis that can never be resolved[83].

The fact that the agent of understanding actively contributes to the meaning that texts acquire raises the question of whether this should be considered as something negative that needs to be avoided. In other words, does Gadamer's realization of the role that our horizon of meaning plays in understanding strives for the implementation of techniques for this not to occur? The answer is negative. Even though Gadamer recognizes that some skepticism and distance concerning our own horizon of meaning is healthy in hermeneutics (especially historical distance), he also acknowledges that this—the horizon or paradigm from which we apprehend reality—is not something we can get rid of. As Schmidt explains, for Gadamer

> understanding or interpretive experience begins with these inherited prejudices within the hermeneutic circle and proceeds towards completion. Human beings exist within history. Each particular consciousness has been effected by history through inheriting a set of prejudices and so is a historically effected consciousness[84].

---

understand is to put something into words and to seek to understand is to search for words, for the right words". Grondin, 26.

83 Gadamer, *Truth and Method*, 321. We will come back to this subject when analyzing Schmitt's thought.

84 Lawrence K. Schmidt, "Experience," in *The Gadamerian Mind*, eds. Theodore D George and Gert-Jan van der Heiden (Routledge, 2021), 105.

In other words, prejudices (previous judgments), which are located in our horizon of meaning, are a condition that makes understanding possible[85]. And what about the precious objectivity that is tirelessly sought by science? Gadamer's answer is simple and direct: it is merely a prejudice among many others[86]. The idea that the eradication of the interference of human subjectivity in knowledge is equivalent to progress, which is present in the core of modern thought, is a prejudice after all. In the words of Gadamer, "there is one prejudice of the Enlightenment that defines its essence: the fundamental prejudice of the Enlightenment is the prejudice against prejudice itself, which denies tradition its power"[87]—although this does not mean that this prejudice has no legitimacy at all. This topic, that of the prejudice of enlightenment, will be an aspect in Schmitt's philosophy which we will carefully scrutinize, so we'll leave the topic here for the time being[88].

Before delving into Gadamer's exploration of law and its exemplary nature, it is essential to address a complex question: does Gadamer's acknowledgment of the influence of the horizon of meaning label him as a relativist?[89] While we have previously explored this

85 Gadamer, *Truth and Method,* 261.

86 For more information on Gadamer and the problem of objectivity, see: Günter Figal, *Objectivity: The Hermeneutical and Philosophy.* (Albany: State University of New York Press, 2011). Morton Thaning, *The Problem of Objectivity in Gadamer's Hermeneutics in Light of McDowell's Empiricism* (Cham: Springer, 2015).

87 Gadamer, *Truth and Method*, 283.

88 For those readers seeking further insight, we recommend Zimmermann's work. He grapples with this issue by arguing that: "Understanding is the fusion of horizons. It begins with the translation of the horizon of the text into one's expanding horizon. In the work of art, one is taken up into the world of the work in the sense that one projects a horizon of meaning in experiencing the work. As the ideality of the word permits this translating of the text into one's horizon of meaning, in art the increase in being of the work permits this translation. It is as if one were brought into a conversation with the work of art, which is able then to express its knowledge to us". Zimmermann, "Gadamer's Century: Life, Times and Works," 21.

89 There have been some, as Krämer, who have argued that the natural conclusion to Gadamer's philosophy is relativism. Others, as Habermas and Grondin, argue that Gadamer's philosophy has a universal and metaphysical character that does

topic elsewhere[90], we will provide a summary of the key points of this discussion:

1. The idea that a "world" cannot be conceived as independent of the being that inhabits it leads to the conclusion, at least according to Gadamer, that the prejudices of the knowing subject are projected onto the world. In this sense, there would be no possibility of "cleansing" the lens of the knower to obtain a purified version of the world, one that is free from distortions.

2. Does the fact that all knowledge is relative to man imply that we are dealing with a relativistic conception of knowledge? According to Gadamer, the answer is negative. This author is of the opinion that stating that knowledge is relative to the *Dasein* is not the same as saying that it depends on the will or caprice of the subject. In Gadamer's words, "the fact is that meanings represent a fluid multiplicity of possibilities (in comparison to the agreement presented by language and a vocabulary), but within this multiplicity of what can be thought i.e., of what a reader can find meaningful and hence expect to find not everything is possible"[91].

3. That is, reality cannot be stretched beyond its inherent possibilities through interpretive efforts. To give an example, while it is possible, and often the case, that someone who reads Antoine de Saint-Exupéry's *The Little Prince* multiple times may discover new meanings with each reading, they will never be able to convince themselves that they are actually reading Miguel de Cervantes's *Don Quixote*, no matter how deeply immersed they are in Cervantes's text.

---

not allow the discussion of relativism to be treated in a simplistic manner (as is often the case). See: Hans Krämer, *Kritik der Hermeneutik Interpretationsphilosophie und Realismus* (München: Beck, 2007). Jürgen Habermas, "The Hermeneutic Claim to Universality," in *Contemporary Hermeneutics: Hermeneutics as Method, Philosophy and Critique*, ed. Joseph Bleicher (London: Routledge & Kegan, 1980), 181–211. Jean Grondin, "The Metaphysical Dimension of Hermeneutics," in *Hermeneutics and Phenomenology Figures and Themes*, ed. Saulius Geniusas and Paul Fairfield (London: Bloomsbury, 2020), 125–37.

90 Pérez-Lasserre, Diego. "Gadamer y la hermenéutica jurídica: ¿un insumo útil?" Vniversitas 68, no. 138 (2019). Pérez-Lasserre, Diego. "El 'Otro Juez' y La Hermenéutica: El Ficcionalismo Como Criterio Legitimador de La Decisión Jurídica." Revista Chilena de Derecho 45, no. 2 (2018): 363–80.

91 Gadamer, *Truth and Method*, 281.

4. In sum, we, as humans, are beings who perceive the world from our own relative horizons. However, we direct our understanding toward a common truth, which can be unveiled through various viewpoints. That is why engaging in dialogue, in an existential sense, is essential for us to expand our horizons and deepen our collective understanding. This form of dialogue represents not just a conversation, but a subjective disposition characterized by its *openness* to the horizon of the "other". This "other" may be a person, a text, a tradition, art, nature, death, or any other entity and phenomenon. In the end, this approach to dialogue is beyond being just a method; it's a mode of being deeply rooted in the relational nature of the *Dasein.*

In fact, in *Truth and Method*, Gadamer articulates his stance on relativism by stating that

> If we examine the situation more closely, however, we find that meanings cannot be understood in an arbitrary way. Just as we cannot continually misunderstand the use of a word without its affecting the meaning of the whole, so we cannot stick blindly to our own fore-meaning about the thing if we want to understand the meaning of another[92].

Furthermore, Gadamer goes beyond simply claiming the finitude of human knowledge. His aim is not just to deny the charge of relativism, but to undermine the very foundations upon which relativism rests. The argument he formulates to achieve this is more or less the following: the idea that human beings can achieve universal and necessary knowledge, the fundamental prejudice under which modern enlightenment is built, is incomatible with the recognition of the unitary character of *Dasein.* To speak of relativism it is necessary that its antinomic pole—absolute knowledge—is attainable. So, if the possibility of absolute knowledge is eliminated, the relative of it becomes the rule. If this is so, the fact that knowledge is relative to the *Dasein* loses its negative connotation—as long as it is not understood as a synonym of arbitrary—and the discussion concerning absolute truth becomes meaningless and therefore ends. In Gadamer's own words:

92 Gadamer, 281.

> Historicality is no longer a limitation of reason and its claim to grasp the truth, but represents a positive condition for the knowledge of the truth. As a result, the argument of historical relativism loses any real foundation. A criterion that demands absolute truth reveals itself as an abstract metaphysical idol and loses all methodological significance. Historicality ceases to evoke the specter of historical relativism[93].

In other words, the recognition of the finitude of our understanding and the denial of the possibility of accessing universal and necessary knowledge, although it implies the impossibility of carrying out the scientific philosophical project of modernity "to institute a court of justice, by which reason may secure its rightful claims while dismissing all its groundless pretensions"[94], does not necessarily lead to the conclusion that *anything goes*.

While Gadamer's philosophical approach indeed broadens the range of possibilities for unveiling the world, it's important to note that this doesn't mean it can encompass or "endure" everything. Instead, things can only be understood and made present when they are engaged within the context of their own possibilities. For Gadamer, then, anyone who reads and interprets a text, including a judge, must be cautious not to impose their own prejudices to such an extent that it obscures the true meaning of the text. The interpreter's task is, from his horizon, to be open and understand the text in its own context, rather than through the lens of their personal biases or dogmas.

---

93 In the German edition it reads: „Die Geschichtlichkeit ist nicht länger eine Grenzbestimmung der Vernunft und ihres Anspruchs, die Wahrheit zu erfassen, sondern stellt vielmehr eine positive Bedingung rur die Erkenntnis der Wahrheit dar. Dadurch verliert die Argumentation des historischen Relativismus jedes wirkliche Fundament. Ein Kriterium für absolute Wahrheit verlangen enthüllt sich als ein abstrakt-metaphysisches Idol und verliert jede methodologische Bedeutung. Die Geschichtlichkeit hört auf, das Gespenst des historischen Relativismus heraufzurufen, vor dem noch Husserls Programm-Aufsatz von Philosophie als strenge Wissenschaft so leidenschaftlich gewarnt hatte". Hans-Georg Gadamer, *Hermeneutik II: Wahrheit und Methode*, 2nd ed., Gesammelte Werke (Tübingen: J. C. B. Mohr, 1993), 103.

94 Kant, *Critique of Pure Reason*, A XI-XII.

In short, even though Gadamer acknowledges a greater interference of subjectivity in the act of understanding, this does not categorize him as a relativist. Reality, particularly in the case of texts, possesses its own truth that opens up numerous possibilities for its revelation, but there are limitations to the manner in which it can be unveiled. This concise overview of Gadamer's thematization of human understanding provides sufficient context for us to explore why this author immerses himself in the realm of law.

At the beginning of the chapter of *Truth and Method* dedicated to the *Recovery of the Fundamental Hermeneutic Problem*[95], Gadamer says:

> In both legal and theological hermeneutics there is an essential tension between the fixed text—the law or the gospel—on the one hand and, on the other, the sense arrived at by applying it at the concrete moment of interpretation, either in judgment or in preaching. A law does not exist in order to be understood historically, but to be concretized in its legal validity by being interpreted. Similarly, the gospel does not exist in order to be understood as a merely historical document, but to be taken in such a way that it exercises its saving effect. This implies that the text, whether law or gospel, if it is to be understood properly—i.e., according to the claim it makes—must be understood at every moment, in every concrete situation, in a new and different way. Understanding here is always application[96].

That is, Gadamer dives into legal (as well as theological) hermeneutics because of the dynamic that it is possible to observe in them, namely, that which occurs between the abstract and immutable text and the constantly changing concrete cases to which they must be applied.

Gadamer's philosophical–philological gaze clearly distinguishes that these types of texts (the canonical books of religions and legal statutes) do not exhaust their purpose in isolation but are intended for specific applications. In other words, they are not meant to be comprehended solely on an intellectual or theoretical level, but are designed to have a tangible impact on practical reality—to incarnate or *bring into flesh* justice and salvation. In that sense, Gadamer asserts that

95 Gadamer, *Truth and Method*, 318.

96 Gadamer, 319–20.

understanding these types of texts is not something different from their application. As Kögler explains,

> Gadamer invokes the hermeneutic operation of executing the law vis- à- vis particular cases and the theological practice of actualizing the message of scripture in sermons: in both hermeneutic applications, the validity of what is being handed down is assumed, but the concretization of its truth, its ultimate realization as meaning, is achieved in the applicative interpretive acts[97].

In other words, it's not a sequential process where the text is first understood in an abstract manner, independent of the specific details of the case that requires a juridical or theological solution, and then applied separately. Instead, understanding these types of texts inherently involves their application. Kaufmann, who shares a similar perspective with Gadamer, elucidates this concept as follows: "[W]hen law is 'applied', it is realized. A mediation of two worlds occurs: the world of everyday reality with its legally relevant life circumstances and the world of law with its rules that contains an ought to be. Through the realization of law, the ought to be and what is come into contact; *law is the correspondence between what ought to be and what is*"[98].

In legal interpretation, Gadamer contends, "[T]he law as a statute or constitution always needs interpretation for its practical application and this means, conversely, that all practical application already implies interpretation"[99]. Since the hermeneutical process of determining the meaning and scope of a legal text necessitates consideration of the specific case to which the text is to be applied, legal interpretation is not a merely a process of fitting the case into a predefined rule. Instead,

97 Hans-Herbert Kögler, "Dialogue on Dialogue: Gadamer and Habermas," in *The Gadamerian Mind*, ed. Theodore D George and Gert-Jan van der Heiden (New York & London: Routledge, 2021), 294.

98 Arthur Kaufmann, *Rechtsphilosophie* (München: C.H. Beck Verlag, 1997), 224.

99 In the original German it reads: „Daß sie wie ein Text ist, ob kodifiziert oder nicht, liegt in dem Geltungsanspruch der Rechtssetzung. Das Gesetz wie die Satzung bedarf für die praktische Anwendung stets der Interpretation, und das bedeutet umgekehrt, daß in jede praktische Anwendung Interpretation bereits eingegangen ist". Gadamer, *Hermeneutik*, 346.

for legal interpretation to be genuinely just, it must consider the unique circumstances of the situation that require the judge's intervention. As Grodin explains, blindly or indiscriminately applying the law (statute) to all cases, according to Gadamer, would entail a profound ignorance of the present situation, resulting not in legal certainty but in a lack of objectivity and justice[100]. In simpler terms, legal statutes don't acquire meaning when considered in isolation, as you might say in physics, but rather in *relation* to the specific case to which they are to be applied. What Gadamer seeks to reject is the notion that the correct application of a statute is solely dependent on the knowledge of the text, reducing every judgment to a mere act of subsumption[101].

This overcoming of the distinction between different moments or stages of the hermeneutical process is a logical consequence of the appropriation of Heidegger's thematization of the *Dasein* as a relational entity, and of Gadamer's emphasis on the need for the recognition of our finitude and its consequent elimination of the enlightened chimera of the possibility of obtaining "pure knowledge", completely detached from human subjectivity. This leads Gadamer, although not surprisingly, back to Aristotle's idea of *phronesis* (practical wisdom). In his words,

100 Jean Grondin, *The Philosophy of Gadamer.*, trans. Kathryn Plant (Hoboken: Taylor and Francis, 2014), 108.

101 On this matter Schmidt claims that Gadamer presents the interpretation of texts as a form of reflective judgment as explained by Kant in his *Critique of the Power of Judgment.* In his words, "It has long been a central concern of hermeneutic theory insofar as juridical decisions, the 'application' of a universal law to a particular case that is not unproblematically subsumed under that law, have been defined as hermeneutical problems. However, when he describes judgment in this section of Truth and Method, Gadamer does not reach back into this long tradition of legal hermeneutics but refers instead to what Kant calls 'reflective judgment', 16. In other words, Gadamer turns to the problematic of aesthetic judgment as exhibiting a form of thinking that does not obey the laws of conceptual reason and does not operate according to the logic of conceptual determination and subsumption". Denis J. Schmidt, "Gadamer. Humanism, and the Humanities," in *The Gadamerian Mind*, eds. Theodore D George and Gert-Jan van der Heiden (Routledge, 2021), 43.

> *For the hermeneutical problem too is clearly distinct from pure knowledge detached from any particular kind of being.* [. . .] The alienation of the interpreter from the interpreted by the objectifying methods of modern science, characteristic of the hermeneutics and historiography of the nineteenth century, appeared as the consequence of a false objectification. My purpose in returning to the example of Aristotelian ethics is to help us realize and avoid this. For moral knowledge, as Aristotle describes it, is clearly not objective knowledge i.e., the knower is not standing over against a situation that he merely observer; he is directly confronted with what he sees. It is something he has to do[102].

How does Aristotelian ethics intersect with the philosophical concepts we've been exploring? The link becomes clearer when we consider Aristotle's perspectives on prudence and practical wisdom.

Aristotle sees these virtues as pivotal in ethical decision-making and navigating human affairs. He asserts that prudence, or practical wisdom (*phronesis*), is deeply engaged with matters that are human and subject to deliberation. This reflects a keen understanding of human nature, as it captures the relational character of our being and, therefore, the variabilities in moral choices that individuals face in their daily lives. Practical wisdom or prudence is not solely about grasping universal truths; it involves being attuned to the particulars of each situation. It recognizes that practical truth emerges in application, which means that openness to varied and specific contexts is necessary. That is why Aristotle emphasizes that *phronesis* (practical wisdom)

> is concerned with things human and things about which it is possible to deliberate; for we say this is above all the work of the man of practical wisdom, to deliberate well, but no one deliberates about things that cannot be otherwise, nor about things which have not an end, and that a good that can be brought about by action. The man who is without qualification good at deliberating is the man who is capable of aiming in accordance with calculation at the best for man of things attainable by action. Nor is practical wisdom concerned with universals only—it must also recognize the particulars; for it is practical, and practice is concerned with particulars[103].

---

102 Gadamer, *Truth and Method*, 324.

103 *NE*, VI, 1141b8-1141b20. For this reference, we have utilized the following edition of Aristotle's Nicomachean Ethics: Aristotle, "Nicomachean Ethics," in

Simply put, practical wisdom or prudence cannot be taught in a way that allows to perfectly apply it to any specific situation after learning it. It depends on the unique characteristics of the situation that requires a prudent solution. A prudent person must consider the contingent circumstance of the world for arriving at a correct solution. Similarly, Gadamer argues that what is legally or theologically correct can only be determined attending to the specific that requires salvation or a just solution. In practical knowledge, application is not a distinct process that takes place *after* comprehending an abstract rule. Instead, the specific case codetermines the understanding of the rule as a whole from the beginning[104].

In the same vein as Aristotle, Gadamer asserts that the process of understanding and applying the law cannot be neatly separated into two distinct moments. As previously mentioned, comprehending legal statutes is not a process where the correctness of a legal decision hinges on the fine and precise understanding of the letter of the law. Instead, in order to reach a just legal, a judge often

> will have to refrain from applying the full rigor of the law. But if he does, it is not because he has no alternative, but because to do otherwise would not be right. In restraining the law, he is not diminishing it but, on the contrary, finding the better law. [. . .] Clearly legal hermeneutics finds its proper place here. The law is always deficient, not because it is imperfect in itself but because human reality is necessarily imperfect in comparison to the ordered world of law, and hence allows of no simple application of the law[105].

In essence, the accurate interpretation of the law does not depend on its alignment with the ideal of perfection as defined by legal doctrine. Instead, it is heavily contingent on the specifics of the individual case. It's essential to note, nonetheless, that this interpretation is not arbitrary; it is firmly rooted in positive legal texts in some form or another.

Complete Works of Aristotle, ed. Jonathan Barnes, vol. 2, 2 vols., The Revised Oxford Translation (Oxford: Princeton University Press, 1991).

104 Gadamer, *Truth and Method*, 333.

105 Gadamer, 328.

In synthesis, practical rationality, the dimension in which Gadamer argues law unfolds, is thus characterized by an apparent oxymoron: it is an openness that adheres to rules. There are rules—in the case of law, the statutes—so it is not a matter of acting freely based on mere opinions or ideas. At the same time, however, openness is necessary, for delimiting with precision the meaning that the rules will acquire in *relation* to the infinite and diverse cases that demand their application is something that is beyond the possibilities of finite and precarious beings like humans.

d. *Some conclusions regarding Gadamer's thought*

This brief analysis of Gadamer's thought allows us to understand that through the thematization of legal hermeneutics we can further understand the human condition, one which seems to be located in the middle of the abyss between knowledge and ignorance. The essence of what Gadamer tries to convey is that, while we can obtain knowledge from the world, our finite nature prevents the modern desire for achieving absolute and objective knowledge from coming to fruition. A phrase that we believe encapsules Gadamer's quest towards finding the middle way between absolutism and relativism in hermeneutics is the following:

> [O]f course the reader before whose eyes the great book of world history simply lies open does not exist. But neither does the reader exist who, when he has his text before him, simply reads what is there. Rather, all reading involves application, so that a person reading a text is himself part of the meaning he apprehends. He belongs to the text that he is reading[106].

In other words, hermeneutics allows us to realize that we, as human beings, are inevitably covered by a veil of ignorance, which Gadamer refers to as finitude. This veil obscures our ability to see the "full picture". However, it is still possible for us to catch glimpses of the truth

106 Gadamer, 349.

of the world through this veil. Despite the limitations imposed by our finite, historical and discursive human nature, some light can penetrate. Nonetheless, we cannot perceive this light directly. The veil of human understanding is akin to a blurred window. While the other side may be clear and undistorted, we can only perceive it in a fuzzy manner.

Law, according to Gadamer, is a phenomenon that remarkably highlights the characteristics of the veil through which human understanding operates. The tension between legal statutes that originated from a past horizon, and a new, unique and exceptional case that presents contemporary "place" from which the world is understood, enables us to elucidate the ontological structures that underlie human understanding. This is due to the fact that, in legal hermeneutics,

> the interpreter dealing with a traditionary text tries to apply it to himself. But this does not mean that the text is given for him as something universal, that he first understands it per se, and then afterward uses it for particular applications. Rather, the interpreter seeks no more than to understand this universal, the text i.e., to understand what it says, what constitutes the text's meaning and significance. In order to understand that, he must no try to disregard himself and his particular hermeneutic situation. He must relate the text to this situation if he wants to understand at all[107].

In other words, the application of a legal text presents the judge (or the one who applies it) with the challenge of reconciling an apparently unchanging text with countless and constantly varying specific real-world situation.

Simultaneously, the application of legal texts demonstrates that the fragile and finite horizon from which we comprehend the world can be expanded. Gadamer views the hermeneutic legal process as a form of dialogue, in which the text and the interpreter engage in a conversation for the sake of truth. And, as in any genuine dialogue—where the participants are dedicated to truth rather than their own positionalities—all individuals involved emerge enriched by what others have said. This occurs because their horizon merges with those presented by others in

---

107 Gadamer, 333.

the dialogue, and their limited perspective of the world is broadened as a result. Legal hermeneutics provides an exemplary experience of this process. In the act of interpretation, both the text and the interpreter "present" their horizons to each other. The case to which the text must be applied already carries a pre-existing meaning that must be unveiled in the hermeneutic process. Consequently, a mediation between all these elements becomes necessary, and this mediation is none other than the process of interpretation itself. The meaning that legal statutes acquire, then, arises from a kind of "interaction" among these three elements: the text, the case, and the characteristics of the agent that bridges both realms. The question that arises is: how can we determine the correctness of a legal decision? In the following chapter, we will explore how Schmitt uses this question as a starting point to delve into the nature of human understanding.

§ 3. Conclusions to the first chapter

We began this part of our journey by clarifying our definition of the theory of understanding. Within this context, we emphasized that this concept does not aim to address, as epistemology does, the constitution of reality through the subject-object dichotomy (i.e., how something external becomes an idea in our minds). Instead, its focus is on elucidating how reality gains meaning. In other words, a theory of understanding is not concerned with how we form the idea of an apple through our senses, but rather with how it acquires, for example, commercial or artistic significance (such as the meaning behind Apple's logo).

The specificity of what we term a "theory of understanding" lies in the fact that it focuses not only with the concrete pole, what we commonly call reality, and the ideal one, the conceptual articulations of the mind that allow us to elucidate that same reality, but also on the particular characteristics of the agent who knows the world. This is because it takes as a premise that the knowledge acquired of reality is not necessarily a reliable correlate of it, but is often a projection of the characteristics of the agent who understands the world (and it is this particular issue to which we have given, and will continue to give, most of our attention). A theory of understanding, then, must therefore be concerned not only with the real and ideal pole but also with the particular characteristics of the agent who articulates both.

This chapter allowed us to see how an elucidation of the dynamics and nature of human understanding can lead to a scrutiny of the legal phenomenon. Additionally, throughout it, we provided a rational justification that strongly asserts an idea introduced at the beginning of this manuscript, namely, that a perspective of a theory of understanding is preferable to a merely epistemological one. This preference stems from the fact that, as clearly shown throughout this text, an epistemological perspective commendably thematizes the way in which the human mind is capable of collecting, processing and ordering data gathered through the senses. However, it falls short in explaining the *meaning* of all that chaotic data that is synthesized by the human mind. That is, while describing human mind as a machine that processes the data provided by the senses, as posed by epistemology, represents an impressive mass of information, it does not answer the most basic question humanity has sought for eons: what does it all *mean* (i.e., hermeneutics)?[108]. A theory of understanding, on the other hand, directly tackles the question concerning the meaning of what is presented to our senses (and of existence in general). As we saw with Gadamer, it considers not only the ontic characteristics of the subject and object involved in understanding, but also of a more subtle, yet equally important element: the horizon from which subject and object emerge. In this context, the ontological structures inherent in human nature (the *existentiale*) become of great significance, since they "not only give shape to and allow us to navigate the world of our existential concerns but as placeholders they serve as portals to horizons other than our own. Through the medium of conversation the passing

108 Hawkins, *Transcending the Levels of Consciousness*, 224.

from one framework of meaning to another is an ever-present possibility"[109]. That is, they enable us to transcend our ontological limitations through dialogue.

In short, an epistemological approach is unable to thematize a path to truth that accounts for the interaction between conscious subjects, as its concern lies elsewhere: the configuration of the world. A theory of understanding appears more apt for this task, since it is founded on the premise, as we saw with Heidegger and Gadamer, that human existence (*being-in-the-world*) is relational in nature. Dialogue, therefore, is but the conceptualization of the method through which human beings relate and give meaning to its existence. A theory of understanding is, thus, a questioning of the conditions that enable human beings to engage in existential dialogue with themselves and the world—which is the same as saying that it questions the way of being human *per se*.

In the following section we will see how another philosopher, Carl Schmitt, travels a similar path to that of Gadamer (that of the dialogue between interpreter, text, and a particular case to which the written word is to be applied). Schmitt, as Gadamer, starts by thematizing law and the problems he observes in the modern way of understanding this phenomenon, to then rise to an ontological elucidation of how human understanding operates in general.

---

109 Nicholas Davey, "Dialogue, Dialectic and Conversation," in *The Gadamerian Mind*, ed. Theodore D George and Gert-Jan van der Heiden (New Yor & London: Routledge, 2021), 68.

2 Carl Schmitt "the soldier"

§ Methodological warning concerning Schmitt's text selection

Before addressing the matters that correspond to this section of the manuscript, we would like to warn the reader about a methodological issue. Even though in the introduction of this work we explained the general structure of the second and third chapters, we would like to insist on it so there is no confusion. In the second chapter, we will analyze two of Schmitt's early works: *Statute and Judgment* (1912) and *The Value of the State and the Significance of the Individual* (1914). Not only will we focus solely on these two texts, but the perspective (horizon) from which we will read them is specifically legal. By this we mean that we will focus on how Schmitt provides theoretical and practical arguments to "demolish" the concept of law, and of the legal phenomenon in general, that the school of thought that takes the name of "legal positivism" provides. That is why in the title of this section we have described Schmitt as a "soldier".

In the third chapter, on the other hand, we will see how Schmitt, after clearing the "intellectual construction site" of law, aims at building a more adequate horizon from which to understand the legal phenomenon, one that takes into account the human element and its existential characteristics (such as its finitude and historicality, among others). The adjective "artist" that we add to Schmitt's identification as a subject is indicative of this. It must be noted, however, that in this third chapter we once again return to the two texts revised in the second chapter (*Statute and Judgment* and *The Value of the State and the Significance of the Individual*), but from a different perspective. The horizon from which we will read Schmitt's early legal works, the ones in which he addressed legal matters and wrote between 1912 and 1922, in the third chapter is one that seeks to elucidate the concept of law that Schmitt seems to propose through his reflections on the matter. Our conclusion, which is the main hypothesis that we defend throughout this manuscript, is that through his thematization and conceptualization of the legal phenomenon Schmitt provides a theory of understanding with general scope. So, even though in both chapters two of Schmitt's text recur, the horizons from which they are analyzed in each segment are radically different, so the reflections that emanate from our scrutiny of them are also distinct.

§. Between the universal and the concrete: Carl Schmitt's early legal thought

In 1912, Carl Schmitt published one of his first academic works: *Gesetz und Urteil* (Statute and Judgment). In this work, Schmitt sets out to answer the question "when is a judicial decision correct? (*Richtig*)"[110]. He then adds, "the investigation is a juristic one. It asks when a decision that has been taken in today's legal practice is to be regarded as juristically correct"[111]. In other words, in the first page of one of his early juridical works, he affirms quite clearly that his writings must be understood in strictly legal terms.

A few years later, however, in 1968, the editorial C. H. Beck publishes the second edition of this book. For this edition, Schmitt writes a new prologue. What strikes us the most is that in this text the German jurist contradicts his statement that his legal thought should be understood strictly in juridical terms by saying:

110 Schmitt, "Statute and Judgment: An Investigation into the Problem of Legal Praxis," 47.

111 Schmitt, 47.

> Further reflection on the independent significance of the decision as such (*Dictatorship* 1921, *Political Theology* 1922, *The Guardian of the Constitution* 1931, *On the Three Types of Juristic Thought* 1934) later led me to the general insight that the domain of law as a whole is structured not merely by norms, but also by decisions and institutions (concrete orders)[112].

That is, in his late years Schmitt recognizes that the fundamental ideas that he brought forth in his early legal thought are present and, in a sense, sustain, all his posterior work. This statement makes the study of Schmitt's legal texts even more relevant, since it gives grounds for justifying that it is precisely in his legal thought that one may find a key to reading his work. In other words, Schmitt's 1968 prologue to *Gesetz und Urteil* gives way for arguing that for the German jurist "[l]aw is a form of understanding [. . .] that extends to existence as such, because its problem and its methodological approach to it coincide with the question of the relationship and the general tension between conceptuality and reality"[113].

Before analyzing his legal texts, we find it prudent to formulate and answer the following question: what is Schmitt's objective when studying the legal phenomenon? Schmitt's purpose, as we shall argue in the course of this research, is twofold. On the one hand, he wants to demonstrate the weakness of positivism, a theory which understands law as mere technology. On the other, he wishes to provide a better understanding of the legal phenomenon, one that takes into account not only the "pure" legal texts but also the concrete human life that it regulates.

We must bear in mind, however, that the Schmittian analysis of positivism must not be understood in isolation, but rather as part of his general critique of the prevailing thought in late modernity: technology. As Ojakangas explains,

> in Schmitt's view [. . .] an outstanding characteristic of this epoch [late modernity] is the dissolution of political struggles and social conflicts into a neutral

112 Schmitt, 42.

113 Hugo Herrera, "Carl Schmitt como jurista," *Derecho y Humanidades*, no. 28 (2016): 59–60.

> sphere, above all into the sphere of the technical rationalizations [. . .]. Schmitt sees manifestations of this tendency everywhere. He finds it in modern jurisprudence and especially in the formalism and normativism of legal positivism, which confuses legitimacy and thereby political authority with legality, identifying law (*Recht*) with "objectively valid" legal rules and norms (*Gesetz*). He discovers it in the juristic life of the liberal bourgeois "constitutional state" (*Rechtsstaat*), which subjects the power of the state to the rule of law and dismisses the immediate and revolutionary constituent power of the people, reducing it to a mere concept[114].

Differently put, the German jurist sees the reduction of the legal phenomenon to positive texts that normative positivism promotes as a manifestation of a type of scientism, a thought which ignores the practical and political existence and aims towards the rationalization and "neutralization" of all aspects of what is human. In short, through his critique of legal positivism, Schmitt is actually criticizing the fundamental characteristic of late modernity: the neutralization of everything in existence.

Another characteristic of Schmitt's legal thought that must be considered before analyzing his texts is that he sees in the legal phenomenon a constant tension between two dichotomous and irreconcilable poles of existence: one being abstract and general (represented by norms), and the other being concrete and real (pertaining to everyday human life)[115]. In the words of Herrera, "the exceptional, the singular, the peculiarity of reality, the situations, the individuals in them, are in tension with the rules and concepts and determine, as Schmitt points out, that between the concrete and the abstract there is an 'insurmountable abyss'[116]". That is, Schmitt recognizes the necessity of a general

114 Mika Ojakangas, *A Philosophy of Concrete Life: Carl Schmitt and the Political Thought of Late Modernity*, 2nd ed. (Bern: Peter Lang, 2006), 30–31.

115 As previously noted, Schmitt employs the domain of law in an exemplary manner. This implies that the tension he identifies within the legal phenomenon mirrors the tension present in human existence at large.

116 Herrera, "Carl Schmitt como jurista," 60. Herrera is making a reference to Schmitt's *Der Wert des Staates und die Bedeutung des Einzelnen*. Carl Schmitt, *Der Wert des Staates und die Bedeutung des Einzelnen* (Berlin: Duncker und Humblot, 2004), 80.

framework (legal statutes) that transcends the particularities of empirical situations. However, the challenge lies in the fact that reality is immeasurable and incalculable, rendering it impossible for a few (or many) legal texts to comprehensively regulate every aspect of it. Some aspects of reality elude legal regulation, manifesting themselves in what we commonly refer to as the "exceptional".

The foregoing creates tension: on the one hand, we have legal statutes that are unable to provide a solution for the exceptional case, and on the other hand, a particular case that requires a legal remedy (and often urgently so). So, who can resolve this tension? Who, as Derrida suggests, can "reconcile the act of justice that must always concern singularity, individuals, irreplaceable groups and lives, the other or myself *as* other, in a unique situation, with <the> rule, norm, value or the imperative of justice which necessarily have a general form, even if this generality prescribes a singular application in each case?"[117]. Schmitt answers that the judge, through his decision, is the only one who can perform this task. It is the irreplaceable "flesh-and-bone"[118] judge, the only one who can grapple with the exception (although he can never fully reconcile the dichotomous poles that come into play). Now, as we will see in the following chapters, this does not imply that Schmitt advocates for arbitrary judicial decisionism. Quite the opposite, his primary concern is to strike a balance between the legal certainty that positive law provides and the justice demanded by the specific case. This explains why Schmitt is always oscillating between the universal and the particular. However, this is not something for which he ought to be intellectually condemned. On the contrary, here lies, as Ojakangas well explains, the richness of his thought:

> [O]n the one hand, the acuity of Schmitt's thought lies in his ability to avoid universals and abstractions, which have no reference to a concrete instance or

---

117 Jacques Derrida, "Force of Law: The 'Mystical Foundation of Authority,'" in *Deconstruction and the Possibility of Justice*, ed. Drucilla Cornell et al. (New York: Routledge, 1992), 17.

118 By this we mean, as we will explain when examining *Gesetz und Urteil*, that a machine could never perform such a task by itself.

> to the concrete state of things. On the other hand, it lies in his capacity to make immediately comprehensible conceptual distinctions, yet without forgetting the demands of generality posed to theoretical thinking. This dual intention becomes manifest already in the name of his approach, combining philosophy *and* life: "A philosophy of concrete life"[119].

In other words, it is precisely due to his ability to articulate both domains that Schmitt's philosophy succeeds in offering a legal theory that, to the extent possible, encompasses the diversity of the legal phenomenon.

In this chapter, we will analyze the initial two academic works authored by Schmitt concerning the legal phenomenon: *Gezets und Urteil* (1912) and *Der Wert des Staates und die Bedeutung des Einzelnen* (1914). Our objective in doing so is to establish that even in his early works, Schmitt's exploration of the legal phenomenon leads him toward an elucidation of how human understanding functions. Specifically, we will contend that both his critique of positivism and his proposal for a new understanding of law are grounded in a prior clarification of certain fundamental ontological structures inherent in all human understanding.

§ 1. *Statute and Judgment* (1912)

As we mentioned at the beginning of this work, Schmitt's first academic works, aside from his doctoral dissertation (*Über Schuld und Schuldarten. Eine terminologische Untersuchung*), is *Gesetz und Urteil* (*Statute and Judgment*). He commences this book by posing the question of whether a judgment arising from judicial praxis (*Rechtspraxis*) is correct (*richtig*) from the perspective of legal praxis itself[120]. In other words, he explicitly outlines the objective of his work: to establish a

119 Ojakangas, *A Philosophy of Concrete Life*, 12.

120 Cf. Schmitt, "Statute and Judgment: An Investigation into the Problem of Legal Praxis," 47.

criterion for assessing the correctness (*Richtigkeit*) of legal judgments that is not rooted in legal theory but in judicial practice. While it becomes evident by the end of the text that Schmitt accomplishes his initial goal, it also becomes clear that his analysis goes beyond that objective. In this book, he introduces an alternative way of comprehending law that differs from the prevailing perspective of his time, which was legal normative positivism. In fact, Schmitt implicitly acknowledges this shift himself in the prologue to the second edition of *Statute and Judgment*, written in 1968. He states that the ideas presented in this work, particularly concerning judicial decisions, ultimately led him to recognize that the domain of law is not solely structured by rules but also by concrete orders.[121]. As Herrero comments,

> in the prologue to the 1968 edition of *Statute and Judgment*, that is to say, at the moment in which his last great work on *The Nomos of the Earth* had already seen the light, and with the perspective that it gives him having already developed his intellectual itinerary, Schmitt clarifies that the meaning of this work of 1912 is to delimit the specific meaning of the decision regarding positive norms [. . .]. That is the political philosophical issue that is at stake in that book[122].

Now, the challenges that Schmitt's *Statute and Judgment* confronts can be summarized as follows: the legitimation of legal decisions (i), and how to address the tension between a general and abstract text that pertains to a past historical, and a legal situation that presents a contemporary issue requiring resolution (ii). In other words, Schmitt's text addresses two fundamental philosophical questions: (using Kantian terms) the *quid juris* of legal decisions, which aims "to establish the entitlement or legal claim"[123] associated with them, and the central problem that all philosophy of law must grapple with—the mediation between the universality of law (statute) and the singularity of particular cases[124]. Even though the philosophical questions with which

121 Cf. Schmitt, 42.

122 Herrero, "Estudio preliminar," XXVII–XXVIII.

123 *Critique of Pure Reason* A 84/ B 116. We have used the following translation: Kant, *Critique of Pure Reason*.

124 Cf. Herrero, "Estudio preliminar," XIX.

Schmitt is dealing in *Statute and Judgment* are colossal, his objectives are rather modest. On the one hand, he wants to demonstrate the weaknesses of the positivist way of understanding the legal phenomenon; on the other, and through the formulation of a legitimizing criterion for judicial decisions, he proposes a new approach towards law grounded on legal practice.

Having already contextualized the thematic focus of *Statute and Judgment*, let us now specify the questions that will guide our investigation in this section. These questions encompass two main aspects: does Schmitt effectively demonstrate the theoretical and practical weaknesses of the positivist perspective on law? Furthermore, does he succeed in establishing a legitimizing criterion for judicial decisions rooted in legal practice? We will address these questions within the following structure: First, we will examine Schmitt's critiques of legal positivism (1). Then, we will delve into his legitimizing criterion for judicial decisions based on legal practice (2). Subsequently, we will argue that through his criterion, Schmitt is formulating a concept of law that stands in opposition to positivism (3). We will also analyze the role of the exception in his legal philosophy (4). Finally, we will explore whether, as some Schmittian readers have suggested, *Statute and Judgment* can be interpreted in terms of what Kant refers to as "reflective judgments" (5) and draw some conclusions (6).

Before commencing our analysis, we deem it prudent to initially highlight two aspects (to ensure these factors remain present throughout the reading of these chapters). First, the tangible judge, as the sole mediator capable of bridging the chasm between the general and abstract realm of positive legal texts and the specific concrete existence through their decisions, occupies a pivotal position in Schmitt's legal philosophy. Second, this does not imply, as some scholars have suggested[125], that we are confronted with arbitrary or capricious decisionism.

125 Such as Heinz Laufer, Karl Löwith, Helmut Kuhn and Leo Strauss. Heinz Laufer, "Das Kriterium Politischen Handelns. Versuch Einer Analyse Und Konstruktiven Kritik Der Freund Feind-Unterscheidung Auf Der Grundlage Der Aristotelischen Theorie Der Politik; Zugleich Ein Beitrag Zur Methodologie Der Politischen Wissenschaften" (Thesis doctoral, Würzburg, Würzburg, 1961).

a. *The irrationality of "rational" legal positivism: ignoring the facts of life*

In the opening lines of his *Pure Theory of Law*, Kelsen asserts that his legal theory is a science and not what he terms "legal politics". That is why it is referred to as "pure", since it only "describes the law and attempts to eliminate from the object of this description everything that is not strictly law: It aims to free the science of law from alien elements. This is the methodological basis of the theory"[126]. In other words, Kelsen initially confines his scope of study to positive law and subsequently contends that any analysis that incorporates "alien elements" (such as ethics, politics, empirical data, etc.) lacks scientific rigor. In essence, he applies Kant's assertion in his *Critique of Pure Reason* that metaphysics should adhere to the secure path of science (basing its model in the methodology used in mathematics, physics, and biological sciences)[127] to the domain of law. Kelsen believes that this approach is the only means by which law can shed the mysticism associated with Natural Law and Theology, thus becoming "rational".

Kelsen's premise is not surprising when one considers that even in his early works, the Austrian thinker contended that the jurist must approach law from the perspective of *formal relations*. In his own words,

> If one wants to juridically understand the relationship of the state to the subject who behaves lawfully, on the one hand, and to the subject who acts unlawfully and on whom the state's will to punish and execute is realized, on the other, then one must not regard the state as the master and the subject as the obeyer, but must see nothing but the *legal obligations* that exist in both cases. [...] For the jurist, human behavior comes into consideration only from the point of view of

---

Karl Löwith, "Der Okkasionelle Dezisionismus von Carl Schmitt," in *Sämtliche Schriften*, vol. VIII (Stuttgart: Metzler, 1984), 32–71. Leo Strauss, "Anmerkungen Zu Carl Schmitt, Der Begriff Des Politischen," in:: *Carl Schmitt, Leo Strauss Und «Der Begriff Des Politischen». Zu Einem Dialog Unter Abwesenden*, ed. Heinrich Meier (Stuttgart & Weimar: Metzler, 1998).

126 Hans Kelsen, *Pure Theory of Law*, trans. Max Knight (New Jersey: Lawbook Exchange, 2005), 1.

127 Cf. Kant, *Critique of Pure Reason*, B XXIII-XXV.

whether it forms a prerequisite to which the state's will to punish or to execute is linked or not. For him, right and wrong stand only in this *formal relation* and not as obedience or disobedience to an order, as fulfillment or thwarting of a purpose. The legal proposition, then, is for the jurist only the determination of those preconditions to which a will of the state is attached, and not the purpose-pursuing commandment of a power [128].

In other words, legal scholars should not take into account the facts of concrete human life. Neither the content nor the purpose of norms should be regarded as relevant to legal science. Instead, the jurist's attention should be directed towards legal statutes and their structure.

This brief reference to Kelsen's thought helps us to understand Schmitt's conceptualization of legal positivism. According to him, "positivism identifies statutory governing with *Recht*; it recognizes—also when it makes concesion [sic.] to the possibility of prescriptive law—instead of *Recht*, only the normative fixed legality"[129]. In other words, it reduces the entire spectrum of the legal phenomenon to mere positive norms (the texts containing legal prescriptions). Legal positivism, especially that of the nineteenth century, typically manifests itself in two forms (although it often presents itself as a combination of both): normativism and decisionism. In his words,

> depending upon the situation at hand, it permits positivism to be sometimes decisonist and sometimes normativist in order to satisfy the sole authoritative positivist requirement for certainty and calculability. That positivity always lies in the interest of the real certainty, firmness, and calculability of that which is actually realizable, whether that be the decision of the legislator or whether it be the statute emanating from his decision and the legally calculable decision emanating from that statute[130].

In other words, for legal positivism, the legal text or statute is the most crucial element to be taken into account by juristic thought.

128 Hans Kelsen, *Hauptprobleme Der Staatsrechtslehre* (Tübingen: J. C. B. Mohr, 1923), 8.

129 Carl Schmitt, *On the Three Types of Juristic Thought*, trans. Joseph W Bendersky (Westport: Praeger Publishers, 2004), 64.

130 Schmitt, 68.

Nevertheless, the content of this text is not always straightforward. In certain instances, it seems that the letter of the law, the text itself, should be regarded as superior, absolute, and everlasting[131] (in these cases, the inclination is toward normativism). In others, it appears that the substance of the statute is determined by the content of the legislator's or lawmaker's will (in these situations, we lean closer to decisionism). Nonetheless, in both scenarios, there exists a reverence for the written text and its purity, emphasizing its detachment from concrete reality[132].

Schmitt seems to doubt that "purity" is a synonym of rational. As McCormick well explains, Schmitt "asks how 'positive' can positivism be if it ignores what it is supposedly concerned with, namely, the 'fact'? [. . .]. How rational or scientific can Enlightenment rationality be if it ignores such a facet of concrete reality, if it is too afraid to, as it were, face the facts of life?"[133]. And what is the primary aspect that legal positivism opts to overlook? It is the reality of the *fact* that "there will always, and inevitably, be an unforeseen or unexpected occurrence that can never be predicted or for which accounts or plans can never be made"[134]. In other words, legal positivism fails to consider that reality is never constant and uniform, as in mathematics, but rather that the unexpected and unforeseeable will always disrupt the regularity of what is deemed "normal". Regardless of the quantity and complexity of legal statutes, they can never comprehensively regulate every aspect of human existence. The "exceptional" is an integral part of human reality, and, according to Schmitt, a legal theory that aspires to effectively encompass the complexities of the legal phenomenon in its entirety and seeks to be useful for judicial practice, must acknowledge and be shaped by the exception. As Herrera puts it,

---

131 Cf. Schmitt, 21.

132 Joseph W Bendersky, "Introduction: The Three Types of Juristic Thought in German Historical and Intellectual Context," in *On the Three Types of Juristic Thought*, ed. Carl Schmitt (Westport, Conn.: Praeger Publishers, 2005), 8–9.

133 John P. McCormick, *Carl Schmitt's Critique of Liberalism: Against Politics as Technology*, Modern European Philosophy (Cambridge ; New York: Cambridge University Press, 1997), 224.

134 McCormick, 224.

> the realization concerning this background of exceptionality from which existence emerges allows the human being to be aware of its condition, as well as of the scope and limits of thought and knowledge. The articulations of the mind—the words, concepts, and rules—discern existence. They are, however, heterogeneous with respect to the exceptional, the depth, the alterity betrayed by concrete reality and the particular situations within it. In virtue of this indetermination and depth, the situations, the cases before the human mind, differ from mere examples-of-a-rule, and cannot fully be reduced to the articulations of the mind. The situations possess a depth from which they arise, a depth that makes each of them to be also a specific and peculiar case"[135] .

In essence, the exceptional backdrop from which reality arises provides an opportunity to explore the enigmas of human understanding and the very essence of existence. Given that in law the exceptional is vividly evident in the relationship between rules and cases, it serves as an ideal avenue for investigating these aspects.

Although the fundamental idea we have just discussed regarding the exception and the incommensurability of human existence underpins Schmitt's critique of legal positivism, in *Statute and Judgment* he primarily directs his inquiry towards the conceptual-theoretical and practical inadequacies of this perspective. On one hand, Schmitt contends that the concepts upon which positivism is built (such as "legality") are ambiguous and obscure. On the other hand, he demonstrates that, given the theory's failure to consider concrete reality as a significant factor, it proves to be ineffectual for legal practice. In the following sections, we will delve into Schmitt's conceptual and practical critiques of legal positivism.

The first conceptual error that Schmitt identifies in legal positivism is its claim to universality. He argues that this perspective is built on an impossible premise (at least for mortals), namely, the belief that we, as human beings, can elevate ourselves above our own finite nature and attain absolute, necessary, and therefore timeless knowledge. As Ojakangas explains, for legal positivism "all non-normative concepts and conceptions, all considerations concerning, for instance, the concrete

135 Hugo Herrera, *Carl Schmitt. Between Technological Rationality and Theology* (New York: State University of New York Press, 2020), 83–84.

sources of law, have to be set aside including the existential concept of a people and the personified concept of the sovereign"[136].

Specifically, positivism intents to provide a conceptual framework that is ablet to explain, legitimize, and solve every legal and conceptual problem within all legal systems, regardless of their diversity or uniqueness. In Kelsen's words, "it is a theory of positive law in general, not of a specific order. It is a general theory of law, not an interpretation of specific national or international legal norms; but it offers a theory of interpretation"[137]. According to Schmitt, positivism does not, and will never, achieve its goal due to a simple, yet fundamental, fact: it fails to acknowledge that human beings are not gods. This means that, due to the limitations inherent to our human condition, we are incapable of attaining knowledge of eternal nature. Therefore, we must content ourselves with and aim for knowledge that is within our reach. As Gadamer reminds us, we should always be aware of the fact that

> history does not belong to us; we belong to it. Long before we understand ourselves through the process of self-examination, we understand ourselves in a self-evident way in the family, society, and state in which we live. The focus of subjectivity is a distorting mirror. That is why the prejudices of the individual, far more than his judgments, constitute the historical reality of his being[138].

In a similar vein to Gadamer, although several years earlier, Schmitt postulates that for a theory of law to be useful for legal praxis, it must take into account concrete reality[139]—which is inherently singular and contingent. In his words, "any derivation from an idea of law that claims

---

136 Cf. Hans Kelsen, *General Theory of Law and State* (Cambridge: Harvard University Press, 1949), xvi.

137 Kelsen, *Pure Theory of Law*, 1. It is important to recognize that Kelsen asserts his theory of interpretation as universally applicable across all legal systems. In doing so, he seemingly disregards the unique specificities inherent in each system, opting instead to subsume them under a singular, overarching hermeneutic theory.

138 Gadamer, *Truth and Method*, 288–89.

139 In this sense: Ernst-Wolfgang Böckenförde, "Konkretes Ordnungsdenken," in *Historisches Wörterbuch Der Philosophie*, ed. Joachim Ritter and Karlfried Gründer, vol. 6 (Basel: Schwabe Verlag, 1984), 1312–13.

atemporal validity is either hostile to any content and thus devoid of value for practice, or it surrenders itself in order to become useful to practice"[140]. That is to say, if a legal concept that positions itself above historicality wants to be of any use in concrete reality, which is situated in time and history, it must relinquish its abstract and universal characteristics and become *immersed* in concreteness.

When formulating this critique, Schmitt is specifically addressing positivism's inability to offer a criterion for legitimizing legal decisions (which his primary focus on *Statute and Judgment*). Concerning this particular matter, Schmitt asserts that legal philosophy should not seek an absolute and timeless answer to the question of the correctness of a decision. Instead, it is imperative that the inherent dynamism of reality to be accounted for when elaborating such a criterion. Only with such awareness can progress be made in legal theory. In his own words, "it is the task of the doctrine of the method of the application of law to find the guiding idea of *contemporary* practice, and to be of use to the latter by helping it to become aware of its own purpose and means. There is scientific progress in a practice becoming aware of its own sense"[141]. In that sense, as Rasch points out, it is important to bear in mind that in this text Schmitt is not concerned "about the relation of natural to positive law, but about the relation of positive law to the empirical facticity of the particular case"[142]. In a similar way, Ojakangas argues that "although Schmitt conceived it as his task to outline the method of legal positivism, which has become the dominant doctrine of law in the bourgeois 'constitutional state' (*Rechstaat*), he did not want to return to natural law either"[143]. That is, he is focused not on the meta-positive foundation of law (in which he believes[144]) but on the most concrete

140 Schmitt, "Statute and Judgment: An Investigation into the Problem of Legal Praxis," 109–10.

141 Schmitt, 48.

142 William Rasch, "Judgment: The Emergence of Legal Norms," *Cultural Critique* 57, no. 1 (August 12, 2004): 98.

143 Ojakangas, *A Philosophy of Concrete Life*, 46.

144 See Schmitt, "Statute and Judgment: An Investigation into the Problem of Legal Praxis," 67–68.

aspect of legal practice: judicial decisions. In sum, Schmitt demonstrates the fragility of the "abstract" basis upon which legal positivism is constructed and then affirms that his criterion for legitimizing legal decisions will not make the same mistake.

The former leads us directly to examine the second theoretical-conceptual weakness that Schmitt identifies in positivism: its hermeneutical criterion for the correctness of a judicial decision. Legal positivism typically operates under the notion that a legal decision is deemed correct when the presiding judge can appropriately categorize (subsume) the case within the established legal framework[145]. That is, as long as the judge can align the specific case with the general description outlined in legal statutes. The equation, metaphorically speaking, is already provided; the judge's sole task is to substitute the variables. Hence, a legal decision is to be considered correct if the judge has followed this procedure thoroughly.

Schmitt believes this logic to be flawed. He argues that while subsumptivist logic provides a hermeneutical procedure for judges, it does not establish a criterion for confirming the correctness of those decisions. That is, it does not propose a means to verify if the subsumption was done correctly. It merely describes how the procedure is to be performed. Furthermore, Schmitt contends that even if it were able to furnish such a rule, it would result in an infinite regress. In his own words, it is necessary "to recognize that the problem concerns the *correctness* of subsumption and one cannot determine the correctness of a subsumption in further subsumption"[146]. This is because that rule would necessitate another rule to validate that the subsumption of the case under positive law was executed correctly (and so forth). Schmitt, then, seems to be appealing to the Kantian argument that states that

> to a concept of understanding, which contains a rule, must be added an act of judgment by which a practitioner distinguishes whether or not something is the

---

145 Cf. *Giusnaturalismo e positivismo giuridico* (Madrid: Editorial Trotta, 2015). Bobbio is referring specifically to positivism a *Formal theory of interpretation.*

146 Schmitt, "Statute and Judgment: An Investigation into the Problem of Legal Praxis," 96.

> case of the rule; and since judgment cannot always be given yet another rule by which to direct its subsumption (for this would go on to infinity), there can be theoreticians who can never in their lives become practical because they are lacking in judgment[147].

Put differently, the inevitable regress to infinity (*unendlicher Regress*) that subsumption as a criterion for ensuring that law was correctly applied to a particular case leads to its impracticability. As Neumann explains, the norm must refer to the concrete case, which poses a problem that the text itself does not have the ability to solve: that of specifying the conditions under which it can be considered that the case was correctly subsumed under the norm[148].

A few years later, Hans Kelsen seems to confirm Schmitt's suspicion. In his *Pure Theory of Law* he explains that positive legal texts function as "schemes of interpretation". This implies that they enable the determination of whether an event that can be perceived through the senses (because it occurs in time and space) is to be deemed legal or illegal. If the law assigns a legal consequence to a situation that has unfolded in accordance with the natural laws of causality, which Kelsen refers to as concrete reality, the judge must then proceed to enforce the sanction stipulated in the law[149]. However, when addressing "legal interpretation", Kelsen makes the following statement:

> Jurisprudential interpretation must carefully avoid the fiction that a legal text admits only of one as the "correct interpretation". Traditional jurisprudence uses this fiction to maintain the ideal of legal security [. . .]. It is, from a scientific and hence objective point of view, inadmissible to proclaim as solely correct an interpretation that from a subjectively political legal viewpoint is more desirable

147 Immanuel Kant, "On the Common Saying: That May Be Correct in Theory, but Is of No Use in Practice," in *Practical Philosophy*, trans. Mary J. Gregor, The Cambridge Edition of the Works of Immanuel Kant (Cambridge & New York: Cambridge University Press, 1996), 279.

148 Cf. Volker Neumann, *Carl Schmitt Als Jurist* (Tübingen: Mohr Siebeck, 2015), 21. In a similar sense, Hasso Hofmann, *Legitimität gegen Legalität: der Weg der politischen Philosophie Carl Schmitts* (Berlin: Duncker & Humblot, 2010), 59.

149 Cf. Kelsen, *Pure Theory of Law*, 3–4.

> than other, logically equally possible, interpretation. For in that case a purely political value judgment is falsely presented as scientific truth [150].

In other words, if normative texts offer two or more logically possible interpretations, it is impossible, solely through logical analysis, to ascertain that one of them is superior to the others. This is because the same logic that leads to the conclusion that multiple legitimate interpretations exist also implies that if logic were to determine one interpretation as correct, it would indicate that the initial logical reasoning, which suggested the existence of multiple reasonable interpretations, was flawed. That is why Kelsen argues, at the end of his discussion on the interpretation of the law, that "the question of which of the possibilities within the frame of the law to be applied is the 'right' one is not a question of cognition directed toward positive law we are not faced here by a problem of legal theory, but of legal politics"[151]. In essence, he concludes his chapter on interpretation by highlighting that legal positivism lacks the capacity to address the question of the correctness of an interpretation. In sum, as early as 1912, Schmitt identified what Kelsen would later acknowledge: that the excessive reliance on logic within legal positivism renders it useless for legal praxis.

The third and last theoretical problem that Schmitt identifies in positivism is its concept of "legality". In *Statute and Judgment,* he states that, according to legal positivism, "the judge, thus, ought to be subject to statute [. . .] [but it] does not say what is to be regarded as a statute and what as its content"[152]. In other words, he criticizes that this legal theory is constructed upon the concept of "legality", but never actually explains what is meant by it. In that sense, the statement that legal decisions are correct when they are legal is an empty one; it does not provide content to which the judge can resort when ruling a case.

Schmitt explains that to address this conceptual vacuum, positivism includes two concepts in its criterion for verifying the correctness

150 Kelsen, 356.

151 Kelsen, 353.

152 Schmitt, "Statute and Judgment: An Investigation into the Problem of Legal Praxis," 52.

of judicial decisions, namely, the will of the statute law and of the legislator[153]. Concerning the first of these concepts, the will of the law, Schmitt explains that it is obscure and, therefore, that it further complicates the elucidation of what is to be understood by legality. He argues that "will" is a quality that belongs solely to individual human beings; therefore, it would be absurd to attribute it to an inert piece of paper, no matter how many formalities it had to comply with to come into the life of the law. Moreover, even if we accept that there is a "will of the statute", positivism does not explain how we are to identify it and then verify if a judge has applied it correctly.

Regarding the "will of the legislator" as a means to define what is meant by legality, Schmitt argues that it also further complicates the task of judges. Before explaining this, let us describe the logic behind the idea of the "will of the legislator": "legality" is an attribute conferred upon positive law by a concrete legislator at a specific historical moment. In that sense, a decision will be correct when it is legal, and it will be legal only if it is in harmony with the will of a specific legislator. As Calvo García explains it,

> by identifying the objective meaning deposited in the letter of the law as the will of the legislator or a deep rational instance, the authoritative or correct interpretation would express without opacity or distortion the thought or the intention incorporated as a spiritual instance to the text, to the letter of the law[154].

Schmitt argues that this postulate contradicts the fundamental idea upon which positivism is built, namely, that this theory of law must remain "pure" and "eliminate from the object of its description everything that is not strictly law"[155] if it wants to follow the secure path of science[156]. Introducing the will of a concrete and historical legislator results in the inclusion of something belonging to the empirical world in the concept

153 That is, it tilts the balance towards decisionism.

154 Manuel Calvo García, "La voluntad del legislador: genealogía de una ficción hermenéutica," *Doxa*, no. 3 (1986): 115.

155 Kelsen, *Pure Theory of Law*, 1.

156 This is a reference to Kant's *Critique of Pure Reason*. Cf. Kant, *Critique of Pure Reason*, B X.

of legality; that means that the statute, and therefore the "science" that is built upon it, loses its purity. Moreover, the inclusion of the "will of the legislator" not only seeks to explain the origin of a positive norm in causal terms, in which case the normative purity of the text could still be preserved, but it also subordinates every future judicial decision to that concrete will. In Schmitt's words, if it is approached "with the means of historical interpretation, one will have to conclude that it was the 'will to the statute' or 'the will of the legislator' to bind the judge to the clear meaning of the statues. The judge was to do nothing further than to subsume under statutes"[157]. In other words, it reduces the task of the jurist first to identifying as precisely as possible the will of a specific legislator and then ensuring that this will is applied to concrete reality throughout history. The inclusion of this concept transforms law not into a normative-conceptual science but instead into a causal-explanatory one that aims towards clarifying the origin of a norm in causal terms. In short, the inclusion of concepts that refer to concrete historical moments to fill the conceptual void of "legality" results in legal positivism collapsing on itself because it contradicts the basic idea upon which this theory is built. Due to its inability to maintain a conceptual coherence in its reasoning, legal positivism fails to provide a legal science that is free from "alien elements"[158].

Schmitt also claims that this theory [legal positivism] is not only theoretically flawed, but that it is also ultimately useless for legal praxis. The fundamental idea behind Schmitt's "practical critiques" of positivism is that this theory seeks to explain an immeasurable concrete reality using limited legal categories. In other words, it asserts that legal reality is confined to abstract normative texts without verifying whether this is true in legal praxis. This omission is not a minor one, because it is evident that in the best-case scenario the

157 Schmitt, "Statute and Judgment: An Investigation into the Problem of Legal Praxis," 52.

158 Cf. Kelsen, *Pure Theory of Law*, 1.

> content of statute, so understood, could regulate only very few of the cases that are put to a judge for decision. It is unthinkable that life, in all of its facets, could find an exhaustive regulation in a few paragraphs, which one would merely have to read out of the statute in concrete cases[159].

In other words, no matter how much this theory strives to conceptually encompass concrete reality conceptually, it cannot tame it; it consistently emerges irregularly and in unexpected ways. The exceptional is part of legal reality, and this must be considered by legal theory. The problem with legal positivism is precisely, as McCormick explains, that it "avoids the reality of jurisprudence by denying the existence of 'gaps' within the law and consequently demotes judges to the status of mere vending machines that mechanically dispense the law, without intellectual reflection or active contribution"[160]. Schmitt's practical critiques precisely aim to demonstrate that the complexity of legal praxis proves that legal positivism's approach, since it denies the dynamism of concrete reality, is reductionist.

The first practical flaw that Schmitt identifies in legal positivism is that it provides a criterion for legitimizing legal decisions that is impracticable. As mentioned before, positivism's solution to the conceptual void of "legality" was to introduce two criteria into its content: the will of the statute and of the legislator. The impracticability of the "will of the statute" as a criterion for determining if a decision is legal becomes evident if we consider the absurdity already indicated when analyzing the theoretical problem that the inclusion of this concept generates, namely, that legal texts have no will, so it is impossible to articulate a way of applying them to practical reality. The "will of the legislator", on the other hand, requires further explanation.

As explained, the use of the will of the legislator as a criterion for verifying the legality of a decision and, consequently, its correctness, implies that the judge must refer to an act of will of a specific legislator in a determined historical moment. The question that naturally

159 Schmitt, "Statute and Judgment: An Investigation into the Problem of Legal Praxis," 52.

160 McCormick, *Carl Schmitt's Critique of Liberalism*, 207.

emerges is: what procedure should judges follow to uncover the content of this will? Is such a task even feasible? Schmitt argues that if there is only one legislator, and they are alive, obtaining the content of their will is straightforward; you simply need to ask them. However, when there are multiple individuals involved in the legislative process (such as a Congress), or if the sole legislator has passed away (which is typically the case), implementing this criterion appears to be impossible. It is not feasible (unless one relies on the art of the *mediums*) to ascertain the will of a legislator and its implications for the interpretation of a particular case when the creator of the statute is no longer alive. Even more challenging is attempting to elucidate the will of a collective body (such as Congress) whose members' opinions are often far from homogeneous [161]. Consequently, judges who employ this criterion often fail to recognize that they are not adjudicating in accordance with the legislator's intention but rather based on an idealized construct of it. In Schmitt's words, judges construct an "ideal legislator, who only ever wills what is **reasonable** and who pushes aside the historical legislator"[162]. That is, they attribute to the historical legislator an idea of justice that, though it originates in themselves, they assume would be shared by him.

What Schmitt criticizes about the criterion of the "will of the legislator" is not the "construction" of this ideal lawgiver but positivism's refusal to acknowledge its artificial nature. In his words,

> the contradictions and practical inconsistencies of the doctrine of the will of the legislator had their ground in the fact that one did not wish to admit to oneself that one was operating with a mere fiction. Had one been consciously aware of the fact that one treated a number of "transpositive" moments and contents as though they were the will of the legislator, and had one—always remaining conscious of this fiction and proceeding from it—tried to develop a theory of

161 Moreover, the methodological challenge extends to substantiating the existence of this will and elucidating its attributes.

162 Carl Schmitt, *Gesetz Und Urteil* (Berlin: Verlag von Otto Liebmann, 1912), 24. The highlight is ours.

> interpretation, one would have arrived at theoretically and practically valuable results[163].

That is, if positivism recognized that through the concept of the "will of the legislator" judges are actually referring to a sense of justice that they assume is common to all human beings, then it would be useful and helpful for legal praxis. However, by insisting that this concept refers to a real statement of intention, this theory turns this criterion into an illusion. Now, before delving into another Schmittian critique of positivism, it is important to note that even though he asserts that legal interpretation does not depend on the will of the authors of the law, Schmitt believes, and clearly states, that it is crucial for there to be prudent lawmakers and, consequently, good legislation. In other words, for judges to be able to provide some legal certainty, legal statutes must possess conceptual precision, a unified terminology, and a certain degree of linguistic consistency (within the limits of what is feasible)[164].

Schmitt formulates two more "practical critiques" against legal positivism. It is important to bear in mind that through these critiques, Schmitt is not attempting to prove the impracticability of legal positivism, as he did before. Instead, he argues that legal positivism overlooks certain practical aspects of reality that are fundamental to the law. His first critique is that, in its theoretical elaboration, positivism deliberately ignores the fact that in legal praxis it is possible to identify two kinds of positive legal texts: those that are applied by judges and those that are not. In Schmitt's words,

> it is a matter of fact that there is "effective" and "ineffective" law, that legal practice understood the content of statutes at times in wider and at times in narrower terms, and that it consequently conceived of a decision's "conformity to statute" as a relation to a content that did not lie open in a statute, without further ado, but which has to be read into it through complicated constructions[165].

163 Schmitt, 25.

164 Cf. Schmitt, "Statute and Judgment: An Investigation into the Problem of Legal Praxis," 122.

165 Schmitt, 52–53.

In other words, legal positivism, due to its conceptual shortsightedness, fails to recognize that the fact that judges do not apply every valid legal text is an essential aspect that legal theory must consider if it aims to thoroughly explain its subject matter.

The question that naturally arises is: what does Schmitt mean when he says that it is a fact that there is effective and ineffective law? Well, through this statement he is arguing that the formal validity of a positive legal text is not sufficient for it to haver an impact on concrete reality. In other words, he is asserting that the "survival" of statutes does not depend solely on its "legality". On the contrary, the elements that enable a legal text to survive and maintain its legitimacy are not limited to legality (although it is also necessary), but also encompass the continuous revisions of the text of the law, the modifications imposed by the emergence of an infinite number of new scientific concepts, the accumulation of precedents in legal libraries, among other factors[166]. In simple terms, there is a variety of circumstances that come into play in determining whether a particular statute is legal or not (within a broader conceptualization of "legality" that includes its ability to impact practical reality). Positivism, by reducing the legal phenomenon to statutes, chooses to overlook this aspect and, therefore, is unable to provide a satisfactory account of what law actually is. In sum, and as Croce and Salvatore explain, Schmitt's "meta-theoretical criticism is that Kelsen's theoretical purity risks being tantamount to blindness, or even intentional inaccuracy"[167].

His second practical critique is that positivism operates with an abstract concept of justice that overlooks any consideration of individual cases (singularities of the real pole). According to this line of thought, legal texts—and not judges—are tasked with delivering justice. In Schmitt's words, "justice is not immediately decisive for the judge; what he has to work with is, in every case, a form of second-hand justice—something that has been transformed—whether he simply

166 Cf. Schmitt, 53.

167 Mariano Croce and Andrea Salvatore, *The Legal Theory of Carl Schmitt* (New York: Routledge, 2013), 86.

performs a smooth subsumption under the statute or [. . .] grants a suit for cessation that has developed only in practice"[168]. In other words, lawmakers are the ones who must concern themselves with the sense of justice they intend to impart through their legislation. The judge's role is simply to apply that concept of justice to concrete cases.

Schmitt believes this approach to be flawed. While he acknowledges that the aspiration of both the legislator and the judge is to be fair[169], he also maintains that the primary challenge facing the science of law (*Rechtswissenschaft*) is not solely the justice of legal texts (although it is also an important aspect) but rather the justice for the particular case and how to achieve it. In his own words, the central concern of law is the gap between substantial justice, particularly in the context of concrete cases, and its realization in everyday life[170]. In other words, the primary focus of a theory of law should be on how to bridge the gap between the abstraction of positive law and the specificity of individual cases, allowing justice to prevail. According to Schmitt, in this context, the role of the judge is paramount because they are the ones tasked with mediating between the general and abstract content of legal texts and the unique circumstances of the case presented to them. Positioned between these two poles (abstract and concrete), the judge must resolve the tension that arises between them through their decision.

In conclusion, Schmitt's theoretical and practical critiques reveal that legal positivism, as an approach to understanding the legal phenomenon, is incapable of two essential things: firstly, maintaining a conceptual coherence. This is because it frequently departs from its supposed "purity" to address conceptual challenges, resulting in the collapse of this theory's theoretical foundations. Secondly, legal positivism falls short in furnishing judges with a practical criterion for assessing the correctness of legal decisions. In its pursuit of purity, positivism disregards concrete reality, focusing solely on abstract normative concepts.

168 Schmitt, "Statute and Judgment: An Investigation into the Problem of Legal Praxis," 87.

169 Schmitt, 87.

170 Schmitt, 87.

b. *"The other judge": Schmitt's criterion for the correction of legal decisions*

Having highlighted the shortcomings of legal positivism, Schmitt proceeds to offer what this theory lacks—an explicit criterion for judges to determine the correctness (*Richtigkeit*) of their legal decisions. However, his proposal is distinct from normativism, as Schmitt emphasizes that his criterion is firmly rooted in and designed for legal praxis[171]. In this section, we will provide a brief overview of this topic. In Chapter Four, we will revisit this matter and delve into it more comprehensively.

As we already explained, the "insufficiency" of positive law and logical procedures in explaining the legal phenomenon leads Schmitt to assert that in every legal problem (a particular case that requires solution), many extra-legal elements come into play (such as principles, customs, an idea of justice, etc.). In this regard, there is an inevitable moment of indeterminacy. In his words: "[A]part from very rare exceptions, every statute contains such a moment of indifference, which a civil lawyer might refer as aleatory. Up to certain degree, it is always more necessary that there be a statute at all than that the statute have a particular content"[172]. Now, the issue at hand is that this "indifference" or "indeterminacy" must be resolved for justice (or something akin to it) to emerge. The question, then, is how to transition from this indeterminate or stochastic moment to one of legal certainty. For these purposes Schmitt proposes what he terms the "principle of determination of law". According to this principle, what enables the law to move from an abstract and indeterminate state to determination is the judge. He is the one who resolves this tension through his decision (in the context of a trial, of course). Judges are tasked with determining the meaning and scope of law for a particular case.

The emphasis that the German jurist places on the judge's decision raises the following question: does this imply that judges can arbitrarily select the elements (law, customs, principles, etc.) they deem

171 Cf. Schmitt, 47.

172 Schmitt, 84–85.

relevant for a particular case? Put differently, does this procedure lead to judges being able to establish their own "legality"? Schmitt's answer is negative. He argues that legal decisions must be correct (*richtig*), and to achieve this, it is essential to steer clear of two equally harmful extremes: (1) disregarding the singularities of the real pole and concentrating solely on the preconceived justice offered by legal texts, and (2) entrusting the decision solely to the subjectivity of the judges.

In *Statute and Judgment* Schmitt furnishes a method for ensuring that a particular decision of a judge is, in fact, *richtig*. He affirms that it is feasible for a judge to say that "a judicial decision is correct, today, if it is to be assumed that another judge would have decided in the same way. 'Another judge', in this context, refers to the empirical type of modern, legally trained jurist"[173]. In other words, he argues that, when deciding about a case, judges should asses whether the judicial community would endorse that specific decision. The aim of this criterion, Schmitt explains, is to establish, to the extent possible, legal certainty—meaning a certain degree of predictability in legal decisions. Legal praxis, says Schmitt, "is governed by the aspiration to provide *calculable* decisions"[174].

This Schmittian proposal, while intriguing, raises several questions, such as: what is meant by the "other judge"? How would a judge secure the endorsement of their colleagues? Does this imply that the correctness or justice of a particular decision relies on judicial convention? In the following discussion, we will explore Schmitt's responses to these inquiries.

First, it should be noted that with his criterion, Schmitt is not asserting that all judges must make identical decisions when adjudicating similar cases, or that they must seek the endorsement of their colleagues (in the sense of directly requesting it) before making a decision[175]. On the contrary, he explicitly says that if his criterion were interpreted in that manner, it would involve delving into other fields of

173 Schmitt, 103.

174 Schmitt, 99.

175 Particularly noteworthy is the consideration that achieving genuinely universal agreement is an overly ambitious expectation, even within the confines of a small community. In that sense, see Robert Brandom, *Making It Explicit: Reasoning,*

knowledge that, in his view, are unrelated to the legitimation of legal decisions—such as the study of collective or social psychology concerning the magistracy, its interactions with the legal profession, or the objectives of a law within a community[176]. More importantly, the issue with interpreting *Statute and Judgment* in this manner would be that it aligns with what Robert Brandom criticizes of "descriptive regularism", namely, that if the lines that separate *what happens* and *what ought to* happen are erased, then the normative (and practical) essence of decision disappears[177]. Schmitt firmly disagrees with this notion. In this text, he explicitly asserts that "from what happens, one certainly cannot infer what ought to happen. [...] This means to say: what is correct cannot be derived from what actually happens in modern practice"[178]. Furthermore, if such were the case, this criterion would lose its effectiveness, as it is widely acknowledged that different judges do not arrive at identical decisions when faced with similar cases[179].

Another option would be to interpret Schmitt's criterion in terms of the methodology employed in *common law*, a legal system where judges are required to make decisions based on the precedents established by previous judges. However, this would not accurately represent Schmitt's proposal. The idea of making legal decisions communicable to other judges, which the German jurist aims to achieve through reasonableness and predictability, differs from validating judicial decisions solely based on precedents established by other judges who have

Representing, and Discursive Commitment (Cambridge: Harvard University Press, 2001), 39–40.

176 Schmitt, "Statute and Judgment: An Investigation into the Problem of Legal Praxis," 50.

177 This is because, then there would "be no regress or circularity in appealing to them as part of an account of knowing-that, of expressing norms explicitly in rules and principles. For the only one who needs to understand how to apply correctly the rule conforming to which makes performances count as regular is the theorist who describes the regularity in terms of that rule". Brandom, *Making It Explicit*, 26–27.

178 Schmitt, "Statute and Judgment: An Investigation into the Problem of Legal Praxis," 48–49.

179 Cf. Schmitt, 48–49.

previously encountered similar cases. Schmitt's criterion, on the other hand, guides judges to validate their decisions according to contemporary legal practice, rather than depending on past precedents. In essence, his solution differs from the system of precedents because its central axis is the adaptability of the content of legal decisions in accordance with the historicality of humanity. He explains this as follows:

> [A] judge who wants to decide correctly does not, therefore, have to codify the views of all other judges, so to speak, and then to subsume under that codification. That, needles to say, would be the old error that regards "conformity to statute" as the criterion of the correctness of a decision. Rather, **the judge has to make an effort to make sure that his decision is conformable to actual practice** and that, if he departs from a dominant opinion, he does so with arguments that are so compelling that the departure remains within the realm of the foreseeable and calculable. The reasons offered for decision therefore can, under certain circumstances, possess a creative significance [180].

In other words, *common law*, due to the binding character of past decisions (precedents), encounters similar methodological challenges as legality when used as a criterion for assessing the correctness of decisions. Furthermore, because it compels current legal judgments to adhere not to an abstract text (statutes) but to a specific and concrete decision, these systems prohibit judges from introducing innovations in their decisions, even more explicitly than *codified* systems. Schmitt's criterion, on the other hand, maintains a level of openness to the historicality of law (we will address this matter in chapter three), allowing legal decisions to adapt to changes in this phenomenon. That is why it enables judges to deviate from prevailing opinions in legal doctrine and jurisprudence if they determine that the judicial community would endorse their decision.

Having already dismissed, based on Schmitt's statements, certain interpretations of this criterion, we will now clarify what he actually means with "the other judge" as a standard for verifying the correctness of legal decisions. Although it may seem evident, it is important to emphasize that he is not referring to an actual, tangible judge.

180 Schmitt, 108–9. The highlight is ours.

Instead, he employs this concept in a normative manner. As Schmitt points out, the term "other judge" pertains to the "normal" juridically educated judge, where the word "normal" is used " in a quantitative sense that refers to the average, not as the designation of an ideal type and not in a qualitative-teleological sense"[181]. Why is this concept to be deemed normative? Because, as Crowell explains, "the normative is found wherever we can speak of rules, measures, standards, exemplars, ideals, concepts, and so on; wherever distinctions between better and worse, success and failure, can be made"[182]. This "other judge", therefore, is a normative concept, one intended to serve as a standard of measurement for legal decisions. More specifically, it is normative in the sense that its legitimacy and enforceability are derived from the legal praxis itself through the hypothetical endorsement of the community of judges. "The other judge", then, represents not the *sein*, but the *sollen*.

Therefore, we are not confronted with arbitrary decisionism in which judges may render judgments based solely on their idiosyncratic notions of justice. Schmitt himself underscores this point by noting that

> the criterion of the correctness of the decision does not lie in the subjectivity of the judge; it is altogether independent of him as an individual. It is practice that decides whether the decision is correct. Practice has its own specific criterion. To this corresponds the formula: a judicial decision is correct in the event that another judge would have decided in the same way[183].

In other words, for a judge's decision to be deemed correct, they must hypothetically persuade another judge that their decision is reasonable for that specific case. In this context, as Herrero explains, it becomes pivotal for "the judge who decides and normatively wants his decision to be correct, its substantiation. This is what the formula proposed by Schmitt demands. That another judge must be convinced is that he

181 Schmitt, 109.

182 Cf. Crowell, *Normativity and Phenomenology in Husserl and Heidegger*, 2.

183 Schmitt, "Statute and Judgment: An Investigation into the Problem of Legal Praxis," 126.

would have decided in the same way"[184]. In other words, it is insufficient for judges to merely declare, after engaging in this hypothetical exercise, that they have concluded that other judges would have reached the same decision. Instead, they must furnish the specific rationales that guided their decision-making process when adjudicating that particular case. That is why Schmitt says that, "[T]he reasons of decision are an essential component of every decision [. . .]; they are not merely important in assessing the scope of a judgment's legal force. They do not merely want to individualize the decision; they want to convince"[185]. In other words, a mere verdict (guilty or innocent, for instance) does not suffice for the "other judges" to endorse their judgment. They must be convinced that their decision was not only correct but also that, if faced with the same case, they would have ruled in an identical manner. Consequently, the presiding judge must provide the compelling reasons for them to believe they would have made the same judgment.

Underlying his critique of positivism and his criterion for determining the correctness of a legal decision, it is possible to discern that Schmitt is operating with a concept of "Law" that diverges from the one embraced by positivism, and even from that of naturalists. In the following discussion, we will illuminate the key features of Schmitt's concept of law and its philosophical underpinnings. Then we will argue that through its articulation, Schmitt is, in fact, shedding light on some of the fundamental structures that operate within all human understanding.

c. Schmitt's concept of law in Statute and Judgment

At this junction, it becomes evident that Schmitt does not equate "Law" with statutes. The fact that judges can decide *contra legem*

184 Herrero, "Estudio preliminar," LXI.

185 Schmitt, "Statute and Judgment: An Investigation into the Problem of Legal Praxis," 112. In the same sense, Rasch, "Judgment: The Emergence of Legal Norms."

(contrary to written law) serves as compelling evidence of this perspective. As Schmitt explains, judges are allowed to rule in opposition to legal texts as long as, following the hypothetical exercise discussed earlier, they conclude that other judges would have reached the same decision when confronted with an identical case. In Schmitt's own words, "a decision that conflicts with the literal meaning of a statute —that is, a decision *contra legem* [...]— is correct under the same conditions as any other: namely, when it would have been taken in the same way by another judge (by practice as a whole)"[186].

However, this does not imply that statutes are unimportant for Schmitt. Instead, it signifies that the concept of "law" encompasses additional elements that, in specific cases, may carry greater significance and thus warrant a deviation from what is stipulated in a positive legal text. Life is dynamic, and if law aims to regulate it (or at least certain aspects of it), it must introduce a degree of openness into its concept. Schmitt argues that the criterion he presents in *Statute and Judgment* precisely achieves that, since

> the positive statute, the cultural norms, the moral opinions of the people are no longer determinate and fixed rubrics under which a complex of events is to be classified—under which the case is to be subsumed—before one can conclude that the decision is correct. They are no longer the vessels into which the judge can pour the facts of the case. They step out of their tranquility and stability. They become the means of grounding an expectation (that this is how the case would, in general, have been decided); they become mobile and acquire a new function. Their static character is replaced by a new dynamism[187].

In other words, statutes, due to their static nature, cannot offer the required dynamism for law to effectively address the constantly evolving cases that require resolution. Schmitt's criterion, on the other hand,

---

186 Schmitt, "Statute and Judgment: An Investigation into the Problem of Legal Praxis," 135. As Herrero points out, "Judging correctly *contra legem* from this point of view, does not suppose an exception, but rather one of the multiple cases that satisfies the criterion formulated". Herrero, "Estudio preliminar," LXII.

187 Schmitt, "Statute and Judgment: An Investigation into the Problem of Legal Praxis," 116–17.

manages to accomplish this by asserting that not only statutes, but a multiplicity of elements influence legal decisions and positing that it is impossible to establish *a priori* the dominance of any one element over the others. This determination is left to the judge in each case, and it is subsequently (or rather simultaneously) legitimized by the community of judges (the legal *praxis*).

Schmittian scholars have interpreted this extension of the concept of law in two ways: as a form of judicial decisionism that justifies its legality *a posteriori*, and as an expansion of this concept that effectively incorporates the dynamism of real-life situations while also curbing judicial arbitrariness. William Rasch seems to belong to the first group. In *Judgment: The Emergence of Legal Norms* he argues, based on his reading of *Statute and Judgment*, "that we look at the emergence of norms as a supplement of legal decisions that retroactively legitimate these decisions by posing as presuppositions"[188]. He then adds that "the judge, by acting the way a judge should act, does not apply the law according to norms, but rather produces the norm in the very act of applying the law. The law, like the work of art, *reveals* the rules that guide its application only *after* it has been laid down"[189]. Although Rasch's primary objective in his paper is to argue that in *Statute and Judgment* the German Jurist operates within the framework of Kantian reflective judgment, his interpretation of this aspect of Schmitt's text still warrants attention. Rasch suggests that positive laws are not that practical for judges when deciding a specific case. Instead, they become useful after the decision is made, since they bestow judicial decisions with a "halo of legality" that legitimizes them before public opinion. Croce and Salvatore, aligning with Rasch's perspective, emphasize the radical nature of Schmitt's portrayal of the decision-making process. This characterization is considered radical because Schmitt notably omits any explanation for the criteria used to "select" the correct decision from among the various possible options. By not delineating the

188 Rasch, "Judgment: The Emergence of Legal Norms," 97.
189 Rasch, 102.

basis of decision-making, they argue, Schmitt leaves a significant gap in understanding how decisions should be judged or valued[190].

Herrero, on the other hand, argues that far from suggesting that judges are free to do as they please with statutes, in *Statute and Judgment* Schmitt affirms that judges must adhere to the law. The difference would be that for him this adherence does imply that judges should become mere mechanical arbiters who simply apply general descriptions from the text to specific cases. The legality to which they must abide extends beyond statutes (though it includes them) and can only be determined intersubjectively by the community of judges in each particular case (through the hypothetical exercise explained in § 2). In her words, "the judge does not create law but appeals to the law. When issuing a judgment, [. . .] he does not perform that task as if he were the legislator or an autonomous entity, but as a subject that participates in a task whose strength and prospective exceed him"[191]. In essence, the "legality" of a ruling is not a matter to be determined arbitrarily by the judge. Rather, it is an appellation that can be ascribed only to those decisions deemed legitimate and reasonable, not just by the individual judge, but also by the community of judges[192].

We believe both positions to be correct and that they are, in fact, reconcilable. Rasch and Croce and Salvatore are correct in their assertion that for Schmitt the judicial decision carries a "productive meaning". Indeed, as Schmitt himself recognizes, "the 'subjection to statute' or the 'conformity to statute' are not suitable criteria of the correctness of decision, for the reason that statute acquires a new content with

190 Cf. Croce and Salvatore, *The Legal Theory of Carl Schmitt*, 17. These authors are focused in the political character of the decision (the sovereign's decision). Their description, however, is also relevant for Schmitt's concept of law and the role that the judge's decision plays in it.

191 Herrero, "Estudio preliminar," LXIII–LXIV.

192 However, it is essential to note that Schmitt does not suggest that judges should literally seek the endorsement of their colleagues—that is, he does not advocate for judges to actively inquire whether their peers deem their decisions rational. The "other judge", as we explained in § 2, refers to a normative dimension.

every decision"[193]. That is, since judges are required to do more than merely subsume particular cases under the existing statute, and instead must offer an interpretation for each specific case that is deemed reasonable by "other judges", the legal text inevitably gains a new meaning each time it is applied to a particular situation. In this specific context, the judge acts, to some extent, as a "creator of law", albeit not as radically inventive as the legislator. This, however, does not imply that judges can regard the work of application of law as making free with the text[194]. On the contrary, their decisions must be according to legal statutes. The problem, however, is that if the legal phenomenon is not reducible to positive legal texts (statutes), determining if a decision is correct or not becomes an arduous task, and that is why Schmitt comes up with his hypothetical exercise (which, as we explained in § 2, manages to avoid, within the limits of what is possible, arbitrariness in judicial sentences). The thorough substantiation of legal decisions that the German jurist demands from judges also points in this direction, since it compels them to base their decision not solely on their perception of fairness, but on the normative elements at hand. In that sense, Herrero correctly asserts that the judge is not at liberty to interpret the normative elements as he wishes[195]; he must decide rationally.

Now, Schmitt's concept of law, along with his critiques of positivism and the provision of a criterion for the correctness of legal decisions, aims to provide an understanding the legal phenomenon that supersedes the predominant "scientistic" legal positivism of his time. He pursues this not only since he believes his theory to be superior, but also because he views positivism as an embodiment of a metaphysical approach to understanding the world that neglects characteristically human elements in favor of technological efficiency and calculability. Therefore, "the perspective he criticizes Kelsen from is

193 Schmitt, "Statute and Judgment: An Investigation into the Problem of Legal Praxis," 73. Note N°38.

194 Cf. Gadamer, *Truth and Method*, 341.

195 Cf. Herrero, "Estudio preliminar," XXXIX.

not epistemological but *existential*"[196]. As Ojakangas explains, Schmitt sees in legal positivism "a variant of the modern tendency towards the nihilistic self-propelling machine, for which every question concerning the concrete source and foundation of a system refers back to the system itself"[197].

Schmitt's anti-positivistic project, then, can be read as an effort to illustrate that technology, including its legal manifestations, is anything but "neutral". By this, we mean that Schmitt's legal theory wants to challenge the prevailing modern paradigm, which posits that technology and science can eliminate human caprice and the tendency to err (and therefore paves the way open for rationality and genuine knowledge). As Gadamer later explains, the notion that eliminating the influence of human subjectivity in knowledge equates to progress is deeply rooted in the core of modern thought. In his words, "there is one prejudice of the Enlightenment that defines its essence: the fundamental prejudice of the Enlightenment is the prejudice against prejudice itself"[198]. Schmitt, as Gadamer, firmly believes that technology is far from being neutral. He argues that technology leads to a closure to existence, limiting its alterity. This is because technology attempts to explain all of existence through allegedly "rational" categories created by human beings. The technological paradigm asserts that every aspect of human existence can be explained through science and rationality (with the belief that it's only a matter of time before science can elucidate what is currently unknown). Modernity imposes, via projection, a meaning on existence that transforms it into a self-contained system where everything can be explained using rational categories. This results in the interpretation of existence as stable, manageable, dispensable, and even artificially producible. In essence, it closes itself off to alterity by imposing a static meaning on existence, denying the possibility of its emergence through exceptional means.

---

196 Ojakangas, *A Philosophy of Concrete Life*, 51. In the same sense, Michael Marder, *Groundless Existence: The Political Ontology of Carl Schmitt* (London: Bloomsbury Publishing, 2014). Hofmann, *Legitimität gegen Legalität.*

197 Ojakangas, *A Philosophy of Concrete Life*, 50.

198 Gadamer, *Truth and Method*, 283.

Schmitt's critique of positivism, then, is not solely juridical. He views its pursuit of "purity" and its self-contained, logical, and systematic construction as a denial of the human element. As Ojakangas aptly explains, in legal positivism,

> the philosophical speculation on law was replaced by the scientific research on objective legal rules and norms. Schmitt sees here not only a step forward but also a step back, because in moving into a sphere of propositions and postulates jurisprudence becomes alienated from the concrete reality of man and institutions. In Schmitt's opinion, the transition to legal positivism paves the way for juridical nihilism, because it dismisses concrete origins and foundations, and thereby the concrete sources of the legitimacy of law. Law (*Recht*) is simply identified with legal rules and norms whereupon the mere objective existence of a norm becomes the criterion of its own validity and legality becomes the only form of legitimacy. According to the doctrine of positivism, argues Schmitt, "something is valid if it is valid and because it is valid"[199].

In other words, legal positivism represents a manifestation of modernity's technological paradigm as it aims to suppress the interference of the human element and explain the legal phenomenon solely through abstract statutes.

Therefore, Schmitt's examination of legal positivism serves as a critique aimed at the modern notion of removing human subjectivity from knowledge and the presumed neutrality that results from this removal. That is why his conceptual and practical critiques of legal positivism primarily revolve around the idea that a theory attempting to eliminate any reference to concrete life either implodes upon itself (as human interference can always be detected, even if assumed as an epistemological supposition, as seen in Kelsen's case)[200] or it is ultimately useless for legal praxis. In McCormick's words,

> Judges may be formally restricted by all the ironclad norms in the world, but at the moment of judgment there is always at least a slight leeway in how they

199 Ojakangas, *A Philosophy of Concrete Life*, 46.

200 For a further analysis of this topic, see: Paul Gragl, "The Pure Theory of Law and Legal Monism – Epistemological Truth and Empirical Plausibility," *Zeitschrift Für Öffentliches Recht*, no. 70 (2015): 665–736.

> apply norms. Thus does subjectivity rear its supposedly suppresses head. The reliance on the scientific method ignores the personal, the human element, only to ultimately undermine precisely that scientific project[201].

That is, the intrusion of human subjectivity is unavoidable if law is to exert any influence on concrete reality. Furthermore, every rational mechanism is ultimately driven by a specific individual who imparts purpose to it. Therefore, even a self-propelling machine, whether it be a sophisticated judging apparatus or a basic mechanical device, requires a tangible human presence to define its objectives[202].

Against this "pure" notion of law, Schmitt introduces a conceptualization of this phenomenon that incorporates a pivotal human instance: the deciding judge. In Ojakanga's words,

> Schmitt's concept of legal order includes two basic form-elements, the legal norm and the decision. The state of exception suspends the normative element of legal order and reveals the element of decision in its "absolute purity". However, as a juristic form-element the decision is not equal to the normative element. It is the constitutive form of law as such. This is the cornerstone of Schmitt's decisionism. The state of exception reveals the original non-normative ("free from any normative ties") character of law. It is not law as such (Recht) which recedes in the state of exception but the normative element of law (Gesetz). The state of exception reveals the existential character of law. It reveals that, in the final analysis, the decision is the law[203].

While Ojakangas primarily examines the constitutional state of exception in his reference, his argument is also applicable to *Statute and Judgment*. One of Schmitt's primary concerns in this text is to strike a balance between the legal certainty that is necessary for a relatively peaceful and orderly societal life, and the required dynamism for law to effectively regulate the ever-changing concrete human life. On one hand, Schmitt believes that it is essential for people individuals to have a clear understanding of what is legally permissible and prohibited in advance. On the other, he "argues that law does not have an

201 McCormick, *Carl Schmitt's Critique of Liberalism*, 221.
202 Cf. Ojakangas, *A Philosophy of Concrete Life*, 64.
203 Ojakangas, 55–56.

unchangeable or fixed content, but that it is 'constant living force' "[204]. Hence, it is impossible for legal texts, regardless of their quantity and quality, to comprehensively regulate every aspect of human life. A situation that was not foreseen in a legal text—an exceptional case will always emerge—and it falls upon the judge to provide a legal solution through a decision that is validated intersubjectively. Thus, the exceptional case demonstrates that law is not composed solely of a normative element. The judge's decision regarding the exceptional case would not be illegal due to the absence of a statutory reference, which would be the natural consequence of considering law as purely normativistic science. As there is no legal text to consult, the legality of his decision hinges on the fact that it is made by a judge fulfilling his judicial duties. Nevertheless, and as we have emphasized repeatedly in this work, this does not imply that the judge possess unfettered discretion to determine the content of a ruling when confronted with a legal vacuum. His decision must be just, and for this reason, he is obliged to substantiate it comprehensively, to the extent that another judge would deem it rational.

There is one final issue we wish to discuss in relation to Schmitt's concept of law and his criteria for the correctness of legal decisions: whether it effectively bridges the gap between abstract normativity and concrete facticity. Herrero, for example, believes that Schmitt is unable to propose a clear solution to this problem. In her words,

> from my point of view, Schmitt is not able to find his philosophical position between facticity and ideality. He keeps lurching to one side and the other. He pretends to find a normative criterion and, therefore, to flee from the pure deterministic facticity. The criterion must not simply ratify what actually happens, he argues quoting Hegel; however, when, to avoid the risk of incurring an abstract ideality, he tries to get out of such logic through the "normal type of trained lawyer", [. . .] he falls back into facticity[205].

In other words, Herrero suggests that Schmitt is hesitant when choosing between normativity and facticity. He oscillates between extremes

---

204 Neumann, *Carl Schmitt Als Jurist*, 17.

205 Herrero, "Estudio preliminar," LVIII.

without decisively determining which is more relevant for adjudicating a specific case.
While we acknowledge Herrero's analysis as accurate, we do not perceive this oscillation as a flaw in Schmitt's legal philosophy. As Herrero herself argues, legal "praxis can never aspire to the security of theory. No matter how much it insists on achieving this, it [reality] will always break its molds. [. . .] All these considerations, however, do not suggest a denial of the normative aspect in the criterion formulated by Schmitt"[206]. That implies that achieving mathematical certainty is not feasible, and as a result, we must settle for a more flexible level of certainty than what is offered by the natural sciences. In that sense, Schmitt's criterion offers the maximum level of certainty that a legal theory based on legal praxis can provide. Unfortunately, this means that what matters the most, the normative pole or concrete life, cannot be determined *a priori*, but only after the judge has taken into consideration all the particularities of the case and performed the hypothetical exercise previously explained. It is impossible to go beyond this, so our expectations must consider this premise and not demand the impossible.

In conclusion, Schmitt presents a concept of law that extends beyond statutes and encompasses normative elements. He also argues that it is impossible to determine *a priori* which of these elements is the most relevant to a specific case. This leads him to incorporate a human element that synthesizes and resolves any indeterminacy present in this chaotic phenomenon that is law: the judge's decision, Therefore, Schmitt's concept of law in *Statute and Judgment* consists of at least two components: the normative elements and the judge's decision. In the following section, we will delve deeper into the latter aspect.

206 Herrero, LVII.

d. The exception, history, and finitude: a recognition about how human understanding operates

In all of Schmitt's legal philosophy there is an idea that is often repeated, namely, that in law it is possible to identify a dichotomous and irreconcilable division between an abstract and a concrete world. In *The Value of the State and the Significance of the Individual*[207], published two years after *Statute and Judgment*, he recognizes this when stating that in the legal phenomenon "an opposition of two worlds is given. Should the law be autonomous and independent of power, then entails a dualism that corresponds to the antithesis of ought and is, of the normative and the genetic, of a critical and a natural-scientific inquiry"[208]. That is, on the one hand we have the abstract pole of law that is concerned with what ought to be (*Sollen*) without any consideration to any particular situation; on the other, there is the world of what actually is (*Sein*), of the concrete, where a particular situation needs a solution in light of what *ought to be* (at least in a legal sense). The problem is, as Herrera points out, that for the German Jurist there is an "insurmountable abyss" between the concrete and the abstract[209]. The dilemma that arises from this distinction is how to articulate these two worlds. In Schmitt's words, "the problem consists in connecting both realms to one another, in determining the point from which that which exists can be affected so as to come to conform to legal norms, and in such a way that the primacy of the law over power is preserved"[210].

Before explaining Schmitt's solution, we should first clarify that the need for a liaison between these dichotomous worlds does not arise from mere theoretical interest, but from the fact that concrete people require a legal solution for their problems. In other words, it is the contingent and complex nature of human life that, on the one hand, necessitates factual consideration to rise from the empirical realm and

207 The subsequent section will be devoted to a detailed analysis of this text.

208 Schmitt, "The Value of the State and the Significance of the Individual," 177.

209 Cf. Herrera, "Carl Schmitt como jurista," 60.

210 Schmitt, "The Value of the State and the Significance of the Individual," 188.

be examined in the context of abstract normativity, and, on the other hand, pressures law to abandon its purity and deliver justice for a specific concrete case. How does Schmitt propose that this insurmountable abyss can be resolved? He answers that the judge, through his decision, is the only one that can settle the tension between the abstract and the concrete world. In McCormick's words, "for Schmitt, between the law and concrete reality there will always be a gap that must be mediated by a judge"[211].

Schmitt's answer is not unexpected. In all of his legal, political, and existential thought, the institution of the decision is fundamental. Therefore, it is no surprise that already in one of his early works he addresses it as a way of resolving the aforementioned tension. In other words, as early as 1912, Schmitt began his *phenomenology of the exception*, as referred to by Pardo[212]. In this framework, the decision, particularly that of the judge, is the sole means to resolve the tension between an abstract normative world and a contingent, concrete one. In a similar sense, McCormick's explains that this—the decision—is a notion that Schmitt returns to in his later works:

> Just as Schmitt argues in his early treatises on law that a judge must mediate the gaps between the law and a particular case (gaps whose existence legal formalism denies) with a personal decision, he argues in *Political Theology* that a sovereign must address the political exception the situation for which the constitution does not provide explicit direction with a personal decision as well[213].

In other words, McCormick draws a parallel between Schmitt's political analysis of exceptions and his legal assertion that judges are responsible for reconciling the abstract dimension of normativity with the concrete aspects of everyday human life.

---

211 McCormick, *Carl Schmitt's Critique of Liberalism*, 209.

212 See: Celestino Pardo, "Estudio Preliminar," in *El Valor Del Estado y El Significado Del Individuo*, by Carl Schmitt, trans. Celestino Pardo, Clásicos Políticos (Madrid: Centro de Estudios Politicos y Constitucionales, 2014), XXIII. In a similar sense, Herrero points out that in Schmitt we have a *phenomenology of the decision*. Herrero, "Estudio preliminar," XXX.

213 McCormick, *Carl Schmitt's Critique of Liberalism*, 2013.

Now, what does the concept of the exception have to do with Schmitt's comments about law in *Statute and Judgment*? As mentioned earlier, Schmitt criticizes positivist legal theory, particularly its normativist variant, for primarily constructing its theory at an abstract level, effectively excluding the contingent concrete aspects of life. This implies that this perspective assumes judges are dealing with a stable, predictable reality in which unexpected situations are not a factor to be considered. The issue, however, lies in the fact that reality does not conform to positivism's assumptions.

While it is true that a certain level of "normality" or "stability" exists in concrete life, it is equally correct to assert that the "abnormal" or "exceptional" frequently arises, disrupting the established order of normality. In essence, the "exceptional" is an integral part of human reality. Schmitt argues that a legal theory which fails to acknowledge this fact is ultimately incapable of comprehending the full complexity of the legal phenomenon. Thus, in response to the question posed at the outset of this paragraph, *Statute and Judgment* reveals that, on the one hand, Schmitt demonstrates positivism to be a conceptually flawed and practically ineffective theory due to its neglect of the exceptional case[214]. On the other hand, he offers a legitimizing criterion for legal decisions based on the concept of the exception.

In *Statute and Judgment*, how does Schmitt suggest the exceptional case should be approached? In this work, the jurist from Plettenberg argues that the pertinent question is not *how* these inevitable types of situations are addressed, but rather *who* should be responsible for handling them. As McCormick explains,

> although Schmitt continuously emphasized the limited potency of man, the most important juridical question for him throughout his career was *quid judicabit*: "What matters for the reality of legal life is who decides". For the reality of that life the most central issue cannot be the norm itself, not even the basic

---

214 Bobbio highlights that this is the reason why the belief that judicial interpretations of law are solely logical operations—those that seek to deduce specific conclusions from predetermined premises—is no longer widely held. See: Bobbio, *Giusnaturalismo e positivismo giuridico.*

> norm, insofar as a norm is not an agent. It neither speaks nor acts. As such, it is totally mute and passive [. . .] According to Schmitt, only concrete persons can carry out these tasks. Only a concrete "who" decides on the validity of a norm[215].

In other words, and as Schmitt will later argue in *The Value of the State and the Significance of the Individual,* statutes are an entirely abstract phenomenon and, therefore, are unable to cope with anything that belongs to concrete human life (as is the case of the exceptional). Facticity, on the other hand, is also incapable of addressing the exceptional case without succumbing to unrestrained subjectivism. If the only criterion for judging the exceptional case is the transient and subjective perception of fairness, then a descent into arbitrary decisionism becomes inevitable. Consequently, there is a necessity for an arbiter who can effectively reconcile the normative, abstract dimension with the contingent, and often exceptional, concrete reality. Schmitt contends that the individual tasked with this responsibility — to provide a solution that is both normative, in the sense of being deemed rational and fair by any other judge, and capable of addressing the unique aspects of the exceptional case — is none other than the judge himself.

A final aspect, crucial for comprehending his critique of positivism in *Statute and Judgment*, concerns the relationship between transcendence and the exceptional situation. As previously discussed, Schmitt's critiques of positivism should not be interpreted solely in juristic terms. His criticism of this legal approach stems from the view that it represents a metaphysical perspective on the world, specifically, one centered on technology. Schmitt believes, as Ojakangas points out, that "the modern *Weltanschauung* entails the absolutization of immanence. [. . .]. Against it, Schmitt poeses transcendence, not in the sense of a substantial foundation of order but in the sense of *openness* of every order"[216]. Through his legal philosophy, Schmitt aims to challenge this worldview, asserting that not everything in existence is merely controllable immanence. However, as we have emphasized, Schmitt does

215 Ojakangas, *A Philosophy of Concrete Life*, 52.
216 Ojakangas, *A Philosophy of Concrete Life*, 203.

not advocate a return to classical natural law theory. As explained by Ojakangas, Schmitt regarded the era of traditional natural law—characterized by the belief in a transcendence providing moral normativity to be adhered to by law—as concluded. Consequently, he seeks to demonstrate that certain aspects of existence cannot be fully explained by immanence alone, yet he approaches this using the same methodology as technological thought, that is, without presupposing a transcendent normativity.[217]. In essence, Schmitt's legal philosophy aims to expose the insufficiency of understanding human existence purely in terms of immanence, as evidenced *by immanence itself.* It is in this context that he argues that transcendence manifests within immanence, particularly through the exceptional case.[218]. Schmitt contends that a systematic examination of law reveals that immanence itself indicates the incalculability and uncontrollability of existence. He substantiates this assertion by noting that regardless of how exhaustive and detailed the description of the legal phenomenon as an immanent and self-sufficient system may be, the unforeseen and exceptional will inevitably arise, disrupting the technological framework

The inevitability of the exceptional in law, then, is not simply a recognition of something occurring on the empirical plane that legal positivism overlooked, but an acknowledgment of the impossibility (or naivety) of explaining existence in terms of absolute immanence. In Ojakangas's words, Schmitt's

> concepts are posed as antipodes to absolute immanence. <However,> they do not oppose it from the perspective of the traditional notion of transcendence, that is to say, from the perspective of transcendence beyond immanence. Schmitt fully realized that late modernity is marked by a fundamental loss of such transcendence. [...] Therefore, Schmitt's [...] concepts should not be understood as establishing new transcendent foundations of order beyond immanence. But what are they, then? They denote transcendence *within* immanence. All of

217 Ojakangas, 46.

218 This aligns with Schmitt's depiction of God as being simultaneously transcendent and immanent. See: Carl Schmitt, "Die Sichtbarkeit Der Kirche: Eine Scholastische Erwägung," *Summa*, no. 1 (1918 1917): 71–80.

> Schmitt's central concepts refer to this transcendence within immanence and *it is this transcendence that he calls the concrete*[219].

In other words, in Schmitt's thought the exceptional, that is, the indeterminacy or situation that cannot be grasped by any human norm, emerges as transcendence. As Herrera points out, here law and theology approach one another[220]. This does not mean, however, that Schmitt's legal philosophy fully embraces a theological way of understanding the world. Instead, he believes that an adequate *Weltanschauung* must pay attention both to the transcendent and the immanent. That is why, in latter texts such as *The Nomos of the Earth* and *Glossarium*, Schmitt sustains that law is a phenomenon that is located between technology and theology, between the extremes of "total substantialism" and that of "absolute functionalism"[221].

There is a final point to consider in this section: how does the aforementioned relate to how human understanding operates? We believe that in this text, Schmitt is asserting at least two things about understanding (which he will further develop in his subsequent works): first, that it is historically conditioned, and second, that it is finite (we will revisit this in chapter three).

Regarding the first point, the analysis in this chapter suggests that throughout *Statute and Judgment*, Schmitt develops the idea that in law, a decision that was legitimate twenty years ago may no longer be acceptable today. For instance, a century ago, it might have been reasonable for the community of judges to believe that prostitutes did not have sufficient dignity to enjoy all constitutional rights and guarantees, whereas today, it would be manifestly contrary to the law for a judge to rule that way. In this sense, Schmitt recognizes the historicality of human beings in the development of his legal thought and, more specifically, in his criterion for the correctness of a legal decision. He posits that there must be a certain openness in the legal phenomenon to accommodate the shifts in paradigms that occur throughout

219 Ojakangas, *A Philosophy of Concrete Life*, 33.

220 Herrera, "Carl Schmitt como jurista," 57.

221 See: Herrera, 56–57.

history. Law must take these historical changes into consideration if it aims to dispense justice. Therefore, Schmitt introduces the notion of the mutability of the content of legal decisions according to the historicality of human beings. This recognition of mutability is essential for law to address this aspect of human nature, and that is precisely what Schmitt accomplishes in *Statute and Judgment* with the introduction of the other judge as a criterion for the correctness of legal decisions and his expanded concept of law.

Regarding the second point, we also believe that Schmitt's theory of law in this early text is grounded in the idea that our understanding as human beings is limited. By asserting that we should not aspire, as legal positivism did, to an absolute and timeless criterion for evaluating legal decisions, Schmitt seems to suggest, in line with Gadamer's later insights, that we must always remember our human limitations; we are not gods[222]. It is in this sense that his reflections upon the exceptional—transcendence—always unpredictably emerging immanently in concrete life should be understood. In other words, through these statements we believe Schmitt to be arguing that we must recognize that there is knowledge that our limited minds cannot grasp; thus, any line of thought, be it legal or metaphysical, that attempts to ignore this fact and explain existence by absolutizing immanence, will, sooner or later, be refuted by concrete life itself. Our understanding is finite, and therefore it cannot, by itself, "hope to survey in order to predict how they will operate in any given situation. 'Finitude' points to a dependency of knowledge on conditions that the human knower can never fully know"[223].

In conclusion, we believe, as Ojakangas, Herrero, and Herrera[224], among others, that Schmitt's legal thought, and specifically his 1912

222 Cf. Gadamer, *Hermeneutik*, 40.

223 Brice Wachterhauser, "Getting It Right: Relativism, Realism and Truth," in *The Cambridge Companion to Gadamer*, ed. Robert J. Dostal (Cambridge: Cambridge University Press, 2002), 56. Though Wachterhauser is talking about Gadamer, we believe his analysis is also applicable to Schmitt's legal thought.

224 Ojakangas, *A Philosophy of Concrete Life*. Herrero, "Estudio preliminar."

text *Statute and Judgment*, possesses significance not only from a legal perspective but also from a philosophical point of view. We contend that in this early work, three fundamental notions can be discerned that become pivotal in Schmitt's later writings, especially in *Über die drei Arten des rechtswissenschaftlichen Denkens*. These include the idea that the exceptional situation reveals the inadequacy of understanding existence solely in terms of immanence; the recognition that humans are influenced by historicality, necessitating its consideration in law; and, finally, the acknowledgment of the finitude of our understanding, which implies that our intellectual endeavors must always account for this aspect of human existence.

e. Legal decisions as a type of reflective judgment

A final issue that we believe is pertinent to analyze concerning *Statute and Judgment* is its relation to Kantian reflective judgment. We consider addressing this topic to be appropriate in this work because it is commonly discussed in the secondary literature. However, our treatment of it will not delve too deeply into the question of whether legal judgment can be legitimately viewed as a form of reflective judgment from a Kantian perspective. In this section, we aim to establish a connection between Schmitt's legal thought and Kantian reflective judgment before explaining how these two topics provide us with the necessary foundation to argue that Schmitt's examination of law leads him to elucidate some fundamental structures that operate in all human understanding.

In her *Preliminary Study* of her translation into Spanish of some legal works by Schmitt published under the title *Positions before Law*, Herrero states the following:

> The judgment is reflective, Kant says, if from the particular the universal is sought. This is precisely what is at stake in the criterion of correction of the judicial decision proposed by Schmitt. Some universality must exist if we can characterize the judgment about the particular case as correct. This criterion, however, cannot be found in legal theory. [...] Schmitt rejects the two solutions

> implicit in the Kantian approach: one is to consider universality as a norm under which one must subsume to carry out the determination; what Schmitt calls, in the second chapter, the erroneous presupposition that the decision has to be measured solely by statutes. The other, to leave the judgment to the subjectivity of the judge[225].

In a similar vein, Rasch[226] argues that in this text Schmitt employs the logic that underlies Kantian reflective judgment when articulating his criterion for verifying the correctness of a legal decision, since he requires, grounding his demand subjectively and not theoretically, "the other's assent"[227]. Before examining the legitimacy of these claims, we will (once again) provide some context for the argument.

In his *Critique of the Power of Judgment*, Kant "describes two different ways in which judgment can operate: depending upon whether it is first furnished with a universal or a particular, judgment may be 'determining' or 'reflective' "[228]. Determining judgments are responsible for applying the pre-established pure concepts (*a priori*) to specific particulars. In other words, the primary function of these judgments is to subsume intuitions under concepts, thereby enabling the experience of phenomena. Reflective judgments, on the other hand, operate in the following manner: the particular is given, and it is the universal—the concept—that needs to be discovered[229].

Kant's rationale behind this distinction is as follows: determining judgments elucidate a specific aspect of phenomena, namely the conditions that make experience possible, but they do not account for other attributes like beauty or purpose, which remain undefined and undetermined. The

---

225 Herrero, "Estudio preliminar," LIII. Herrero affirms that Kant's third critique has consequences for legal though based on Wieland's article *Kants Rechtsphilosophie der Urteilskraft*. Wolfgang Wieland, "Kants Rechtsphilosophie Der Urteilskraft," *Zeitschrift Für Philosophische Forschung* 52, no. 1 (1998): 1–22.

226 Herrero, "Estudio preliminar." Rasch, "Judgment: The Emergence of Legal Norms."

227 Cf. Rasch, "Judgment: The Emergence of Legal Norms," 101.

228 Paul Guyer, *Kant and the Claims of Taste*, 2. ed (Cambridge: Cambridge Univ. Press, 1997), 35.

229 Cf, CJ, FI, IV, 5:180.

objective of the reflective use of judgment is to furnish the concepts (universals) that govern these facets of existence[230]. However, as we learned from the *Critique of Pure Reason*, human knowledge has its limitations. These concepts—the ones that the reflective use of the power of judgment pursues—are located beyond them. Therefore, we cannot fully grasp and comprehend these concepts and must merely subjectively assume that *if* they exist, they were provided by a supersensible understanding (God). Hence, when discussing the concepts (universals) that the reflective use of the power of judgment aims to grasp, we are subjectively placing our object of study within the realm of the supersensible, a domain where human knowledge is inherently unattainable.

In his third critique, Kant's focus is centered on reflective judgments, particularly in Aesthetic and Teleological ones. He directs his analysis on these types of judgments, not because they are the only form of reflective judgments in existence, but because they serve as exemplars illustrating how this type of judgment, where the particular is given and the universal must be discerned, operates.[231]. In that regard, it is not unreasonable to contemplate that other types of judgments, like those rendered by judges, could also be regarded as reflective.

Now, does Schmitt believe that legal decisions are a type of reflective judgment? Answering this question requires a thorough historical analysis which involves a series of skills that are beyond our reach, which is why we will not delve into it. Nonetheless, from a philosophical perspective rooted in conceptual examination, we posit that there are resemblances between the logic employed by Schmitt in *Statute*

230 In this sense, in the *First Introduction* of the *Critique of Judgment*, Kant states that "particular experience, thoroughly interconnected in accordance with constant principles, also requires this systematic interconnection of empirical laws, whereby it becomes possible for the power of judgment to subsume the particular under the general, however empirical it may be, and so on, right up to the highest empirical laws and the forms of nature corresponding to them, and thus regard the **aggregate** of the particular experiences as a **system** of them; for without this presupposition no thoroughly lawlike interconnection, i.e., empirical unity of this experiences can [be] (sic) obtained". CJ, FI, II, 20:203.

231 Douglas Burnham, *An Introduction to Kant's Critique of Judgement* (Edinburgh: Edinburgh University Press, 2000), 40.

and Judgment and the manner in which Kant delineates the operation of reflective judgment. We believe the similarities to be the following: in *Statute and Judgment* Schmitt expands the concept of law (as we already saw in § 3) and includes numerous (and diverse) normative elements. This results in the situation where numerous crucial elements for the resolution of a case are left unspecified by legal statutes. We contend that in *Statute and Judgment*, Schmitt's objective is to provide a certain unity to this multifaceted legal phenomenon (after demonstrating that legal positivism is incapable of achieving it), and he accomplishes this through the normative concept of the "other judge". Scattered throughout Schmitt's explanation of the hypothetical exercise he requires judges to undertake, one can discern a surprisingly "reflective" notion, namely, that judges must, albeit subjectively, assume that there is a certain rationality in legal judgments that should be shared by all magistrates. That is, he argues, in a similar manner as Kant did in his third critique when addressing the *sensus communis,* that there exists a rational unity within the "legally manifold" that we subjectively assume to be shared by everyone, but that we are unable to conceptualize because, *if* such a rationality does indeed exists, it resides beyond the possibilities of our understanding as human beings.

In conclusion, we believe that Schmitt's characterization of the procedure judges must follow when ruling in *Statute and Judgment* can be read in terms of Kantian reflective judgments. This is based not only on how they function (the judge is confronted with a specific case and must seek to identify a suitable universal for it) but also on the concept of the "other judge" that Schmitt encourages judges to gravitate toward. Schmitt urges judges to embrace a supersensible idea of justice that is assumed, albeit subjectively, to be shared by all other judges. Furthermore, the fact that Schmitt explicitly mentions Kant's *Critique of the Power of Judgment* in this book when asserting that his criterion does aim to serve as a guide for producing aesthetic genius[232] seems to confirm Rasch's and Herrero's suspicions. It should be noted, however, that while it is admissible to contemplate Schmitt's portrayal of legal

232 Schmitt, *Gesetz Und Urteil*, 73.

judgments in terms of Kantian reflective judgment, there is a feature of these types of judgments that sets them apart from those examined by Kant (aesthetic and teleological). Namely, the requirement for a decision that determines what is just in a particular case.

f. Some conclusions regarding Statute and Judgment

We began this chapter by stating that Schmitt has two purposes in *Statute and Judgment*, namely, to demonstrate the weaknesses of the positivist way of understanding the legal phenomenon, and to offer a new way of understanding law grounded on legal practice by posing a criterion for judges to verify whether their decisions are or not correct. Consequently, the questions that guided our research in this chapter were the following: does Schmitt succeed in demonstrating the weaknesses of this line of legal thought? And, is he able to provide a legitimizing criterion of judicial decisions grounded in legal practice? There also was another question that, even though we did not explicit in the introduction to this chapter, quietly guided our examination of the early work of Schmitt, namely, the general inquiry that this work addresses: is Schmitt saying something concerning the way human understanding operates through his legal philosophy in *Statute and Judgment*?

In §a, we focused on the first question, that is, whether Schmitt is able to establish the shortcomings of legal positivism. Specifically, we explained that in this early text the German jurist sets himself to prove that, on the one hand, legal positivism is incapable of maintaining a conceptual coherence, and, on the other, fails to provide a criterion for verifying the correctness of legal decisions that is useful in legal praxis. Schmitt's primary argument is that legal positivism faces both theoretical and practical issues that result in the theory crumbling under the weight of its conceptual foundations, rendering it incapable of comprehending the tangible and practical aspects of law. The jurist from Plettenberg argues that legal positivism consistently compromises its "purity" in order to address the conceptual challenges it encounters. In pursuit of this very purity, it sets aside concrete reality and deals solely with abstract normative concepts.

After reviewing Schmitt's critiques of legal positivism, we proceeded to analyze Schmitt's proposal of a criterion for judges to verify whether their decisions concerning particular cases are correct or not (in §b). That is, we addressed our second question, namely, whether the German jurist is able to provide a legitimizing criterion of judicial decisions grounded in legal practice. As we explained in that section, Schmitt's proposal is the following: "[A] judicial decision is correct, today, if it is to be assumed that another judge would have decided in the same way. 'Another judge', in this context, refers to the empirical type of the modern, legally trained jurist"[233]. Put differently, when making a decision in a case, judges should hypothetically validate it (their decision) by asking themselves whether the judicial community would endorse it. After posing his proposition, we explained that:

a. Schmitt's own words prevent us from interpreting his criterion in terms of a psychology or sociology of masses, or as a methodology similar to the *Common Law.*
b. The "other judge" should be understood as a normative concept. That is, it refers to the "normal" juridically educated judge, where "the word 'normal' is used here in a quantitative sense that refers to the average, not as the designation of an ideal type and not in a qualitative-teleological sense"[234].
c. The notion that legal reality is incommensurable underlies his criterion for the correctness of legal decisions. That fundamental characteristic renders it impossible to reduce legal methodology to a set of rules that guarantee mathematical precision (and the fact that positivism did not grasp this is the main reason for its failure). This leads Schmitt to contend that the effectiveness of such a criterion should not be judged solely by its conceptual precision but rather by its utility in legal

233 Schmitt, "Statute and Judgment: An Investigation into the Problem of Legal Praxis," 103.
234 Schmitt, 109.

practice. In this regard, we posited that even though Schmitt's criterion is not flawless, it is sufficiently effective.

While in sections §a and §b, our primary focus was on the legal aspects of Schmitt's early work, in §c, we began to explore the philosophical implications of Schmitt's juridical theory. Specifically, we argued that:

a. In this text, the German jurist employs (or more precisely, formulates) a concept of law that differs from the one upheld by legal positivism. He argues that law is not constituted solely by legal texts but rather by two fundamental ingredients: the normative elements (which include statutes, principles, and custom, among others) and the decision of the judge.
b. The Schmittian rationale behind this notion is that it is impossible for legal statutes (regardless of their number) to regulate every facet of human life. A situation that was not anticipated in the legal text, namely, an exceptional case, will inevitably arise. In such instances, it is the judge, through a decision validated intersubjectively (as we elaborated in §b), who must o a solution.
c. The aforementioned has implications in Schmitt's thinking, since now legal decisions possess a certain "creative significance". That is, given that judges must not only subsume particular cases under the statutes, but rather provide an interpretation for a particular case that must be deemed reasonable by "other judges", legal texts inevitably acquire new meaning each time they are. Nonetheless, this does not suggest that judges can perceive the process of applying the law as an opportunity for unrestricted text interpretation[235]. Instead, they must make rational decisions[236] (which is precisely the objective of Schmitt's criterion).
d. With this "broad" conception of law, Schmitt not only seeks to supplant the one maintained by legal positivism but also

235 Cf. Gadamer, *Truth and Method*, 341.
236 Cf. Herrero, "Estudio preliminar," XXXIX.

aims to combat the scientific and metaphysical interpretation of existence. He views this positivistic perspective as a manifestation of a metaphysical worldview that omits what is distinctly human and substitutes it with the efficiency and predictability of technology. In this regard, his critique of legal positivism takes on an existential dimension.

e. The manner in which Schmitt "challenges" technology as a framework for comprehending existence is by asserting that the involvement of human subjectivity is unavoidable if law is to exert any influence on the concrete reality.

In §d we ventured beyond the juridical aspect of *Statute and Judgment* and delved into some of the philosophical implications that can be derived from thit text. We began to elucidate the central question addressed by this work: namely, whether Schmitt's legal philosophy is, in fact, making assertions about the way human understanding operates. Specifically, we sustained that:

a. Throughout Schmitt's legal philosophy, the following notion is consistently present: within the realm of law, there exists a dichotomous and irreconcilable division between an abstract and a concrete world. On one hand, there is an abstract aspect concerned with what ought to be (*Sollen*), without regard for any specific situation (the domain of law); on the other hand, there is the world of the concrete (*Sein*), where a particular situation demands a solution. This distinction brings about Schmitt's main dilemma, namely, that of articulating and reconciling these dichotomous realms.
b. The German jurist argues that this insurmountable abyss can only be resolved by a concrete and empirical judge. It is only through the judge's decision that the tension between the abstract and the concrete world can be reconciled.
c. From the concept of "the exceptional" situation that statutes did not anticipate, we contend that Schmitt is asserting the historicality of the legal phenomenon. We argued that this idea

can already be discerned in this early Schmittian text when he asserts that the factors enabling a law to endure and uphold its legitimacy over time are not solely its legality but also the ongoing revisions of the text carried out by legal literature and jurisprudence.

d. Through his legal philosophy, Schmitt seeks to challenge the technological way of understanding the world. The exceptional situation plays a pivotal role in this endeavor. Through this perspective, it becomes apparent that the German jurist is endeavoring to assert that existence is not solely immanent—such a view would imply that humans can control it by unveiling the mechanistic laws governing immanence. Instead, Schmitt suggests that the exceptional, representing the form that transcendence assumes within immanence, is always inherently present *within* immanence.

The aforementioned considerations that we explored in §d have led us to the conclusion that even in this 1912 text, Schmitt, through his legal philosophy, is conveying at least two aspects regarding human understanding (elements that he will expand upon in subsequent texts): firstly, that it is historically conditioned, and secondly, that it is finite.

In sum, we believe the inquiry conducted in this chapter enables us to discern that in 1912, certain foundational ideas for Schmitt's philosophy, such as the historicality of law, the limitation of our understanding, and the significance of the exception, were already beginning to take shape. While some of these ideas, like the historicality of humanity, may have been in an early developmental stage in *Statute and Judgment*, we contend that their fundamental aspects were already present in this early text. As we will argue in the subsequent chapters, acknowledging this fundamental human dimension for a comprehensive understanding of the legal phenomenon sets the stage for the incorporation (in law) of the *openness* that characterizes existential hermeneutics. In the forthcoming section, we will explore how Schmitt undertakes a similar endeavor to that found in *Statute and Judgment*, but this time from the perspective of political law.

§ 2. Power, law, and people: *The Value of the State and the Significance of the Individual* (1914)

In 1914, Schmitt published his habilitation work under the title *The Value of the State and the Significance of the Individual* (*Der Wert des Staates Und die Bedeutung Des Einzelnen*). In this text, Schmitt analyzes the relation between "Power", "law", and the "state". He also reflects on the consequences that the articulation of these concepts holds for individuals. In his words,

> the investigation restricts itself to several definite questions: that concerning the relation between law and state, [as well as] that concerning the definition of the state and of the consequences that result for the individual in the state. The numerous questions, in particular, which are connected to a definition of the law [*Recht*] are discussed only to the extent that this was requisite to laying out the essence of the state in order to find the path through a plethora of problems and to provide the context for a complete legal-philosophic theory of the state[237].

While the aforementioned is Schmitt's primary concern in this work, he also explores the abstract nature of law, the concrete aspect of individual human life, and the challenge of reconciling both of these realms through the agency of the state. That is, in *The Value of the State and the Significance of the Individual* Schmitt revisits the tension between the abstractness of law and the concreteness of human life. However, this time he does so from a different perspective, namely, that of political law.

The Value of the State and the Significance of the Individual is divided into three chapters. The first is dedicated to "Law and Power"; the second to "The State"; and the third to "The individual". Schmitt's primary objective is to clarify whether the state precedes and subsequently establishes law, or if law precedes and the state is one of its creations (Schmitt holds the second position to be true). He also expresses

237 Schmitt, "The Value of the State and the Significance of the Individual," 173.

concerns about the repercussions of this discourse for the individual who is subject to both the state and law.

The structure of Schmitt's text facilitates the formulation of the questions that will guide our research throughout this chapter. They are the following: is Schmitt able to sufficiently justify the primacy of law over the state? (1); what are the consequences that he believes his position holds for the individual? (2). Does this 1914 text contribute to Schmitt's concept of law? (3); and is Schmitt saying something about the manner in which human understanding operates? (4).

Before addressing the questions posed above, two topics need to be explored. The first pertains to Schmitt's approach towards the subject. Given that he discusses the state and its relationship with law and individuals, one might assume that Schmitt approached this issue from a political standpoint. The fact that his next significant work is *Political Romanticism* (1919) seems to corroborate this suspicion. However, in *The Value of the State and the Significance of the Individual*, the jurist from Plettenberg explicitly states that while his research explores certain political aspects of law, this book constitutes a legal-philosophical inquiry[238]. He also emphasized that "the present book is only justified because it recognizes the State's rationality, and, therefore, does not attempt to draw political conclusions"[239].

Should we believe Schmitt? As will be demonstrated throughout this chapter, Schmitt's primary concern revolves around the tension between the abstract nature of law and the concreteness of facticity. Therefore, it appears that there is some truth in his statement. Nevertheless, he also addresses, mainly in the chapter dedicated to the individual, some political issues, such as the role politicians should play given the premise that law is the cause and foundation of the state. Therefore we disagree with Schmitt because this book cannot be easily categorized solely as either legal-philosophical or political. Instead, it appears to be more of a "transitional book", one where Schmitt is

238 Schmitt, 165.
239 Schmitt, 166.

beginning, perhaps unconsciously, to bridge his theory of law with the realm of politics.

The second issue that needs to be addressed before delving into Schmitt's work is whether, in his examination, Schmitt is merely describing a factual reality or actually pouring some of his substantive thought. That is, if he is merely "drawing a picture" of how modern state relates to law and the individual, or if he is arguing how, from a theoretical point of view, this relation ought to be considered. Although she does not extensively explore this issue, in her translation to Spanish of some legal works by Carl Schmitt, Herrero points out that in this book Schmitt is merely describing the position of the individual in the modern rule of law[240]. In other words, she suggests that we are dealing with a primarily descriptive work. Volker Neumann, on the other hand, believes that even in this 1914 text, Schmitt is developing certain ideas about the state that will become fundamental in some of his later works (such as *Dictatorship* and *Political Romanticism*)[241]. In this discussion, we align ourselves with Neumann's perspective. As we already mentioned, *The Value of the State and the Significance of the Individual* seems to be a book where Schmitt's transitions from a legal philosophy that is strictly legal, to a legal philosophy with political repercussions. In that sense, while it is true that Schmitt describes the modern state within the framework of legal positivism, he also suggests a political solution, a method for restoring dignity to the individual in the era of the modern state.

One last point we'd like to address before delving into this analysis is that Schmittian secondary literature has generally overlooked this 1914 text. Furthermore, the limited references made to *The Value of the State and the Significance of the Individual* typically serve as an introduction to Schmitt's exploration of the legitimacy of the state over

240 Herrero, "Estudio preliminar," XXIII.

241 For instance, Neumann asserts that in *The Value of the State and the Significance of the Individual*, a concept of legality—extending beyond mere legitimacy—which justifies a suspension of the constitutional state is notably present. Neumann, *Carl Schmitt Als Jurist*, 24.

positive legality in his later works. Consequently, our discussion will be more focused than in the previous section.

Our road map for analyzing Schmitt's 1914 book and addressing the questions posed above is: first, we will explore the intricate relationship between law and the state (a), followed by a review of Schmitt's differentiation between abstract and concrete law (b). Subsequently, we will elucidate the implications of the preceding discussion for the individual (c), before concluding this section with what we consider to be some valuable insights (d).

a. The state and law: a complex relationship

It is in *The Value of the State and the Significance of the Individual* where Schmitt thematizes with remarkable clarity within law, two poles of (legal) existence are in constant tension: one normative/legal and another factual and concrete. The statement made by Schmitt in the opening pages of this text, that "Science [of Law], according to its concept, stands in fundamental opposition to active life"[242], serves as evidence for this assertion.

Schmitt contends that the normative/legal pole is inherently devoid of any reference to the empirical world. Furthermore, if, by any chance, law were to "descend" to the specific and contingent issues of concrete reality, that transition would imply a grave deficiency within it[243]. In this regard, the classic argument that posits the difference between moral and legal obligations as the potential for coercion in the latter contradicts the fundamental nature of legal normativity. In Schmitt's words, "a complex of norms to whose essence it pertains to have a 'tendency towards enforceability' would be a paring of heterogeneous things, since the norm retains its validity and value independently of reality, and therewith also independently of its realization and its

242 Schmitt, "The Value of the State and the Significance of the Individual," 170.
243 Cf. Schmitt, 172.

enforceability"[244]. Law is a mandate, an "ought to be" (*sollen*), against which man, as an object of the "real world", follows[245].

At the same time, nothing normative is inherent in the existence of concrete life. It is a realm where things simply are (that of the *Sein*). Therefore, any reference to normative concepts, such as good or bad, just or unjust, permitted or prohibited, is incongruous in this context. A possible objection to this distinct juxtaposition between both worlds could be that law frequently references "factual assumptions" in its regulation (e.g. if you kill an innocent, you will be punished with...), which appears to be a direct reference to the empirical realm. Schmitt, however, argues that these factual assumptions are not events that transpire in real life but rather typifications prescribed in legal norms[246]. In other words, they are hypothetical situations to which law assigns legal consequences, but they are not *real*[247].

The problem, as Schmitt himself points out, is that, even though law possesses an abstract nature, it is intended to produce effects on concrete reality. Therefore, the primary challenge this phenomenon must grapple with is how to bridge both domains, how to connect the *sollen* with the *sein*[248]. Schmitt's problem, as Neumann correctly explains, is

244 Cf. Schmitt, 187.

245 Cf. Schmitt, 187–88.

246 Cf. Schmitt, 187–88.

247 In his 1933 text *On the Three Types of Juristic Thought* Schmitt seems to contradict himself, because he then stated that "without persistent, unavoidable, and indispensable concrete suppositions there is neither jurisprudential theory nor jurisprudential practice. These legal suppositions, however, develop directly out of the concrete assumptions of a presumed normal condition and of a presumed normal type of man". That is, he argues that legal normativity arises from concrete reality, assuming, therefore, that reality already provides us with normative content. Though this matter justifies a rather long treatment, for now we will venture that in this early text Schmitt still poses existence as dichotically structured (the abstract vs the concrete). However, in his later though he seems to recognize that there is a certain unity between the ideal and the concrete. Therefore, there is a shift on his thought concerning this topic. Schmitt, *On the Three Types of Juristic Thought*, 46.

248 Cf. Schmitt, "The Value of the State and the Significance of the Individual," 187–88.

that "on the one hand, law must not contain a single molecule of social reality; on the other, it must nevertheless press for its realization"[249]. The elucidation of the relationship between law and the state, argues the lawyer of Plettenberg, enables us to understand how the connection between the normative world and factuality operate (which is why he undertakes the task of examining these concepts in this 1914 book).

Schmitt explains that the state is not an entity that belongs to the world of abstract normativity. On the contrary, because the exercise of power requires reference to the empirical realm, the state necessarily operates within the concrete sphere. However, the concept "State" is not entirely empirical; instead, it derives its "dignity," as Schmitt terms it, from legality. Let's elaborate on this: If the state were mere facticity then it "would only be a violent power, unjustified and irrational, of which it could only be said that it is a 'will', a terrorism, to which we have become habituated, and from which some know how to profit"[250]. If that were the case, we would have a multitude of distinct states subject to various forms of normativity, each legitimized solely by the passage of time[251]. However, we can observe that there are, at least in some fundamental respects, normative similarities among different states. It could be argued that this is not necessarily due to a reference to some form of transcendent normativity, but rather because we derive the concept of the "State" by considering all existing states and identifying what is common among them. In this sense, the concept we use to describe these entities would be contingent, and therefore subject to change.

While this argument may seem plausible at first glance, a closer examination reveals that it involves a logical fallacy. As Schmitt points out, "the concept attained via an abstraction from one hundred imperfect things cannot yield the concept of a perfect thing, not 'the' concept of the state, which must form the basis of philosophic considerations"[252].

249 Neumann, *Carl Schmitt Als Jurist*, 23.
250 Schmitt, "The Value of the State and the Significance of the Individual," 190.
251 Cf. Schmitt, 175–76.
252 Schmitt, 193.

In other words, this procedure would be riddled with contradictions because it aims to derive a concept in which different objects must be categorized from the same objects that are to be categorized[253]. Therefore, it appears that there must be something more than mere facticity at play in these public entities. In Schmitt's words,

> the concept of the state can only be ascertained by assigning the state a position in a system of values, one from which its authority follows. The state that is to be something other than the cumulative effect, conceived as independent essence, of the actions of individual humans, a point of intersection of causes and effects, [that is to be] more than senseless power [. . .] The state owes its dignity to its conformity to a norm [*Gesetzlichkeit*] can only be found in the law, the law that is not to be defined from the state but rather the state from the law, the state is not the creator of the law, but rather the law is the creator of the state: the law precedes the state[254].

Differently put, the conceptual analysis that Schmitt conducts in the first chapter of *The Value of the State and the Significance of the Individual* leads him to the conclusion that law precedes the state and is actually responsible for its creation. Therefore, it appears natural that in the second chapter of that text, the jurist from Plettenberg analyzes the legal phenomenon to specifically elucidate the legality that constitutes the entity we recognize as the state.

Before proceeding with Schmitt's examination of law, it's worth noting that the clarity of the argument presented by the German jurist in the first chapter of *The Value of the State and the Significance of the Individual* makes Wolin's interpretation of it quite surprising. In his article on Schmitt's "political existentialism", this author contends that

> in this phase [1914], Schmitt's early Catholicism is to the fore, as he takes up the question of the relation between the state and civil society. Unsurprisingly, in Schmitt's conception the balance must be totally resolved in the state's favor.

253 Schmitt, 190.
254 Schmitt, 193.

> Here, the individual is merely "a means to the essence, the state is what is most important". Law itself has no validity prior to the state[255].

In other words, Wolin believes that Schmitt's logic in this text leads him to the conclusion that the state comes before law. However, upon closer examination of this 1914 book, particularly the last reference we made to it, one could plausibly argue that Wolin's interpretation appears to be incorrect or, at the very least, incomplete. However, as we will explain shortly, Schmitt distinguishes between the legality that the state produces and the one that constitutes the state in the first place. Therefore, there is indeed a type of legality that comes after the state. Nevertheless, Schmitt's primary argument in *The Value of the State and the Significance of the Individual* is that law comes before the state. If that were not the case, then all the subsequent analysis that the German jurist makes on law would not make sense[256].

The philosophical problem that Schmitt's addresses in the *The Value of the State and the Significance of the Individual*, then, is quite specific: that of the legitimation of public power (that of the state)[257]. It is in this context that Schmitt argues that law comes before the state. The problem is that if we look at positive legal texts, it is obvious that they emerged from political institutions and procedures that were established *by* the state. So, the question that naturally arises is: to what kind of legality is Schmitt referring to? The next section will provide an answer to this inquiry.

---

255 Richard Wolin, "Carl Schmitt, Political Existentialism, and the Total State," *Theory and Society* 19, no. 4 (1990): 395–96.

256 It must be noted, however, that Wolin is right regarding the individual.

257 Cf. Hofmann, *Legitimität gegen Legalität*, 10–11. It must be noted that this author argues that the problem of legitimacy of power is key to the reading of Schmittian philosophy as a whole, and not just for *The Value of the State and the Significance of the Individual.*

b. Abstraktes Recht and Staatliche Recht: a fundamental distinction

In *The Value of the State and the Significance of the Individual* Schmitt distinguishes between two types of law. On one hand, there is what he calls "abstract law" (*abstraktes Recht*), which "was there before the state and which, as a thought, is independent of the state"[258]. On the other hand, there is "State law" (*Staatliche Recht*) "which does not stand to the originary law in the relation of means and end, whose purposiveness, rather, consists in its inclusion of the empirical world as the field of its effects"[259]. In this section, we will argue that, although somewhat cryptic or obscure, this distinction is fundamental for understanding this 1914 Schmittian text.

As we explained, in this early work the German jurist argues that "the law is abstract thought, which cannot be derived from facts and cannot have any effect on facts"[260]. In other words, law is pure abstraction; and it cannot be derived from the empirical, nor is it possible to include anything empirical in it. The problem, however, is that this phenomenon is intended to be applied in practical reality. The question then arises: how is it that an absolutely abstract phenomenon, inevitably distant from concrete reality, manages to generate an effect on the latter? The distinction between "abstract law", "State law", and how they both relate to the state (considered as an empirical entity) allows us to understand how Schmitt overcomes this "insurmountable abyss".

The short answer to the previous question is that the state is the only entity that can bridge the gap between the normative and concrete poles. As Schmitt explains, the state "signifies the point at which theory and practice touch, because the theory of practice turns into the practice of theory"[261]. Why? Because law, as a purely abstract phenomenon, is incapable of applying itself. In fact, if we argued that what is characterizes law is its coercibility, we would be introducing something

258 Schmitt, "The Value of the State and the Significance of the Individual," 211.
259 Schmitt, 211.
260 Schmitt, 188.
261 Schmitt, 170.

empirical into it, causing it to lose its normative and pure character[262]. Thus, law needs the state to achieve its purpose[263]. But what kind of legality is he talking about? If he were referring to legal statutes (which emanate from the state), we would be reducing the sphere of the legal to pure facticity. This is because, in that case, the state would be responsible for both creating and executing law, implying that the law originates from the same power that then applies it[264].

According to Schmitt, a position like the one just described is unacceptable. It ignores the normative aspect of this phenomenon and reduces law to an empirical force that can be explained merely in causal terms[265]. Law, argues the German jurist, is not pure facticity[266]. If that were the case, one would not be able to inquire about the justice or injustice of an action. Everything belonging to the legal sphere would be pure contingency that has been legitimized by the mere passage of time. The problem is that an explanation that reduces legality to positive law, and ultimately to power, collapses on itself for the simple reason that it is unable to explain the origin of the norm that legitimizes all subsequent norms. Differently put, the causal explanation cannot logically extend itself to infinity. There must be a legality, different from that created by the state, that establishes the conditions under which legal statutes acquire such character[267]. Here is where the distinction

262 Cf. Schmitt, 185–86.

263 Cf. Schmitt, 185.

264 For a more profound analysis on Schmitt's political ideas concerning the application of positive law see: Joseph J Bendersky, *Carl Schmitt. Theorist for the Reich* (Princeton: Princeton University Press, 2016). Heiner Bielefeldt, *Kampf und Entscheidung: Politischer Existentialismus bei Carl Schmitt, Helmuth Plessner und Karl Jaspers* (Würzburg: Königshausen & Neumann, 1994).

265 Cf. Schmitt, "The Value of the State and the Significance of the Individual," 177–82.

266 Hofmann argues that Schmitt does reduce law to facticity. In the following pages we will refer to this matter more profoundly. Cf. Hofmann, *Legitimität gegen Legalität*, 99–100.

267 Schmitt, "The Value of the State and the Significance of the Individual," 177.

between abstract law (*asbtraktes Recht*) and state law (*Staatliche Recht*) shows its usefulness.

The analysis conducted by Schmitt leads him to deduce that there are two distinct types of legality: one of an abstract nature, devoid of empirical elements, and another capable of translating normativity into effective reality. The former, which Schmitt terms *abstraktes Recht*, is what constitutes the state in the first place. According to the German jurist, the reason for the need to create such an entity is that law, positioned at the ideal pole of existence, must "become human" or "become flesh"[268] to be effective in the real pole of existence. This entails that "the giving up of timeless correctness and the reception of a moment of indifference with regard to content are consequence of the εναθρωπηςις (becoming human) of law, the sacrifice that must be offered because a pact was made with the powers of the real world of appearances"[269]. In other words, just as the *invisible* church must renounce its abstract nature for it to have a salvific effect on humanity (as argued by Schmitt in *The Visibility of the Church*[270]), law must shed its timelessness and ahistoricality so that its normativity can produce practical effects on concrete reality. The state, in turn, creates its own law (*Staatliche Recht*) with the objective of ordering the chaos that is reality and facilitating the "practical landing" of normativity (i.e., to achieve its end). In Schmitt's words, "the legal thought, which is to serve as a yardstick for the transformation of reality, must become positive, that is, its content is *set* by an act of sovereign decision, it becomes a statute and is articulated in a concrete version"[271].

Now, given that both the state and its law (*staatliches Recht*) originate from abstract law, they are inevitably subject to it. Consequently, the state and positive law cannot be regarded merely as products of

268 Schmitt uses the Greek concepto εναθρωπηςις, which, according to Vinx and Garrett, should be translated as "«the becoming human», «the becoming flesh»". This can be found in note xcvi of the English translation of this 1914 text. Schmitt, 238.

269 Schmitt, 214.

270 Schmitt, "Die Sichtbarkeit Der Kirche: Eine Scholastische Erwägung."

271 Schmitt, "The Value of the State and the Significance of the Individual," 213.

convention. They are bound to adhere to the abstract normativity established by *abstraktes Recht*, while simultaneously integrating its content into concrete reality, thereby allowing the former to influence the latter.

Regarding the state, the German jurist contends that its subordination to law implies that the state is inevitably under the "rule of law". In his words,

> the term "rule-of-law state" [*Rechtsstaat*] likewise indicates the primacy of the law, since it signifies a state, for a legal-philosophic inquiry, that lets the law be the measure for the state, as a principle which has antecedent validity. **The constitutive elements of the concept of the state can only be derives from the [abstract] law**, as the labelling as a "rule-of-law state" does not signify the confirmation of a mere accidental agreement of the factual state of affairs in an empirical state with a complex of legal norms; rather, in combining the state with the law, the state is wholly seized and determined by the law, completely raised into the sphere of the law[272].

Differently put, since the state is established by abstract law, it is inherently incapable of contradicting that normativity. As Schmitt articulates, the state's sole purpose is the realization of (abstract) law[273]. Should a discord arise between abstract law and the state, the latter would cease to function as a state (in the proper sense). This hypothetical scenario introduces a political-philosophical dilemma, which we will discuss shortly. Consequently, Hofmann suggests interpreting Schmitt's political philosophy as "an attempt to affirm the ideal of an anti-individualist and transpersonal state, as well as a search for a foundation that justifies a post-positivist law"[274]. In what follows we will delve into how Schmitt navigates through this turbulent waters.

Concerning *staatliches Recht*, Schmitt argues that it is not independent from *abstraktes Recht*. That is, what characterizes legal rules and distinguishes them from other normativities is that they rest on an element of original, non-state law[275]. In order to explain this, Schmitt

272 Schmitt, 195–96. The highlight is ours.

273 Cf. Schmitt, 191–92.

274 Hofmann, *Legitimität gegen Legalität*, XXXI.

275 Cf. Schmitt, "The Value of the State and the Significance of the Individual," 210–11.

uses the example of the determination of the sentence when a crime was committed. The setting of the penalty and its duration is a matter of state law. The determination of conducts, such as murder or theft, that are blameworthy and should be penalized, is a matter of abstract law[276]. Schmitt's primary argument in this chapter, then, is that the state and positive law find their source, their principle of existence, in abstract law, and therefore cannot be considered as phenomena that exist and are determined by human convention. The most important consequence of this, as we mentioned above, is that *abstraktes Recht* sets the limits within which the state and law can operate. What happens if the state ignores abstract law or goes beyond its limits? This question leads Schmitt to examine, for the first time, the political impact of exceptional situations.

Using the dualism embodied by the Catholic Church as an example, Schmitt argues that a methodology for "protecting" *abstraktes Recht* is necessary. Control over the positivization of law is indispensable if one is to avoid mere conventionalism in the legal sphere. If this is not instituted, then relativity becomes the core upon which modern democracies are built. In these matters Schmitt seems to be engaging in a discussion with Kelsen, who argued that

> he who views absolute truth and absolute values as inaccessible to the human understanding cognition must deem not only his own, but also the opinion of others at least as feasible. The idea of democracy thus presupposes relativism as its worldview. Democracy values everyone's political will equally, just as it gives equal regard to each political belief and opinion, for which the political will, after all, is merely the expression. Hence, democracy offers every political conviction the opportunity to express itself and to compete openly for the affections of the populace[277].

Schmitt suggests that regardless of its political structure (be it monarchy, democracy, or others), the state and its laws require a guardian to

276 Schmitt, 211.

277 Hans Kelsen, *The Essence and Value of Democracy*, ed. Nadia Urbinati and Carlo Invernizzi Accetti, trans. Brian Graf (Lanham: Rowman & Littlefield, 2013), 103.

set inviolable boundaries. In other words, Schmitt does not equate the acknowledgment of finitude with relativism[278]. Thus, there must be an authority that prevents the state from straying from (abstract) law; a mediator is needed between law and the state to safeguard the law from being overridden by mere factual power[279].

According to Schmitt, the adequate control mechanism is none other than the state of emergency. In almost all philosophies from Plato to Fichte, he argues, he notes the existence of an *ephorate*, a magistrate tasked with monitoring the use of power. This archetypal image of the "guardian of law and justice", in instances of fundamental law violations, is exceptionally authorized to suspend government power and to hold accountable those who breach the foundational principles of the state. In all these philosophies, the rationale behind the "state of emergency"—which is an embodiment of this archetypal image—is rooted in the fear of the state's factual power being abused, a distrust in the people's malice or weakness, and serves as a measure to prevent such occurrences[280].

In this 1914 work Schmitt argues that, although the embodiment of the archetypal image of the *ephorate* in the legal recognition of the "state of emergency" works in theory, it contains a methodological error. No law, not even those permitting the suspension of the government in exceptional cases, can execute itself. It must be applied by a person, and there is no guarantee that this individual will not abuse their power. Thus, a guardian of the *ephorate* is necessary. However, this guardian is also human and is likewise prone to succumbing to power. Consequently, an infinite number of guardians would be required, rendering this system logically infeasible[281]. Even though Schmitt doesn't delve deeply into the state of emergency or *siege* until his work on *Dictatorship*, it is interesting to note that as early as 1914 the topic was already of theoretically concern to him.

278 We will come back to this in Chapter Three.
279 Schmitt, "The Value of the State and the Significance of the Individual," 215–16.
280 Schmitt, 215–16.
281 Schmitt, 215–16.

Returning to the distinction between *abstraktes Recht* and *staatliches Recht*, Neumann views its consequences in the context of the state of emergency as a means of theoretically legitimizing decisionism. In his words,

> the two legal complexes, the abstract and the state law, are as Schmitt continues not two closed masses that are opposite, but both are to be found and divorced in each legal sentence. Thus, the bridge to decisionism is struck: the state can claim in any legal act an authority that does not follow from the substantive appropriateness of the regulation, but from the invisible-abstract law. [. . .] Simply put, the state is always right when and for as long as it acts[282].

In other words, Neumann argues that the introduction of the concept of abstract law is merely intended to serve as a legitimizing mask for blatant decisionism. We, on the other hand, believe that through this distinction, Schmitt is merely recognizing, as we will delve into in the next section, the finitude of positive law (and of human understanding). The possibility of a state of siege is not due to a failure of the law. It simply happens that, because of its own finite nature, it cannot foresee all possible cases. Therefore, *abstraktes Recht* aims to correct this inevitable lack of completeness of positive law[283], and not to justify an arbitrary exercise of power.

However, we believe that Neumann is correct in asserting that Schmitt never specifies the conditions under which abstract legality enables the sovereign to override the existing state legality and establish a new one. This indeterminacy paves the way for arbitrary decisionism. Schmitt would likely argue, as he does later in *Dictatorship*, that further defining the exceptional situation enabling the establishment of a new legal order is impossible (and if it were possible, it would not be, in the strictest sense, an exception). Although Schmitt's argument is persuasive, we believe Neumann makes a valid point in his critique of the stance taken by the German jurist in *The Value of the State and the Significance of the Individual.*

---

282 Neumann, *Carl Schmitt Als Jurist*, 26.

283 We will deepen in this topic in the next section where we delve into Schmitt's 1921 text *Dictatorship.*

This distinct separation between the abstract pole of legal normativity and concrete life, as well as Schmitt's differentiation between *abstraktes Recht* and *staatliches Recht*, has implications not only for positive law and the state but also for the individual. In the following section, we will explore Schmitt's insights on this matter in his 1914 text.

c. *The individual before the state and law*

In the third chapter of *The Value of the State and the Significance of the Individual*, we identify at least three categories of individuals that Schmitt analyses: judges, public servants and ordinary citizens. Even though all three are ontologically human beings, the different functions they carry out justify an independent consideration of each one of them. In what follows, we will review each of them and see how they relate to the state and law.

Schmitt attributes a fundamental role to judges, namely, that of articulating abstract and immaculate normativity with concrete and contingent human life. A judge, argues Schmitt, is not merely the mouthpiece that recites the words of legal statutes. If that were the case, it would imply that law, and particularly the administration of justice, is subject to the power of the state, reducing law to a mere expression power with additional layers (an idea which Schmitt rejects). Judicial work is far more complex, as it grapples with a "triple tension": that between *abstraktes Recht*, *staatliches Rechts*, and the specificities of concrete cases requiring a legal solution. Schmitt argues that in the application of law, numerous extrinsic factors (distinct from positive law) come into play, such as precedents and arguments derived from ethics, legal principles, and more, which further support this argument[284].

284 Schmitt, "The Value of the State and the Significance of the Individual," 210. It is interesting how, already in 1914, the idea of the "extra-legal" concepts, which are fundamental in *Über die drei Arten des rechtswissenschaftlichen Denkens* (1934), is present in the works of Schmitt.

The exploration of a judge's role in the administration of justice prompts Schmitt to delve deeper into the inevitable gap between the normative pole, where law resides, and the concrete one. In his words,

> between everything concrete and everything abstract there lies an insurmountable cleft that cannot be closed by any gradual transition. It is therefore necessary that this moment of mere fixity, according to which it may turn out to be more important *that* something becomes a positive determination than what concrete content it has, will make itself felt in every positive statute. This indifference with regard to content—and this gives the connection to the discussions in my treatise *Statute and Judgment*—results from the state's striving for realization [of the law]. Its significance for the individual judicial decision is more manifest and more evident, because here the distance between insight and execution is not so great, but its influence is no smaller in the formulation of a positive statute. The judgment must concern a concrete case in order to be executed, the statute is in need of concretization in the judgment before its enforceability becomes a fact, the abstract legal thought must become positive statute before the state can be active for its realization, that is, before it sets its apparatus of coercion in motion[285].

In this rather extensive quote, we can catch a glimpse of Schmitt's more substantive legal thinking (which, as he acknowledges, aligns with what he previously discussed in 1912 in *Statute and Judgment*[286]). *Abstraktes Recht* cannot be applied to concrete life and made effective unless it has been positivized. However, statutes are meaningless if there is no legal decision to apply them to a specific case. The challenge arises from the vastness of *abstraktes Recht* and the constraints of positive law, making it impossible for them to be in perfect alignment. Due to the impracticality of typifying every specific case within positive law, some aspects of positive law are inevitably lost when applied to a particular case, and other elements from the source of positive law, namely, abstract law, may come into play. In simpler terms, achieving complete coherence between *abstraktes Recht*, statutes, and legal decisions is an impossibility (and this is why the gap between the two poles is insurmountable). Sacrifices must be made for this "legal machine" to

285 Schmitt, 213.
286 Cf. Schmitt, 213.

function. As we will explain in the next section, the price to pay is the possibility of achieving timeless justice in concrete life—a claim that must be relinquished.

The one that oversees the articulation of these inarticulable spheres is the judge. Schmitt argues that this is no coincidence but rather an obvious consequence of the incomplete character of statutes. In quite an Aristotelian way, Schmitt argues that the incomplete nature of positive law, in the face of the postulate of unrestricted subjection to legality, means that the judge and his "personality" play a fundamental role when deciding on a particular case. That is, since it is impossible for a positive law, given its inevitable general character, to foresee each and every one of the particularities of the cases to which it is to be applied, the judge must inevitably "take care" of everything that is left undetermined (that is not covered) by the normative text.

Does this imply that when a statute does not encompass all aspects of a particular case, the judge can decide based solely on their unrestrained will? In other words, is Schmitt advocating for a form of decisionism in *The Value of the State and the Significance of the Individual*? Schmitt is aware that his argument could be interpreted this way, and he directly addresses this potential objection by saying that

> [e]ven today the whole independence of the judge from every arbitrary power consists in the judge's absolute dependence upon the law alone. The [judge's] "personality" may find consideration, in this context, only insofar as this word is understood to refer to such characterological qualities as offer a guarantee that the [judge's] devotion to the law is exclusive and complete. If the word "statute" [Gesetz], in the proposition according to which the judge is the mouth of the statute, receives the significance of "law" [*Recht*], then it is still valid today and it asserts that, according to the idea, the judge is a function of the law. Therein lies his dignity and his true independence, and it is difficult to grasp how a degradation of the judge can be found in the fact that one wants to hear the reason of the law that has come to articulated consciousness speak through him[287].

In other words, when legal statutes are unable to cover some aspects of a particular case, then the judge cannot resort to his subjectivity

287 Schmitt, 210.

or personal opinion to provide a solution. Instead, he must turn to a different kind of legality, namely, that of *abstraktes Recht*. That is why Schmitt says that if the word "law" in the classic phrase of Montesquieu is understood not as synonym of positive law but in a more comprehensive way (where *abstraktes Recht* and *staatliches Recht* are included), then the dignity of the judge—his independence (from positive law) and his submission to law and justice—is preserved.

As we mentioned earlier, Schmitt's logic on this matter is quite similar to that of Aristotle. Unlike divinity, argues the Stagirite, finitude characterizes human creations, including something as important for politics as legal statutes. Therefore, due to their necessarily general nature, it is impossible for them to foresee every specific circumstance; reality is always richer and more complex than what even the wisest legislator could have anticipated[288]. That is why the renowned issue of equity (*epieikeia*), addressed by Aristotle in Book V of his *Nicomachean Ethics*, emerges. In the words of the Greek sage

> the equitable is just, but not the legally just but a correction of legal justice. The reason is that all law is universal but about some things it is not possible to make a universal statement which will be correct [. . .]. When the law speaks universally, then, and a case arises on it which is not covered by the universal statement, then it is right, when the legislator fails us and has erred by over-simplicity, to correct the omission—to say what the legislator himself would have said had he been present, and would have put into his law if he had known [. . .]. And this is the nature of the equitable, a correction of law where it is defective owing to its universality[289].

That is, both Aristotle and Schmitt agree, even though they use different terminology to express their ideas, on the fact that positive law, due to its inevitably finite nature, is unable to encompass the complexity

288 For a more in-depth analysis of this subject, refer to: Joaquín García-Huidobro and Diego Pérez-Lasserre, "Acoger la excepción. La prudencia del juez como punto de conexión entre las ideas schmittianas y aristotélicas," *Daimon*, no. 83 (2021): 185–99. Herrera has also delved in this matter in: Hugo Herrera, "Aristóteles y Carl Schmitt Sobre El Derecho Natural," *Kriterion: Revista de Filosofia* 55, no. 129 (2014): 205–22.

289 Nicomachean Ethics, 1137b-1137b32. Aristotle, "Nicomachean Ethics," 750–51.

of concrete life and therefore needs help, such as that of *epieikeia* or *abstraktes Recht*, to correct this existential flaw[290]. In *The Value of the State and the Significance of the Individual*, then, Schmitt is not advocating for or paving the way to decisionism, as many have argued[291]. On the contrary, he claims that judges are bound to a legality different from that of positive law when deciding, namely, what he terms *abstraktes Recht* (which, he asserts, "must emerge as a natural law without naturalism"[292]). As Hofmann explains, Schmitt introduces this concept to limit political power, which had been strengthened by positivism to the point where it could legitimize any type of normativity[293].

The case of the public servant, the second category of individuals we identify in this text, is similar to that of judges. It is the commitment to public service, argues Schmitt, and not the particularities of the person "holding office" that makes a great civil servant. In his words, "the dignity to which he lays claim and which is attributed to him attaches only to his office, not to the mortal human being"[294]. Therefore, when addressing the public servant, we observe that Schmitt revisits his previous argument on the judicial function. However, he introduces a critical notion that will be pivotal for his analysis of "the individual"—someone who does not perform a public function in society. Specifically, he stresses that in the modern world, the uniqueness of each member of a political community holds no relevance for law and the state.

Finally, we arrive at the topic of the common and concrete individual (a category that includes judges and public servants when considered individually and not in terms of their function). One of the initial questions Schmitt addresses is whether the individual is the starting

290 We will come back to the "finitude" of law in the next section.

291 Matthias Kaufmann, *Recht Ohne Regel?: Die Philosopische Prinzipien in Carl Schmitts Staats- Und Rechtslehre* (Freiburg: Alber, 1988). Joseph J Bendersky, *Carl Schmitt* (Princeton: Princeton University Press, 1983). Neumann, *Carl Schmitt Als Jurist*. Wolin, "Carl Schmitt, Political Existentialism, and the Total State."

292 Schmitt, "The Value of the State and the Significance of the Individual," 211.

293 Cf. Hofmann, *Legitimität gegen Legalität*, 99–100.

294 Schmitt, "The Value of the State and the Significance of the Individual," 224–25.

point of the triad state-law-individual. In other words, are individuals the creators of law and the state, or are they, conversely, the last in line, merely entities subjected to the force of legality and public authority? Regarding this issue, Schmitt remarks that

> the focus on the issue at hand, whose recognition amounts to a recognition of objectivity, results from the norm alone; it is therefore, as paradoxical as it may sound to many, the opposite of a mere facticity. The individual as a particular empirical entity, however, is initially nothing but a fact. The law, of which it has been shown that it must precede power as mere fact, thus also precedes the individual and can, if this is so, only be an objective law; it does not have its origin in the opinions of the individual as such and it also does not address it to that individual; it knows no individuals at all. Although one should not fail to recognize the practical usefulness, for matters that arise in the administration of the state and in empirical legislation, of the formula that the statutory law exists for the sake of human beings, and not human beings for the sake of the statutory law, it still remains decisive that a norm that holds because it is good and right cannot hold for the sake of the interests of the sum of individual human beings. What is more important than that there are humans is that there are good and just humans[295].

That is, concrete men do not create either law or the state. Law, as an instance that establishes the "moral" parameters under which an action is good or bad, precedes both the state and concrete people. The state functions as a mediator, transforming the abstraction of law into a phenomenon with practical implications in concrete life. Schmitt posits that the state thus acts as a moral authority positioned above the individual. Its primary objective is to translate abstract law into tangible reality, making individuals subject to both it and its decrees[296].

Regarding the individual, Schmitt appears to align with Kelsen. The Austrian jurist remarks that:

> Yet, from a concrete point of view, there is nothing more problematic than this unity which goes by the name, the People. Sociologically, it is riddled with national, religious, and economic differences and thus represents more a bundle of groups than a coherent, homogeneous mass. Here, one can speak of unity

---

295 Schmitt, 226.

296 Schmitt, 232–33.

> only in a normative sense. [...] The "People" as an element of a particular social order, the state. As such a unity, the "People" is not, as is often naively imagined, a body or conglomeration as it were, of actual persons. Rather, it is merely a system of individual human acts regulated by the state legal order[297].

Schmitt also considers the individual as not a relevant instance for the validity of either the state or law in this 1914. However, it is challenging to determine whether Schmitt believes that this is indeed how the triad law-state-individual should be, or if he is merely describing how this relationship operates in modern societies. In either case, it is evident that the picture painted by Schmitt resembles this: concrete individuals, with varying vital experiences and unique singularities, are inconsequential for law and the state's validity. They are to be regarded merely as facts to be subsumed by the state under the force of law, allowing goodness and justice to emerge. Despite individuals being irrelevant as a legitimizing normative instance, they are nonetheless essential for legal normativity to manifest. Law, due to its abstraction, cannot apply itself. It requires a tangible person, whether a judge or a public servant, for it to come to life, so to speak. Therefore, the concrete individual serves as the only available bridge for law to transition from the abstract pole to the concrete one.

This presents a problem that Schmitt does not appear to resolve. On one hand, he suggests that concrete life should take precedence in legal life—Hofmann even argues that one can observe even a fascination or devotion to concreteness that becomes pathological[298]. However, at the same, Schmitt argues that the concrete individual, with all his particular life experiences, is displaced or even suppressed by the titans of the state and law, rendering him utterly irrelevant for the political structure of society. This appears to create a contradiction in his thought. However, if one considers later works by this author, this inconsistency disappears.

In *Political Romanticism* (1919), Schmitt describes "the romantic", an archetype of a being completely in love with himself and his

297 Kelsen, *The Essence and Value of Democracy*, 36.

298 Cf. Hofmann, *Legitimität gegen Legalität*, 48.

ego, using existence as a playground for his own pleasure, to whom the world is an occasion for his experiences[299]. In his words,

> the romantics did not arrive at the identification with people or with history, and the good conscience of Hegelianism remained alien to them. As a result, they floated from one reality to another: form the ego to the people, the "idea", the state, history, the Church—as long as they remained romantics, always playing off one reality against another and never committing themselves in this game of intrigue that is played with realities[300].

This archetypal image represents an extreme in terms of how understanding operates. It asserts that the totality of existence is comprehended solely through the particular framework of the individual subject, without taking into consideration the sensory aspect of the real world. From the viewpoint of political thought, this is undesirable because if every individual only focuses on self-preservation and subjectivity, then any form of communication that could lead to a "community" becomes impossible[301]. Therefore, we can grasp that Schmitt's proposal, which displaces the subjectivity of the individual in *The Value of the State and the Significance of the Individual*, does not aim to eliminate the individual but rather intends to avoid opening the door to another peril: the irrationality of romantic subjectivism. In simpler terms, Schmitt seeks to prevent the remedy for positivism's excessive idealization from being worse than the ailment.

Nonetheless, Schmitt faces a significant dilemma, one that we will extensively examine in chapter three. In order to transition from the abstract pole of law to the concrete, law must abandon its inherent abstraction and conform itself to the vessel that carries it. In essence, law is compelled to "humanize" itself to attain normative power and effectiveness. Therefore, the individual becomes a fundamental component within the triad of state-law-individual. In the subsequent section of this text, we will elucidate the concept of the "humanization" of

299 Carl Schmitt, *Political Romanticism*, trans. Guy Oakes (Massachusetss & London: MIT Press, 1986), 93.

300 Schmitt, 92.

301 Schmitt, 92.

law and specify the particular human characteristics that this phenomenon entails.

d. Conclusions concerning The Value of the State and the Significance of the Individual *(1914)*

We began by elucidating that in *The Value of the State and the Significance of the Individual* (1914), Schmitt aims to elucidate the relationship between law, the state, and the concrete individual. We also argued that through this analysis the German jurist revisits the same dilemma he encountered in *Statute and Judgment* (1912), namely the tension between the abstract realm of normativity and the concrete sphere of everyday life. The inquiries guiding our interpretation of this early work were as follows: Can Schmitt adequately justify the supremacy of law over the state? (1); What are the implications he perceives his stance has for the individual? (2); What does this 1914 text add to Schmitt's concept of law? (3); and, Is Schmitt offering insights into the functioning of human understanding through his legal analysis in this work? (4).

To attempt to furnish comprehensive answers to the posed questions, we proceeded to elaborate on the following points in detail:

a. In this 1914 text, Schmitt articulates in a distinctly manner that within the legal phenomenon there exist two dichotomous and irreconcilable poles. One is characterized by its abstraction and purity (that of law), while the other is concrete and contingent (everyday life).
b. The normative pole is characterized by an absence of reference to the empirical and factual world. Norms are independent of reality, and thus maintain their validity and value regardless of their actualization and enforcement in factual reality.
c. The same applies to the concrete pole. Nothing normative belongs to factual reality. Therefore, any reference to normative concepts—such as good or bad, just or unjust, permitted or prohibited—is out of place.

d. Schmitt argues that although these two poles of existence are dichotomous and irreconcilable, law is designed to exert effects on concrete reality. For law to achieve practical effect and gain efficacy, a bridge between both realms is necessary.

In other words, Schmitt employs a juridico-political perspective of law as a means to delve deeper into the problem he previously addressed in *Statute and Judgment* (1912): the tension between normativity and factuality.

Schmitt starts by analyzing the state. Among his numerous comments on this entity, the following are particularly noteworthy, especially considering the horizon of understanding from which we engage with the text:

a. The state is not an entity belonging to the realm of abstract normativity. Given that the exercise of power necessitates a reference to the empirical, it is evident that the state is situated in the concrete pole of existence.
b. However, the state is not merely brute facticity to which we, as a society, have become accustomed. It is a phenomenon that gains its existence, legitimacy and dignity from law. In other words, law precedes the state.

This statement, while robustly justified by the German jurist, directs us towards clarifying what he means by "law" and how it can emerge from the abstraction and purity of the normative pole to produce an entity like the state.

Schmitt argues the following concerning law:

a. There are two types of normativity. On the one hand, there is what he refers to as "abstract law" (*abstraktes Recht*), which precedes the state and, as an idea, is independent of it[302]. On the other hand, there is "State law" (*staatliches Recht*) whose purpose is its implementation in the empirical world as its field of action[303].

302 Schmitt, "The Value of the State and the Significance of the Individual," 211.
303 Schmitt, 211.

b. The first type of normativity is entirely situated in the abstract pole of existence, meaning it cannot directly affect practical reality. The second type, *staatliches Recht*, represents the translation of *abstraktes Recht* into the empirical world. That is, it is the inevitably imperfect embodiment of a timeless and spaceless norm within a specific space and time in human history.
c. The bridge between one type of normativity and the other is formed by the state. It is this entity, which comes after law and owes its dignity to it, that attempts to translate the ineffable into words (legal statutes) and then applies them to a society existing in a concrete space and time. The state, therefore, is the creator of *staatliches Recht*—albeit inspired and constrained by *abstraktes Recht.*
d. The state and s*taatliches Recht* owe their existence to, and are consequently subject to, *abstraktes Recht.* The state and positive law should not be regarded as purely conventionally determined. They are required to adhere to the abstract normativity of *abstraktes Recht*, yet simultaneously articulate its content with concrete reality, allowing the former to influence the latter. This, Schmitt notes, is the essence of the "rule of law".

Finally, in the concluding chapter of *The Value of the State and the Significance of the Individual*, Schmitt addresses the concrete individual. His insights about this final element in the triad of legality and power are as follows:

a. There are three categories from which one can approach concrete individuals: judges, public servants, and ordinary citizens.
b. Judges play a fundamental role in the society, that of integrating abstract and pristine normativity with concrete and contingent human life. Contrary to the prevailing thought at the time, the German jurist argues that judges are not merely mouths reciting the words of statutes. Judicial work is far more complex, as it confronts a "triple tension" that must

be synthesized through legal decisions: the tension between *abstraktes Recht*, *staatliches Rechts*, and the particularities of concrete cases requiring a legal solution.

c. It is the judge who, through a legal decision, is obliged to articulate diverse elements and resolve the tension between abstract normativity and the facticity of concrete life. Schmitt argues that this assertion promptly compels us to question the specific conditions under which such a synthesis between diverse and dichotomous elements is correct (which reveals the thematic continuity between *Statute and Judgment* and *The Value of the State and the Significance of the Individual*).
d. The case of the public servant, the second category of individual identified in this text, is similar to that of judges. Schmitt argues that it is the commitment to public service, rather than the personal characteristics of the person that is "holding office", that defines a great civil servant.
e. In his analysis of the concrete individual (regardless of the function they fulfill), Schmitt adheres to a logic similar to that of Kelsen. Within the law-state-individual triad, the latter holds practically no significance. Therefore, in this 1914 text, the individual is not regarded as a pertinent factor for the validity of either the state or the law. Concrete individuals are merely seen as facts to be encompassed by the state under the authority of law, in order for goodness and justice to emerge.

As we argued throughout the chapter, it remains unclear whether, on the topic of the complete obliteration of the everyday life experiences of concrete individuals, Schmitt is merely describing the position of citizens in relation to the modern state, or if he is advocating for a purely normative consideration of the individual. Regardless, the theme of the individual who serves the role of creating a link and articulation between the realms of normativity and facticity (judges and public officials) introduces an element is crucial for our proposed interpretation of Schmitt's work: the human being.

Having already established that a legal decision represents an act of synthesizing both the determined and undetermined aspects of positive legal texts, and acknowledging that normativity, whether abstract or concrete, must relinquish its purity and abstraction to "humanize" itself for practical impact on concrete reality, we are now tasked with elucidating what this "humanization" of the legal phenomenon specifically entails.

3 Carl Schmitt "the Artist"

§ 1. Introduction

In a paper published in 2016, Hugo Herrera argues, against Volker Neumann, that Schmitt's legal texts should not be interpreted exclusively in legal terms. Herrera believes that

> for Schmitt the legal method takes on the character of a way of understanding existence as such and not only the specifically legal aspect of it. The expansion of such a legal method is based on the recognition that the problem of the relationship and the tension between generality and exception, involved in that of the relationship and the tension between rule and case, is ultimately identifiable with the problem of the tension between conceptuality and reality. Law is a form of understanding, then, that extends to existence as such, because its problem and its methodological approach to it coincide with the issue of the relationship and the general tension between conceptuality and reality, and with the explicit thematization of that issue[304].

In other words, he argues that Schmitt uses the legal phenomenon, and more particularly the tension between abstract normative texts and the always exceptional and immeasurable concrete cases, as a paradigm to illustrate how practical knowledge operates.

Although we are of the opinion that Herrera's thesis is correct, we believe that such an assertion—namely, that in Schmitt's legal theory, a theory of understanding with general scope is present—requires prior elucidation. In particular, we believe it is necessary to clarify at least two things: first, what do we mean by "theory of understanding" when we say that it is present in the analysis of the legal phenomenon made

---

304 Herrera, "Carl Schmitt como jurista," 59–60.

by the thinker of Plettenberg? Second, in what specific sense is it that Schmitt develops a theory with such characteristics in his legal works?

The questions just formulated are the ones that will guide our research throughout this section. To attempt answering the first, we will complement what Herrera has already said (in 2016, 2019, and 2020) with an analysis of Schmitt's early works. In this sense, it can be understood that our work complements and specifies that of the Chilean philosopher and jurist.

To the second question, we propose what we believe to be a novel answer. In the following pages, we will justify how Schmitt formulates a general theory of understanding in his analysis of the legal phenomenon through his critique of legal positivism. By demonstrating that a major flaw of legal positivism is its reliance on an ontologically inadequate interpretation of the human being—a topic mainly addressed in chapter two—Schmitt proposes an understanding of the legal phenomenon based on a consideration of concrete human existence, which he argues would be ontologically accurate. By this, we mean that he asserts, sometimes more explicitly than at other times, that a complete, non-reductionist theory of law must acknowledge the fundamental structures inherent in all human knowledge that inevitably play a role in the legal phenomenon. In other words, and as we emphasized in chapter two, Schmitt maintains that for law to effectively impact reality, the abstract normativity of law must adopt certain human characteristics (that is, it must *humanize* itself).

To put it differently, Schmitt contends that any theorization of the legal phenomenon aiming to be practical must necessarily consider and be founded upon these existential structures that operate in all human understanding. Specifically, in his early legal texts, we will argue that Schmitt acknowledges the following structures:

1. The finitude of human understanding
2. Its historicality, or rather, the inevitability of being affected by history
3. Language as a condition of possibility for human knowledge.

As previously mentioned at the outset of this work, our study will concentrate on Schmitt's early texts, specifically those addressing the legal phenomenon. We will particularly focus on the works he authored between 1912 and 1922. This focus is justified for the following reasons: Schmitt states, in the prologue to the second edition of *Statute and Judgment* written in 1968, that his early reflections concerning the decision heavily influenced his later thought[305]. In other words, after a prolific academic career, Schmitt recognizes that ideas present in his early works ideas are foundational for his later legal, political, and existential thought. In this context, it seems prudent to first elucidate the scope of Schmitt's early reflections and then to examine how these ideas manifest and evolve throughout his subsequent works. The cutoff year of 1922, marked by the publication of *Political Theology*, is chosen for two reasons: first, in this work, Schmitt revisits the major juridical themes he had been exploring since 1912, including the decision, the exception, and the state, making it a prudent stopping point for a comprehensive analysis. Second, while our specific hypothesis allows us to focus without delving into all topics Schmitt addressed between 1912 and 1922, the sheer volume of texts and the diversity of subjects covered render a complete analysis unfeasible. Therefore, establishing a criterion to limit our study was necessary, and a chronological one, for quite obvious reasons, seemed to us an appropriate starting point. Hance, we will review the following texts: *Statute and Judgment* (1912), *The Value of the State and the Significance of the Individual (*1914), *Political Romanticism (*1919), *The Dictatorship (*1921), and *Political Theology (*1922).

As we anticipated in the introduction to this book, in this section we will propose a reading of the early legal works of Schmitt (1912–1922) from the perspective of a theory of understanding. More specifically, we will argue that through his legal reflections Schmitt seems to propose not merely a groundbreaking thematization of the legal phenomenon, but a theory of understanding with general scope.

305 Cf. Schmitt, "Statute and Judgment: An Investigation into the Problem of Legal Praxis," 42.

In this chapter, we bring together the perspective we introduced in the first chapter as a "theory of understanding" and Schmitt's concept of law as a multiform and dynamic phenomenon, which we discussed earlier. Specifically, we will explore how Schmitt's early legal works suggest that the "humanization" of law involves a process in which abstract normativity (*abstraktes Recht*) takes on human characteristics to effectively manifest itself in concrete reality. This attributes that normativity acquires to manifest itself in human reality, however, do not originate from the particular subjectivity of an individual. Instead, they arise from of human nature. In other words, abstract law acquires the ontological characteristics that enable human knowledge. In this context, the *existentiale*, those fundamental ontological relations to the world that are inevitably *there* and cannot be removed without the obliteration of the human subject itself, gain significance. We will observe that Schmitt recognizes that these characteristics, which are closely associated with the essence of being human, manifest themselves in an exemplary manner within the legal phenomenon.

Our road map unfolds as follows: we will begin by revisiting Herrera's insights regarding the scope of legal understanding in Schmitt's thought. Next, we will argue that Schmitt appears to suggest that human understanding is finite, influenced by historical context, and mediated by language. Moving forward, we will justify that Schmitt's analysis of the exception highlights the significance of the concrete realm over abstract conceptualizations of the human mind, and we will explore the theme of historicality from both an epochal and metaphysical perspective. Finally, we will draw some conclusions.

§ 2. Carl Schmitt's theory of understanding? Herrera's argument

Herrera argues that Schmitt's legal works can be interpreted in at least two ways. One approach is to view them, as Volker Neumann does in *Carl Schmitt als Jurist*, exclusively within the realm of law[306]. The other perspective, however, is to recognize that, while pouring substantive legal ideas into his texts, the German philosopher employs the legal phenomenon to illustrate how practical knowledge operates in general. That is, to understand that he uses, as Gadamer did years later, law in an exemplary manner.

Herrera insinuates that this second perspective from which Schmitt texts can be approached allows for a more comprehensive understanding. It enables readers to gain a broader perspective, interpret his works holistically, and move beyond labels that result from partial readings, such as those that categorize Schmitt's thought as purely decisionist. Even though we agree with Herrera that Schmitt's work is enriched if it is read from the perspective of a theory of understanding, we believe, as was pointed out in the introduction, that such an approach requires at least two prior clarifications: on the one hand, it is necessary to (1) specify what is meant by a theory of understanding, and, on the other, (2) it is imperative to clarify in what specific sense such a theory is present in Schmitt's legal thought. After examining Herrera's approach, we will argue that Schmitt, when analyzing the legal phenomenon, confronts a more extensive challenge: that of normativity. In essence, he grapples with the task of explaining how an abstract *ought to be* aligns with specific a concrete case. This prompts him to not only inquire into the nature of the abstract pole (normative) but also the contingency of the concrete pole (the cases to which this normativity is applied) and the specific characteristics of the entity tasked with bridging both realms (the human being).

Thus far, there are three works[307] in which Herrera explains the specific manner in which it can be argued that there is a theory of

306 Neumann, *Carl Schmitt Als Jurist.*

307 Herrera, *Carl Schmitt. Between Technological Rationality and Theology.* Hugo Herrera, "Análisis de Los Aspectos Fundamentales de La Comprensión Jurídica En Carl Schmitt y Exposición de Sus Alcances Filosófico-Generales Para La Comprensión," *Kriterion: Revista de Filosofia* 60, no. 142 (2019): 85–102. Herrera, "Carl Schmitt como jurista."

understanding in Carl Schmitt's legal analysis. The fundamental idea behind them is the following:

> In all human understanding there are certain rules and concepts according to which one tries to elucidate reality. That reality responds partly and partly not to rules and concepts. The exceptional, the singular, the peculiar, of reality, the situations, the individuals in them, are in tension with the rules and concepts and determine, as Schmitt indicates, that between the concrete and the abstract, an "insurmountable abyss" exists. [. . .]. The elucidation of the relationship between the rule and the case is the fundamental problem of understanding (and of a theory of understanding)[308].

In other words, Herrera sees that, in approaching the problem of legal understanding, Schmitt is faced with a much greater problem: that of language. In fact, the Chilean philosopher observes that throughout his work, the German thinker identifies, sometimes more explicitly than others, the tension between legal rules and the specific cases judges must apply them to, likening it to the tension between a concept and concrete reality. Although the articulations of the mind, the rules, words, and concepts, Herrera points out, enable us to understand reality, they are not sufficient to completely elucidate existence. The rules and concepts only allow us to understand that which reveals itself under observable and measurable parameters. The problem is that reality is not always revealed to us in a regular manner. On the contrary, the exceptional, that which cannot be categorized by the rules available to the mind, inevitably emerges into existence. It is inevitable that the concrete pole often challenges the generalizations of the abstract pole through exceptions that cannot be grappled by the rule.

The exceptional situation, which cannot be encompassed by the rule, leads not to an oblivion of that which is exceptional, but to a reformulation of the rule in the light of the exception. In other words, in the exception, the normative sense of the rule emerges to deal with what was not initially addressed by the rule itself. In this sense, a "feedback loop" is established between the rule and the case, potentially resulting

308 Herrera, "Carl Schmitt como jurista," 60.

in "a modification of the meaning of the cases and of the rules and concepts"[309].

In a rather similar sense to Herrera, Monserrat Herrero argues, in the *Preliminary Study* to her translation of some early Schmittian works, that since he is faced with the problem of "bridging" the gap between the universal (legal rule) and the particular (concrete cases), Schmitt is, in fact, engaging in practical philosophy. In her words:

> A discipline is practical [. . .] when its purpose is to bridge the gap between the universal and the particular. A practical science cannot disregard the regulation of particular cases, otherwise it would be a simple theory. Nor would it be a practical "science" if it renounced the universal pole, since it would be reduced to a mere enumeration of particular cases without order or agreement. It is therefore a matter of conceiving of the particular as relating to the universal[310].

To put it differently, Herrero shares Herrera's perspective that Schmitt's examination of legal understanding transcends mere legal considerations and has implications for practical knowledge. She also acknowledges, in agreement with Rasch and Ojakangas, that Schmitt's legal analysis delves into a significant issue within practical philosophy, specifically the challenge of normativity.

This is not surprising. As Vigo correctly points out, the issue of normativity deals with how the practical agent is referred, on the one hand, to certain demands imposed to him in the form of universal rules, and, on the other, to specific and particular situations[311]. In this sense, any reflection addressing the problem of the articulation of universal rules and particular cases, inevitably encounters the dilemma of normativity.

---

309 Herrera, "Análisis de Los Aspectos Fundamentales de La Comprensión Jurídica En Carl Schmitt y Exposición de Sus Alcances Filosófico-Generales Para La Comprensión," 95.

310 Herrero, "Estudio preliminar," XLVI.

311 Alejandro Vigo, "Autorreferencia Práctica y Normatividad," in *Practical Rationality. Scope and Structures of Human Agency*, ed. A. Vigo and A. González, vol. 1, Reason and Normativity (Hildesheiml, Zurich, New York: Olms Verlag, 2010), 198.

Following Vigo's insights, a comprehensive treatment of normativity requires not only handling both aspects—the normative and the concrete—but also a thorough consideration of the entity tasked with bridging these realms. In essence, a comprehensive examination of the subject necessitates recognizing the characteristics of the practical agent, which is essentially ourselves in each unique circumstance. Thus, if legal understanding ultimately addresses the issue of normativity, it must necessarily take into account three dimensions: the abstract realm where norms reside, the concrete everydayness of life, and the particular characteristics of the agent tasked with resolving the tension between the first two.

Hence, it is plausible to assert that Schmitt elucidates certain ontological structures in human beings that operate not only in legal understanding but generally in human understanding. In other words, it is not irrational to think that the problem of legal normativity leads Schmitt to attempt to elucidate the way in which human understanding operates (and it is precisely in this sense that there would be a "theory of understanding" in his legal texts). In the following sections, we will elaborate on how Schmitt's works from 1912 to 1922 provide insights into these ontological structures that operate in human understanding.

§ 3. Historicality, temporality, and language

Schmitt's initial academic endeavor following the publication of his doctoral dissertation in 1910 was *Statute and Judgment*. The central inquiry guiding his investigation in this text is as follows: under which circumstances can a legal decision considered to be correct? While we have previously discussed this in chapter two, we will provide some context for the sake of our argument.

Regarding the specific way in which it is possible to see that in *Statute and Judgment* Schmitt is concerned with the characteristics of the agent who is responsible for articulating the rules (abstract pole) with the concrete cases in the legal sphere, we find that in this early text, his concern is not so much with how judges actually decide, but rather he focuses his analysis on *who* is in charge of making such a decision. In other words, the question centers on the entity responsible for bridging the universal (the rule) with the particular (the case).

Furthermore, in the critiques Schmitt formulates against legal positivism in this text, it becomes somewhat clear that the major issue he attributes to this approach to understanding the legal phenomenon is its failure to acknowledge that human understanding is inevitably finite and affected by historicality. The following quote, though lengthy, helps us start to grasp this concept:

> It is contemporary practice that is at issue, in the first place, and therein lies a **historical concretization**. An answer to the question of the absolute, timeless correctness of a decision, as it might be derived from the "idea" of judicial decision, is not to be sought here; it would, in any case, have no immediate practical value. It is the task of the doctrine of the method of the application of law to find the guiding idea of contemporary practice, and to be of use to the latter by helping it to become aware of its own purposes and means. There is scientific progress in a practice becoming aware of its own sense. If, therefore, modern practice is taken as the object of investigation, this object is therewith historically delimited[312].

In sum, Schmitt thus argues that one of the primary issues with positivism is its foundation on an exclusively abstract level, consequently neglecting the contingency of concrete life. This perspective implies that judges are confronted with a stable reality, where the unexpected is not a factor to consider. However, the issue lies in the fact that while there is a certain degree of "normality" or "stability" in concrete life, it is equally essential to acknowledge the normalcy of the "abnormal" or "exceptional" occurrences that disrupt the pattern of normality. In essence, human beings are finite, making it impossible to predict every eventuality in existence. The "exceptional" is an inherent part of human reality, and according to Schmitt, a theory of law that overlooks this fact fails to grasp the full complexity of the legal phenomenon.

312 Schmitt, 47. The highlight is ours.

From the concept of "the exception", which refers to the "abnormal" situation that was not anticipated by positive law, we infer that Schmitt is affirming the historicality of the legal phenomenon. Contemporary philosophers like Heidegger and Gadamer offer tools to contextualize issue. They argue that history is not a foreign object that we approach from time to time; rather, we are history itself. Human existence does not transpire *in* history, but *is* fundamentally historical [313]. In a similar vein, Gerhart Husserl argues that law and legal statutes are fundamentally historical. The son of Edmund Husserl explains that not only is man thrown into time and history, but so is law. That is, even when a statute is enacted at a specific historical moment to address a particular problem facing a community, its existence persists through history[314]. Its "legal life" does not conclude once the issues that led to its creation are resolved. This implies that the legal phenomenon cannot be viewed as static and, therefore, must possess a certain *openness* to the varying circumstances that unfold over time.

Schmitt presents a similar argument when he states that the elements influencing the validity of statutes are

> the voluminous revisions of the words of a statute, their modifying penetration with a thousand scientific concepts, their reshaping into a system, the mountains of books that often weigh on one single word in the statute, the libraries of precedents: elements of all of these are effective in a decision that is to be gathered from the "statute". If one still sees in this a "conformity to statute"—if one still regards the postulate of the subjection to statute as fulfilled, in the face of the "unavoidable departures from statutory law on the part of the law that comes to the fore in adjudication"—then one has the scientific obligation to explain what one understands by the content of statute and by the claim that a judge is bound to this content[315].

313 Refer to Chapter One for a comprehensive analysis of the concept of historicality in the works of Heidegger and Gadamer.

314 See: Gerhart Husserl, *Recht und Zeit* (Frankfurt: V. Klostermann, 1955).

315 Schmitt, "Statute and Judgment: An Investigation into the Problem of Legal Praxis," 53.

However, this does not imply that the work of jurists should consist solely of a historiographic analysis of law. Contrarily, Schmitt argues that the task of determining the correctness of a judicial decision is neither historical nor natural-scientific in nature, but rather practical. It focuses on ascertaining the "correctness of a decision in contemporary legal practice"[316].

Similarly, his critique of legal positivism, which we have already argued is existential rather than merely juridical, seems to follow the same direction. Schmitt contends that by asserting the legal phenomenon is constituted exclusively by positive legal texts, this school of thought neglects the inherent historicality of law. As a result, this theory becomes impractical for legal praxis, primarily because its depiction of law is inconsistent with the actual behavior of the phenomenon. Schmitt's proposed solution is as follows: it is the concrete human being, also influenced by historicality (the "concrete and empirical judge", as he refers to in *Statute and Judgment*), who is uniquely equipped to handle the historicality of law. This individual is tasked with resolving the tension between a general and abstract text, addressing a past historical and legal situation, and a new, specific case presenting a current (and potentially exceptional) problem requiring resolution. We believe that the reason behind this argument is as follows: As Herrera astutely points out,

> for Schmitt, what defines juridical thought, and bestows it with a fundamental character, is the explicit thematization of the hermeneutical conditions. Juridical thought is different in this from other forms of understanding, and in this lies the reason for calling a fundamental form of understanding juridical—namely, it has in view and thematizes the relation and tension between rule and case, the general and the particular, norm and exception. All human understanding operates within the context set by those poles. Moreover, every understanding is faced with the task of resolving difficulties generated by this polarity. Thus, for example, new rules are invented and tried that better account for a series of phenomena, or new uses of language are tested that allow for a more proper expression of the meaning of an experience[317].

316 Schmitt, 48.

317 Herrera, *Carl Schmitt. Between Technological Rationality and Theology*, 73.

Differently put, we as humans are constantly engaged in the task of resolving the tension between abstract rules and concrete circumstances. Even if we are not consciously aware of it, the evolution of language vividly demonstrates this phenomenon. Although concepts appear to have definitive content, referencing specific aspects of existence (be it concrete phenomena, ideas, or emotions), they also possess an inherent *openness*. Their meaning is not entirely fixed, which allows the dynamism of historical human existence to permeate and influence the meanings that these concepts acquire[318]. Schmitt contends that a similar situation arises in the legal sphere. Written rules are tasked with encompassing a myriad of dissimilar cases, a challenge a simple text alone cannot meet. A human being, in contrast, is not only competent to perform this task but also appears to be "existentially made for the job". Their ontological constitution enables them to harmonize static normativity with the dynamism of factuality.

We could even argue that Schmitt's approach to positive law mirrors what Heidegger and Gadamer did with the concept of the human being. As we explained, *Dasein* is thematized as an entity that relates to a plexus or network of meanings (the world) through appropriation. These philosophers suggest that in understanding, we make a potentiality our own and bring it to actuality (we understand ourselves or an entity *as* something). Thus, *Dasein* is portrayed as ontologically privileged, possessing the ability, or perhaps even the freedom, to shape both the world and itself[319]. In a similar vein, Schmitt argues that legal texts should no longer be seen as "vessels into which the judge can pour the facts of the case. They step out if their tranquility and stability. They become the means of grounding an expectation"[320]. This perspective indicates that including the human being as a crucial component in the legal equation introduces existential *openness* in law, which facilitates

318 For instance, the ongoing evolution in the understanding of concepts such as "male", "female", and "gender" vividly exemplifies this characteristic (for good or ill).

319 Within limits, as we explained in chapter one of this text.

320 Schmitt, "Statute and Judgment: An Investigation into the Problem of Legal Praxis," 117.

the flow of historical dynamism that goes through us to be projected onto the legal phenomenon. This is achieved through the judge's task of "fusing the horizons" of a fixed text with an exceptional and novel case. It should be noted, however, that in this 1912 text, Schmitt appears to be only beginning to explore the philosophical implications of the "exceptional", and thus does not delve deeply into the considerations just outlined. Despite this, we observe a certain continuity (and evolution) throughout Schmitt's writings in terms of the historicality and finitude of human understanding, a theme we hope will become apparent in the subsequent sections of this work.

Transitioning to *The Value of State and the Significance of the Individual* and the way Schmitt addresses historicality and finitude in this text, it is at the beginning of it that we first see Schmitt make a direct allusion to time. After characterizing modern man as an individualistic type who seeks to discard everything provided by tradition, he points out that

> The modern human, in his normal empirical type, is of the view that his time is a "free", sceptical, authorityinimical and thoroughly individualistic time, that it is the first to have actually discovered and to have honoured the individual, and to have overcome antiquated traditions and authorities. In view of these achievements, these "results" [might appear to] contain an inexplicable atavism, a relapse into a barbaric and anti-cultural enmity towards life. If in truth this were so, then the critique of the modern human could signify an objection. No author, who seriously concerns himself with questions that arise from the law, the state and the individual, may lightly ignore that which, with any justification whatsoever, can be labelled as the spirit of the times. In this there would lie a frivolous arrogance, the just punishment of which would be impressively executed by enduring ineffectiveness and sterility[321].

Schmitt's brief reference to temporality provides insight into his understanding of time. Like Heidegger, Schmitt suggests that there common misunderstanding of time. Modern man is distinguished by a rejection of all that stems from tradition, coupled with an egoic stance that proclaim him, unlike men of the past, as the first to recognize

321 Schmitt, "The Value of the State and the Significance of the Individual," 166.

the fundamental principles underlying knowledge and human progress. Schmitt views the modern *Weltanschauung* as somewhat immature and adolescent. It fails to acknowledge that the success of its era is attributable to the advancements, experiments, and setbacks of its predecessors. Furthermore, he appears to discern a certain naivety in the modern rejection of the significance of history and the elevation of reason, regarded as a pure abstraction, as the sole legitimate authority. Consequently, his critique, akin to Gadamer's philosophy in later years, strives to restore the value of tradition in human understanding.

In this context, Schmitt's reflections take on a surprising depth. Following the passage we just quoted, Schmitt goes on to state that "a time that presents itself as sceptical and exact cannot call itself individualistic in the same breath; neither scepticism nor the exact natural sciences are capable of grounding an individuality"[322]. In other words, a line of thought that dismisses facticity as unscientific is incapable of adequately addressing the human being. Instead, abstract thought must be infused with humanity, an existential character that combines facticity and ideality, in order to attain knowledge that is meaningful for the unfolding of human experience. As Herrera puts it, "in Schmitt's view, only an understanding that considers the exception can arrive at a consciousness of the tension between the ideal and the real, the rules and the exception, and of the scope and limits of understanding"[323]. It seems, then, that for Schmitt temporality goes beyond being a mere indicator that helps us track the changes in reality. It is a phenomenon through which historicality is expressed in the form of tradition. To clarify this assertion, we can turn to what the German jurist says about language.

In the chapter dedicated to the "State", Schmitt notes that

> admittedly, in every linguistic designation, there are many and important references; language is more than a purely biological tool, a means of understanding, which signified no more to the human than its well-honed sense of smell did to the dog. Every problem has its beginning in an investigation of these relations

322 Schmitt, 167.

323 Herrera, *Carl Schmitt. Between Technological Rationality and Theology*, 80.

> and indications. But the method that aims to determine exact linguistic usage in order thereby to attain a scientific concept ignores precisely this significance of language and regards it merely as a fact, akin to every other fact[324].

Although, once again, we encounter a reference that lacks elaboration (and a topic that the text does not revisit), we believe that Schmitt is alluding to the following idea: concepts are not mere tools that we have readily available for use only when a subsumable case arises. To understand language in this manner would be overly reductionist. Each word possesses multiple meanings, and the one that becomes salient in a specific case depends not only on the precision of language use or the clarity of what is presented to the person attempting to conceptualize a phenomenon but also on the perspective from which the subject approaches it. In other words, every concept is inherently equivocal, meaning it has more than one potential meaning. Therefore, pursuing scientific objectivity in its subject matter would be illusory.

The question that arises from the above discussion is: what determines the specific form in which the meaning of a concept emerges? Unfortunately, at this juncture in Schmitt's work, a clear answer to this question is lacking. Instead, the hermeneutic philosophy of Hans-Georg Gadamer, which in content and context bears a resemblance to Schmitt's approach, provides the key to addressing the issue of the (relative) indeterminacy of concepts. In *Truth and Method* the German philosopher and philologist points out that "long before we understand ourselves through the process of self-examination, we understand ourselves in a self-evident way in the family, society, and state in which we live. The focus of subjectivity is a distorting mirror. The self-awareness of the individual is only a flickering in the closed circuits of historical life"[325]. That is to say, in every act of understanding, which is inevitably mediated by language, the subject carries with him what Gadamer calls the "horizon of meaning". By this, we mean, as we explained in the first chapter, that the cultural, historical, linguistic, and family context in which the subject develops throughout his life forms something like

324 Schmitt, "The Value of the State and the Significance of the Individual," 190–91.

325 Gadamer, *Truth and Method*, 289.

a pair of glasses (which cannot be removed) that "distort" everything that is the object of said understanding. In this sense, the meaning that a concept acquires at the time of its thematization depends, at least to some extent, on the horizon of the subject that carries out said thematization. Put differently, every concept exhibits a certain *openness*, appearing as a spectrum of possibilities whose specific determination depends on the horizon of the subject attempting to elucidate its meaning[326].

Now, while interpreting Schmitt's text from this perspective might seem like an overextension of his ideas, there are two factors that lend some credibility to our argument. First, reading *The Value of the State and the Significance of the Individual* from the angle we propose allows a better understanding of why Schmitt points out, a few paragraphs before his reflection on language, that one cannot derive a concept from the very objects one intends to subsume under it (specifically, he is referring to the concept of "State"). This would be reductive, as it would consider only what occurs in concrete reality for the development of a concept, ignoring the horizon (language, tradition, history, etc.) in which the conceptualized phenomenon unfolds. Second, Schmitt appears to reinforce this idea in his 1933 text *State, Movement, People. The Tripartite Structure of the Political Unit,* particularly when he affirms that

> an extraterrestrial who wants to behave critically and astutely, who wants to read and write books, will think and understand differently, since he is arranged differently, and therefore remains in every line of thought, subject to the existential condition of his own species. <In the same sense,> every human thought is linked to its existence, since every standardization and interpretation of the facts are linked to its situation[327].

In other words, in 1933 Schmitt recognized what we already observed in his 1914 text, namely, that the language in which we, as human

326 For a more in-depth analysis of this subject, please refer to the first chapter of this text.

327 Carl Schmitt, *State, Movement, People: The Triadic Structure of the Political Unity*, trans. Simona Draghici (Corvallis: Plutarch Press, 2001), 45.

beings, develop is inextricably linked to the historical and factual circumstances of our human condition. This notion is further underscored by his analysis of Montesquieu's (1984) statement "the judge is the mouth of the law", where Schmitt emphasizes the need to consider the different "mouths" entrusted with this task, since "the same word on the lips of different peoples not only sounds differently, but also means something else in thought and deed"[328].

In summary, we believe that the analysis just conducted justifies that as early as in his 1914 text *The Value of the State and the Significance of the Individual*, Schmitt acknowledges two fundamental ontological characteristics inherent in all human knowledge: its historicality and the inevitable mediation of language in our interaction with the world, along with the consequent influence of a "horizon of meaning" in that relationship. Adding Schmitt's considerations of finitude and the exceptional backdrop from which existence unfolds, we start to understand the *openness* he expects from judges when deciding on the legal outcomes of specific cases. In the following sections, we will explore how Schmitt delves further into these concepts in later works.

§ 4. The exceptional, finitude, and epochal historicality

In *Dictatorship* (1921), the concept of the decision begins to assume greater importance in Schmitt's thought (although it is in *Political Theology* where it reaches its climax). In this work, the question concerning the decision-maker arises again, but this time from a political perspective, thus shifting the focus from the judge to the sovereign.

As Hoelzl and Ward explain, this 1921 Schmittian text should be understood through the lens of the tension between *is* and *ought* (*sein* and *sollen*). In their words,

328 Carl Schmitt, *Über die drei Arten des rechtswissenschaftlichen Denkens* (Berlin: Duncker & Humblot, 2006), 45–46.

> the methodological struggle (*Methodenstreit*) reflects the *is–ought* dichotomy in the following question: Should the law be detached from any historical, political and sociological context, or does it always emerge from and live within a concrete historical, political and sociological context? We can only understand *Dictatorship* against the background of this fundamental struggle between neo-Kantian positivism and decisionism. The struggle also reflects the conflict between theory and practice[329].

That is, Schmitt continues to address legal thought as a field in which a tension between an ideal and normative pole with a concrete and factual one becomes evident in an exemplary manner. Once again, we see that the entity called to resolve this dichotomy is none other than the human being. However, this time, the decision, considered as an instance of synthesis, is not to be made by the judge but by the sovereign.

The logic Schmitt employs to address the issue of sovereign decision unfolds as follows: he begins by noting that legal norms are designed to maintain a certain regularity or normality. Essentially, they aim to establish a framework of predictability enabling a society to function in relative peace. However, as we have already indicated, while legal norms are finite, the concrete reality they seek to regulate is vast. This discrepancy inevitably results in situations where the concrete reality significantly surpasses existing legal regulations, leading to a loss of their normative meaning (i.e., their efficacy diminishes). This raises the critical question: what should be done when legal norms lose their normative sense? Schmitt's response to this query is what propels his examination of the sovereign's decision.

In situations such as the one just described, the German thinker notes, it is law itself that legitimizes a person, the dictator, to undertake all necessary actions to restore the normality under which legality can prevail. In the words of Schmitt,

329 Michael Hoelzl and Graham Ward, "Translators' Introduction," in *Dictatorship: From the Origin of the Modern Concept of Sovereignty to Proletarian Class Struggle*, by Carl Schmitt (Cambridge: Polity, 2014), 229. This text was extracted from note 17 to the introduction made by the translators.

> the methodological autonomy, as a legal problem, of the problem of law implementation becomes most evident here. The dictator's action should create a condition in which the law can be realized, because every legal norm presupposes a normal condition as homogenous medium in which it is valid. Therefore it is a problem of concrete reality without ceasing to be a legal problem. The constitution can be suspended without ceasing to be valid, because the suspension only represents a *concrete exception*[330].

In other words, legality is temporarily suspended to allow for its re-established through the action of the dictator. It is worth noting that Schmitt argues that what enables the sovereign to suspend legality is concrete reality itself. This means that he acknowledges that concrete reality already emerges endowed with meaning. For Schmitt, then, "the pole of the real is that of given existence, which finds itself revealed, emerging in typical ways and according to a certain meaning. Yet it appears against a background of exceptionality—from an abyss of indeterminacy and mystery"[331]. The task of the sovereign is to determine whether concreteness can be accommodated within the bounds of legality or if it justifies resorting to extra-legal measures.

Although Schmitt's legitimation of dictatorship, as well as its implicit connection to the "abstract law" discussed in The *Value of the State and the Significance of the Individual,* warrant extensive examination in their own right, our research prompts us to consider whether, in this text, he identifies and clarifies some fundamental structures intrinsic to human understanding. Our hypothesis is that in this text, Schmitt continues to emphasize human finitude, but from a political perspective. The reasoning leading to this conclusion is as follows: Schmitt starts by acknowledging, even more explicitly than in his earlier works, a tension

330 Carl Schmitt, *Dictatorship: From the Origin of the Modern Concept of Sovereignty to Proletarian Class Struggle*, trans. Michael Hoelzl and Graham Ward (Cambridge: Polity, 2014), 118. German edition: Carl Schmitt, *Die Diktatur: von den Anfängen des modernen Souveränitätsgedankens bis zum proletarischen Klassenkampf* (Berlin: Duncker et Humblot, 2015), 133–34.

331 Herrera, *Carl Schmitt. Between Technological Rationality and Theology*, 83. In the epilogue we will refer more extensively to this "background" from which reality emerges.

between an abstract normative pole and concrete reality. He contends that situations inevitably arise where the concrete reality exceeds the scope of the normative pole's regulation. This leads to a diminution of the legal norms' force due to their inefficacy, leaving only pure facticity (akin to Hobbes' state of nature[332]). The situation just described recognizes that law, as a human creation, is incapable of handling the infinity and incommensurability of existence. In other words, due to human finitude, everything created by humans bears this same characteristic. The loss of legal efficacy, necessitating the intervention of the dictator, is but one manifestation of this existential trait of humanity.

Schmitt validates the argument just proposed through his analysis of Machiavelli's political philosophy. When examining the Italian philosopher's concept of *arcana dominationis*, the German jurist explains that they "are concerned with the security and defence[sic.] of rulers in extraordinary events, rebellions and revolutions, and with the means by which these events can be dealt with"[333]. Today, we would describe them as extraordinary powers granted to the sovereign during times of crisis in order for him to restore the political community to relative normality. Schmitt goes on to clarify that the *arcana* is conceptually opposed to *iura* (law), which takes the form of *iura imperii* when referring to the power that the sovereign has to pass laws, and the form of *iura dominationis* when indicating the legal prerogatives bestowed upon the sovereign by the legal system[334]. For Machiavelli, argues Schmitt, a dictatorship is a specific *arcanum dominationis* of the aristocracy, and its purpose is to channel political chaos, whether caused by natural or human phenomena, towards normality by means of creating "an institution that frightens the people into believing that it constitutes an authority against which there is no possibility of provocation [. . .]. The *arcana* have to change according to the actual situation; but *the iura* cannot be delegated in the way the *arcana* can. The

332 Thomas Hobbes, *Leviathan*, trans. Richard Tuck (Cambridge: Cambridge University Press, 1996).

333 Schmitt, *Dictatorship*, 12.

334 Schmitt, 12.

iura are **finite**—this is the crucial difference [. . .]. The arcana are the secret plans and practices with help of which the *iura imperii* should be maintained"[335]. That is, by analyzing exceptional situations where the existing legality within a political community fails to address unfolding realities, Schmitt affirms the finitude of legal normativity and the unfathomability of existence. The German jurist suggests that it is natural for what is ordinary and finite, although valuable and useful, to be incapable of handling what is extraordinary and infinite. Consequently, it becomes evident that a legal system needs to incorporate dynamism to effectively manage the exceptional. In the political realm, the role of dictatorship is envisioned to achieve this objective.

In this context, Schmitt argues that the exceptional background from which reality emerges should not be ignored by legal theory. In his words,

> from the standpoint of legal theory, it is not enough here to repeat the formula—no doubt correct—that extraordinary situations require extraordinary means. [. . .] In every legal atom, if I may put it in this way, there remains a pattern that presupposes an abnormal situation, different from the law that ought to be valid in a normal situation. At least the awareness of this difference should not be lost in jurisprudence[336].

That is, the finitude of legality, starkly revealed by the exception, is something that should be embedded in the DNA of every legal statute. In other words, the legitimacy of positive law must be understood as contingent upon the context in which it operates. The normative force of statutory law, therefore, endures only as long as the context for its application remains relatively normal, one in which the unfathomability of reality has not yet risen to disrupt the frameworks of normality that humans have constructed to regulate ordinary circumstances.

335 Schmitt, 12. The highlight is ours.

336 Carl Schmitt, "Appendix: Weimar Constitution, Article 48," in *Dictatorship: From the Origin of the Modern Concept of Sovereignty to Proletarian Class Struggle*, trans. Michael Hoelzl and Graham Ward (Cambridge: Polity, 2014), 219.

Now, when discussing the dictatorial power within the framework of Schmitt's political theory, a pertinent question arises: Does a dictator, especially in the role of a sovereign, wield power akin to divine omnipotence? Schmitt's exposition of sovereign dictatorship in *Political Theology*, whereby he describes the sovereign as the one who decides on the exception and argues that the exceptional cannot be determined *a priori* due to its very nature, might suggest the notion of such absolute power[337]. Saralegui, however, challenges this view. He contends that while sovereignty may seem boundless in its constitutive moment, it is not analogous to the *ex-nihilo* creation power of God. The shift from nothingness to being for God's creation might be a mystery, but the creation of sovereignty follows a discernible, albeit open-ended, criterion. Saralegui suggests, drawing on Schmitt's often implicit arguments, that sovereignty is created, much like Hobbes suggests, as a means of securing survival—power is, therefore, formed to prolong life[338]. From this perspective, sovereign power would disintegrate if it became arbitrary. Therefore, any genocidal behavior inherently contradicts the purpose of sovereignty. The essence of sovereignty is to foster peace and life. If it transmutes political life into indiscriminate graveyards, sovereignty loses its meaning. A sovereignty that adopts the role of mass murder is not political sovereignty; it's merely a dangerous embodiment of state-of-nature violence, made more threatening due to its institutional and legitimate appearance[339].

Still, this interpretation does not diminish the potential dangers of Schmitt's proposal if followed to its ultimate consequences—the "Schmittian shadow". This is particularly relevant when we reflect on the events of the 20th century in Europe, and the rise of Nazism—a movement to which Schmitt himself belonged. Amid political crises, Schmitt recognized the need for a robust state and, being blinded by

337 Carl Schmitt, *Political Theology: Four Chapters on the Concept of Sovereignty*, trans. George Schwab, University of Chicago Press ed (Chicago: University of Chicago Press, 2005), 5–7.

338 Miguel Saralegui Benito, *The Politics of Time: Introduction to Carl Schmitt's Political Thought* (Santander: Cantabria University Press, 2021), 159.

339 Saralegui Benito, 157–59.

his statolatry, failed to foresee the horrifying outcomes this could lead to. Saralegui highlights that Schmitt's complex and conscious defense of sovereignty and authoritarianism, sensible in the mid-1920s, loses its rationale by the 1950s. Again, Schmitt's statolatry prevented him from realizing that during significant periods of the 20th century, the uncertainty of the state of nature was preferable to the lethal randomness of the state. The only explanation for Schmitt's misinterpretation is that his political thought is grounded more in theory than in concrete realities[340]. Therefore, even though his reflections on dictatorship make sense ontologically, one must be careful with the practical consequences to which they may lead.

In conclusion, Schmitt's advocacy for dictatorship in the political sphere is fundamentally derived from the recognition of human knowledge's inherent finitude and how it manifests in juridical phenomena. He sees dictatorship as the only viable means of restoring normalcy, a condition that can be encapsulated by legal normativity. However, this understanding of Schmitt's proposition of dictatorship should not be mistaken as an egotistic posture, where the dictator, professing superior knowledge, is legitimized by the ignorance of the populace. Rather, a certain humility permeates Schmitt's analysis. While this interpretation may have an element of naiveté, we perceive that Schmitt's endorsement of dictatorship stems from a radical acknowledgment of the human existential condition—an impossible endeavor of navigating an infinite, extraordinary, and immeasurable reality using finite tools and concepts. The call for dictatorship, therefore, does not emerge from an attempt to deify humanity but rather from a hard-earned recognition of human limitations in grappling with reality. This insight, while not an easy concession, is an acknowledgment of our inability to fully master or control the vast complexity of the world around us.

The last texts we will examine from the specified period are *Political Romanticism* (1919) and *Political Theology* (1922). We believe that in both texts, Schmitt addresses the same fundamental ontological structures inherent in all human understanding: historicality in an

340 Saralegui Benito, 159.

epochal sense and metaphysics as an inevitable human condition. To elucidate what we mean by "the epochal sense of historicality", we will briefly refer to the insights of one of the philosophers who has delved most deeply into this subject: Martin Heidegger.

The history of being, Heidegger argues, is the most faithful and profound record of the meaning of an epoch. In his words,

> western metaphysics, that is, the reflection on beings as such and as a whole, determines beings in advance and for its entire history as what is conceivable and definable in the respects of reason and thinking. Insofar as all customary thinking is always grounded in a form of metaphysics, everyday and metaphysical thinking alike rest on "trust" in this relation, on the confidence that beings as such show themselves in the thinking of reason and its categories, that is to say, that what is true and truth are grasped and secured in reason[341].

That is, he suggests that the manner in which a specific epoch interprets ontic reality and its truth determines, at least to some extent, how the world is to be understood. Metaphysics establishes the foundation of an era at the moment when the hermeneutics of what is to be understood as an entity and the method by which the truth of that entity is accessed are determined. This hermeneutic decision endows an epoch with its essence, since it exerts complete dominance over all phenomena characterizing that era, and vice versa.[342]. In other words, the prevailing worldview in a given era implies that any epochal phenomena under examination, whether in politics, artistic creation, scientific research, or social investigation, cannot escape the essential and interconnected determinations of its historical context. Therefore, a profound thematization of these phenomena enables the elucidation of the interpretation of the ontic and the truth during that particular time.

Aligned closely with Heidegger' approach, Schmitt follows a similar logic. In *Political Theology,* the German thinker explains that "sociology of concepts", a method through which the foundational

---

341 Heidegger, *Nietzsche*, III:50.

342 Martin Heidegger, "The Age of the World Picture," in *Science and the Quest for Reality*, ed. Alfred I. Tauber, trans. William Lovitt, Main Trends of the Modern World (London: Palgrave Macmillan UK, 1997), 70–88.

concepts of an epoch are deconstructed, "transcends juridical conceptualization oriented to immediate practical interest. It aims to discover the basic, radically systematic structure and to compare this conceptual structure with the conceptually represented social structure of a certain epoch"[343]. In other words, Schmitt suggests that a reflective analysis of law enables one to transcend the everyday practical interests typically associated with this phenomenon, in order to uncover the worldview of an epoch, especially how this worldview manifests in legal contexts. Thus, thematizing the legal phenomenon becomes a means through which the understanding of truth and the metaphysical foundation of an era can be explicitly revealed. This is based on Schmitt's assertion that "the metaphysical image that a definite epoch forges of the world has the same structure as what the world immediately understands to be appropriate as a form of its political organization"[344].

For Schmitt, much like Heidegger, historicality is not only instrumental in shaping the horizon of meaning for individuals but also plays a more fundamental role: that of historicality as the foundation of an epoch's paradigm. This is closely linked to another characteristic that we believe Schmitt identifies as universal in human understanding: metaphysics as an inevitable human condition. To further clarify this point, we will once again briefly refer to Heidegger.

Heidegger contends that metaphysics involves transcending the ontic, a process inherent in the essence of human existence. This act of transcending is precisely what defines metaphysics, and it is fundamentally aligned with human nature[345]. Schmitt, in turn, echoing Heidegger, notes in the 1925 preface he added to *Political Romanticism*, that

> today, many varieties of metaphysical attitude exist in a secularized form. To a great extent, it holds true that different, and indeed mundane factors have taken the place of God: humanity, the nation, the individual, historical development, or even life as life for its own sake, in its complete spiritual emptiness and mere

343 Schmitt, *Political Theology*, 45. German edition: Carl Schmitt, *Politische Theologie* (Berlin: Duncker & Humblot, 2015), 59.

344 Schmitt, *Political Theology*, 46.

345 Martin Heidegger, *What Is Metaphysics?*, 2018.

dynamic. This does not mean that the attitude is no longer metaphysical. **The thought and feeling of every person always retain a metaphysical character. Metaphysics is something that is unavoidable**, and as Otto von Gierke has aptly remarked we cannot escape it by relinquishing our awareness of it. What human beings regard as the ultimate, absolute authority, however, certainly can change, and God can be replaced by mundane worldly factors. I call this secularization[346].

That is, Schmitt concurs with Heidegger that metaphysics involves going beyond the ontic and that it is an activity inherent to human nature. He also shares the Freiburg philosopher's view on the role of historicality in framing metaphysics. Schmitt notes that throughout history, various phenomena have filled the "space" of metaphysics, traditionally associated with God. Each epoch has, or is shaped by, its unique metaphysical thought. For example, the Middle Ages can be characterized by a transcendent God occupying this metaphysical space, while modernity is marked by the shift of metaphysical transcendence and its replacement by reason and technical thought.

While secularization, closely intertwined with metaphysics, warrants a dedicated and thorough investigation, our mention of it in this text is solely to underscore that metaphysics is an inevitable aspect of the human condition and a key element in shaping the paradigm that underpins an epoch. This becomes apparent in *Political Theology,* where Schmitt, in examining the metaphysical image of modernity, notes that following the expulsion of God from the world,

the consistency of exclusively scientific thinking has also permeated political ideas, repressing the essentially juristic-ethical thinking that had predominated in the age of Enlightenment. The general validity of a legal prescription has become identified with the lawfulness of nature, which applies without exception. The sovereign, who in the deistic view of the world, even if conceived as residing outside the world, had remained the engineer of the great machine, has been radically pushed aside. The machine now runs by itself[347].

---

346 Schmitt, *Political Romanticism*, 17–18. German edition: Carl Schmitt, *Politische Romantik.* (Berlin: Duncker & Humblot, 2012), 18.

347 Schmitt, *Political Theology*, 48. German edition: Schmitt, *Politische Theologie*, 61–62.

That is, whatever occupies the position that traditionally belonged to God influences, at least in part, our understanding of the world. For instance, during the Middle Ages, nature was contemplated and respected as a divine creation. In contrast, in modern times—an era where calculating, economizing technical thought has supplanted divinity—nature is viewed primarily as a resource for generating economic profit.

In *Political Romanticism*, Schmitt argues that not every metaphysical image is adequate for understanding reality. As Oakes explains, through this text the German jurist acknowledges that

> in the metaphysics of romanticism, the world has no independent or intrinsic reality. Even an event of world-historical importance such as the French Revolution or the First World War has no inherent ontological significance. This means that nothing can be said to exist because of its own substantive qualities, for example, the properties that can be ascribed to it by virtue of its historical, political, or moral status. Romanticism entails that there are no such properties. An item exists only as an object of an aesthetic interest, and the world is constituted by the essentially capricious states of the individual aesthetic imagination. The content of subjective emotional life determines what is real. This means that reality can be ascribed to an item only insofar as it becomes an occasion for an emotional experience[348].

In other words, the romantic directs his understanding solely towards the factual and real pole of existence, entirely neglecting the conceptual frameworks that seek to shape and imbue the world with meaning. The consequence is an individual so enamored with their individuality that they perceive the world as a multiplicity of phenomena arrayed for their enjoyment. This poses a political problem, as Schmitt points out, "when the genial subject seriously put its divine autarky into practice, it no longer tolerated any community. The incorporation of the subject into community and history meant that the self as creator of the world was dethroned"[349]. Differently put the romantic adopts a positionality

348 Guy Oakes, "Translator's Introduction," in *Political Romanticism*, by Carl Schmitt (Massachusetss & London: MIT Press, 1986), xx.

349 Schmitt, *Political Romanticism*, 65.

characterized by an inflated sense of self. In this perspective, every entity and event within existence is ultimately related back to their own self. Within this framework, considering the perspective of others becomes impossible, and the articulation of a "common good" is even less feasible. The inclusion of another "self" into this worldview would undermine the romantic's self-conception, leading them to avoid any situation that requires transcending their own subjectivity.

The contextualization of Schmitt's reflection on romanticism as metaphysical position, in conjunction with his exploration of juridical thought, offers intriguing insights. As observed in chapter two, Schmitt's intellectual critique of legal positivism must be understood more broadly. His real contention is with the modern *Weltanschauung* that reduces human existence to the abstract pole of existence by confining the concept of "truth" to what is predictable, calculable, and replicable by scientific means. Viewing *Statute and Judgment* (1912), *The Value of the State and the Significance of the Individual* (1914), and *Dictatorship* (1921) through this lens, they can be seen as efforts to reaffirm the importance of the concrete, to move away from a worldview that neglects the fact that concepts do not fully encompass reality. In *Political Romanticism*, on the other hand, Schmitt appears to take a contrary stance, cautioning against the perils of reducing reality to merely factual and real aspects. As Herrera explains it,

> Schmitt views romanticism as a movement that, reacting to rationalism, is inclined toward the pole of the real. [...] In the romantic attitude, there is a surrendering to the real, done either without or without sufficient epistemological control. In this surrendering, reality loses its contours, its consistence, and dilutes. After leaning toward the pole of the real and distancing itself from the conceptual one, romanticism gives, however, a second step. An aspect of such diluted reality is taken as the occasional starting point of a "fanciful construction", of the "playful sorcery of the imagination"[350].

Romanticism, therefore, represents an overcorrection of rationalism and is an extreme that should also be avoided at all costs. The concrete pole of existence requires a balancing force to prevent the world

350 Herrera, *Carl Schmitt. Between Technological Rationality and Theology*, 79.

from being reduced to a mere playground for individual subjectivities. Hence, it becomes essential to incorporate rationality in the existential puzzle.

In sum, Schmitt's early philosophy can be interpreted as an endeavor to uncover a mechanism for achieving a crucial balance between the real and the conceptual. The legal phenomenon, according to Schmitt, serves as an exemplary case of how to find this equilibrium, particularly through the roles of the judge and the sovereign. They act as guardians tasked with maintaining the balance between the real and ideal poles of existence. However, this raises key questions: How will a specific judge or sovereign attain this balance? What specific methods should be employed to prevent the balance from skewing toward one of the poles? How does the judge or sovereign ensure the correctness of their decision? In the next chapter, we will explore how Schmitt addresses these challenges.

§ 5. Conclusions and final reflections

The underlying premise of this work is that Schmitt's legal analysis encompasses not just law but also philosophy (and not necessarily *of* law). Although we have not provided criteria to differentiate the purely legal aspects of his texts from those that are not, we have illustrated how the German author subtly shifts between these subjects. Specifically, we initiated our analysis by examining Herrera's argument justifying a reading of Schmitt's legal work from the perspective of theory of understanding. Complementing what the Chilean philosopher has already articulated, we proposed that one way to specify the sense in which a theory with such characteristics can be identified in Schmitt's thought is by analyzing it through the lens of normativity. This approach enabled us to assert that, when viewing his work from this angle, it is evident that Schmitt addresses not only the antinomic poles in legal understanding but also the unique characteristics of the entity responsible for resolving such tension: the human being.

Having clarified the horizon from which we approach the work of the German thinker, we proceeded with a concise analysis of his early texts to elucidate whether Schmitt identifies some of the inherent ontological structures that operate in all human understanding. In this context, we argued:

1. In *Statute and Judgment* (1912) finitude and historicality emerge as ontological traits that are projected to law by humans.
2. In *The Value of the State and the Significance of the Individual* (1914), the focus is on temporality (intimately linked to historicality), as well as language as a configurator of a horizon of meaning.
3. In *Dictatorship* (1921), Schmitt further explores the finitude of human understanding, but from a political perspective.
4. Finally, in *Political Romanticism* (1919) and *Political Theology (*1922), he examines historicality in an epochal sense and justifies the inevitability of a metaphysical grounding that underlies all human understanding.

The openness that defines the human condition, which is manifested in an exemplary manner in legal thought, can be better understood by considering one of the sources of Schmitt's thought: Helmuth Plessner (1892–1985). A fundamental trait of humanness, argues Plessner, is its *excentric positionality.* As Vydrová explains,

> its starting point is the anthropological difference from which centricity and excentricity, closedness and openness (Plessner 2019, 298–316), develops at the levels of the living: plants, animals, and sphere of human. In *centric positionality* is the organism situated in an environment in the manner of the center, but in *excentric positionality* one defines oneself in relation towards the center and becomes aware of one's situation as a kind of tension, while for human it is impossible to found one's life from the center. This brings into life of human being the effort to resolve this situation, which is always present[351].

351 Jaroslava Vydrová, "Spirituality from the Perspective of Philosophical Anthropology: Against the Background of Helmuth Plessner's Conception," *Spirituality*

That is, unlike plants and animals, the human being is an *aperture* that determines its way of being relationally (as seen with Heidegger in chapter one). The world presents us with various entities, situations, and circumstances which urge us to decide about how we engage with them. Each thought and decision, as well as the context from where they emerge (rationality, egotism, love, etc.), is then incorporated into our being. Even though we are not capable, due to our existential finitude, of determining the manner in which reality (facticity) emerges, we are free to decide the way we relate to such worldliness. Human existence, then, is a *groundless existence*, one which has no center and is defined through the resolution of the constant tension between its being and the world. Simply put, due to our existential openness, human life is a constant *becoming*. In Vydrová's words, "as an excentric positionality, one becomes oneself in the performances of one's own life. Human being is open, not pre-fixed or derived from an instance, but constituted in relation to the boundaries of one's world, the possibilities of own corporeality, in relation to other people and one's own activity in the sphere of culture in the broadest sense of the word"[352]. Schmitt's concerns, then, align with those of Plessner: existential openness, the synthesis of the constant becoming that is life through a decision, and the incommensurability of existence (which emerges in exceptional form).

This existential openness identified by Schmitt in human understanding, along with the consequent portrayal of human existence as a continuous process of becoming, highlights the significance of the dynamics at the moment of determining one's own existence; specifically, the moment of existential appropriation. In this context, it appears that another of Schmitt's sources of inspiration during his years in Köln, Wilhelm Dilthey (1833–1911), helps us understand the importance Schmitt places on decision-making as an instance of such appropriation. Dilthey argues that the tension between different realms of existence, so to speak, is a fundamental condition for the existence

Studies 8, no. 1 (2022): 44.

352 Vydrová, 44.

of hermeneutics[353]. Two different worlds, each with its own unique peculiarity, must collide for a hermeneutical relationship to materialize. However, for this relationship to arise, there must be something that articulates and connects these dichotomous realms, that bridges the gap between them. In Dilthey's thought, this articulating instance is referred to as the *structural nexus*, which is an essential prerequisite for the emergence of the teleologically oriented content of law and theology in concrete reality. In his words,

> a hermeneutics is possible here because a relation exists between a people and a state, between believers and a church, between the life of science and a university, that allows a common spirit and a uniform way of life to find a structural nexus in which they are expressed. Thus there exists here a relationship of parts to whole in which the parts receive meaning from the whole and the whole receives its sense from the parts; these categories of interpretation have their correlate in the structural nexus of the organization by which it realize a purpose teleologically[354].

That is, hermeneutics becomes possible due to the mutual feedback between the parts and the whole, which is synthesized through the organizing and unifying activity of the structural nexus. According to Dilthey, this nexus is represented by the psychic life of the human being.

If we follow Dilthey's thematization of human understanding as hermeneutical, then the danger of relativism inevitably comes forth. If the psychic life of the perceiver becomes the unifying instance between the part and the whole (the structural nexus), then it is possible (and probable) that different individuals, which participate in different dimensions of the part, engage with the whole in distinct manners. In this scenario, that which is perceived as real by different individuals will vary. In Dilthey's words, "the truth is that precisely in these properties of psychic life, according to which it is a structural nexus, rests the difference between what is given to us in lived experience and in

353 See: Wilhelm Dilthey, *The Formation of the Historical World in the Human Sciences*, ed. Rudolf A Makkreel and Frithjof Rodi, vol. III (Princeton & Oxford: Princeton University Press, 2002).

354 Dilthey, III:284.

reflection upon it, on the one hand, and physical objects that we construe on the basis of given sense complexes, on the other hand"[355]. Differently put, we must distinguish between things as they are in themselves (*res externa*) and how they are perceived by a concrete human being (*res interna*). We human beings, due to the finite nature of the synthesizing instrument used in the context of perception (mind), perceive an incomplete image of what is present to our senses. Therefore, the image of the world that is presented to the human mind is not necessarily a reliable correlate of the reality of the world itself. What is more problematic is that different minds, influenced by their unique contexts in apprehending the world, generate diverse interpretations based on the same phenomena. Given this context, it becomes natural to question the validity of the concept of truth, as well as to wonder whether humans are even capable of accessing it (assuming it exists).

The acknowledgment of the hermeneutical nature of human understanding consequently lays the groundwork for a relativistic view of truth and reality. It's important to note that a hermeneutical perspective doesn't inherently lead to relativism, but it does allow for an interpretation of the world in this light. Recognizing the existential openness that characterizes human understanding is immensely valuable, as it permits an approach to reality that accommodates abstract conceptuality, facticity, and the human element, without reducing existence to merely one of these facets. However, this openness also, to some extent, undermines the possibility of certainty, as it is difficult to ascertain *a priori* the outcome that will emerge from the interplay of these elements.

Schmitt seems to be aware of the shadow of relativism cast by his hermeneutic thematization of law and human understanding, which is why he emphasizes mechanisms to avoid, as much as possible, a drift toward dogmatic existential positionalities[356]. In the realm of legal praxis, Schmitt strives to embed legal certainty through a fiction that

---

355 Dilthey, III:43.

356 As Herrera notes, the German jurist consistently seeks a middle ground between technological rationality and theology throughout his work. Hence the title of his latest work: Herrera, *Carl Schmitt. Between Technological Rationality and Theology*.

he requires judges to employ. They must decide *as if* there is a common sense of justice inherent in the mind of every judge, guiding their reasoning in rulings on particular cases. It appears that during his time in Strasbourg, Schmitt was significantly influenced by Hans Vaihinger (1852–1933), who is widely known for his philosophy of *Als Ob* (as if). In the context of legal thought, Vaihinger contends that a fundamental fiction is essential for the application of legal statutes. In his words,

> the psychological mechanism of their application consists in subsuming a single case under a conceptual construct not properly intended for it, so that the apperception is, in consequence, merely an analogy. The basis for this method is as follows: since laws cannot include within their formulae all particular instances, certain special examples of an unusual nature are treated as if they belonged to them. Or else, because of some practical interest, an individual instance is brought under a general concept to which it does not really belong. Anyone conversant with the method of jurisprudence will easily understand how important this artifice is for legal practice[357].

That is, in legal matters lawyers and judges rely on a fundamental fiction: the belief that statutes have the capacity to encompass all the circumstances and events that may require a legal solution in both the present and the future. This fiction isn't a mistake made by naive jurists but rather serves as an essential assumption without which the law couldn't function in practical reality. Without this assumption, where legal statutes are considered unable to conform to the complexities of reality, the worlds of abstract normativity and concrete life would exist as separate dimensions, never intersecting. To facilitate the task of judges in bridging these two seemingly separate worlds, legislators often incorporate extra-legal elements into statutes. These elements may include examples, principles, and abstract concepts like prudence or the common man, among others. These additions provide some flexibility to interpreters when applying a legal text to a specific case. Vaihinger offers insight into this by stating:

357 Hans Vaihinger, *The Philosophy of "as If". A System of the Theoretical, Practical and Religious Fictions of Mankind*, trans. C.K. Ogden (London: Routledge & Kegan Paul, 1935), 33.

> “From a **practical** standpoint, the importance is great and almost incalculable. **Theoretically**, however, not only has nothing been gained thereby, but there has been a **deviation from reality**. Without such deviations thought cannot attain its purpose [. . .]. It is just the deviation that, in the end, appears to be the natural procedure, and it is absolutely necessary constantly to stress this fact and draw attention to it”[358].

In other words, these extra-legal elements are not meant to enrich or extend the theoretical underpinnings of the law. Instead, their purpose is to establish the necessary conditions for legal principles to manifest in practical reality and be applied effectively.

Schmitt appears to have discovered in Vaihinger’s ideas a solution to the problem of relativism he encountered when recognizing the existential openness of human understanding within the legal domain. While it is essential to incorporate extra-legal elements into legal thinking, it is equally crucial for judges to make decisions as if there were a common principle of justice guiding the specific application of these elements to individual cases. In the next chapter, we will explore how Schmitt employs the philosophy of *as if* to navigate a prudent path in legal thought, avoiding extreme and dogmatic positionalities.

358 Vaihinger, 35.

4 Towards the *middle way* in legal thought

§ 1. Introduction

> The eye of the philosopher is thereby able to recognize more readily the tremendous difference between the formal processes of thought and the objective reality of external events[359].

The issue of determining the specific conditions under which a particular decision can be considered correct (*richtig*) takes us back to the beginning of our exploration of Schmitt's ideas. In his first academic work, *Statute and Judgment* (1912), Schmitt directly addresses this matter. The perspective from which we approach this topic in this chapter allows us to delve deeper into the meaning and significance of Schmitt's proposition. We now understand that Schmitt views the juridical phenomenon as one where a multitude of elements come into play, not limited to legal statutes alone. He also recognizes that for legal normativity to have a practical impact on reality, it must relinquish its purity and abstraction and become *humanized*. This transformation is carried out by the judge or the sovereign through a decision, which Schmitt presents as an instance of synthesis between the ideal and real poles of existence.

Schmitt's demand of an existential openness in the realm of law, however, does not entail an absolute freedom for the judge and the sovereign in the context of decision-making. Instead, the acknowledgment of legal decisions as instances of synthesis between two opposing poles leads Schmitt to identify two existential positions that he considers highly perilous and which should be avoided: the romantic and

359 Vaihinger, 35.

technical. In both cases, existence is reduced to only one aspect of reality, but they differ in terms of the pole that is chosen to define truth comprehensively. These existential positions manifest in legal thought in the following ways: the technical position takes the form of normative legal positivism, a line of thought which asserts that written rules exhaust the object of study of the legal phenomenon, and any external element, whether ethical or factual, must be eliminated from legal discourse. The romantic, on the other hand, is a positionality that in law manifests itself in law in the form of capricious decisionism. In this stance, judges use the decision as an instance for deploying their subjectivity without restrictions, thus becoming a quasi-divine legal instance in which the functions of the legislator and judge are merged into one person. To avoid falling into these positionalities, Schmitt emphasizes the importance of making legal decisions based on rationality. In this context, he encourages the human element included in the legal process to engage in a reflective exercise, which we argue can be seen as a form of "reflective endorsement" (as we will explore further in this chapter).

As we saw with Heidegger, understanding is an openness towards existence as *Being-possible.* To understand oneself from a possibility is to be able to *be* that possibility, to project oneself existentially as that possibility. For Schmitt, legal understanding seems to be an instance of appropriation of a possibility. That is, positive legal statutes present the judge with a range of possible interpretations. The judge must then decide which of these hermeneutic possibilities he will "bring to life" through his decision. The hypothetical exercise he demands judges to perform, that is, to understand "a judicial decision is correct if it is expectable for another judge to have decided in the same way."[360], is to be considered as a mechanism for ensuring that this appropriation of a legal possibility is done in a rational manner.

Schmitt, then, could be read as a "legal mystic": he demands jurists to understand law as an aperture towards the concrete. At the same time, he is pragmatic: he does not wish the legal phenomenon to turn into a

360 Schmitt, *Gesetz Und Urteil*, 68.

tool for the dogmatic deployment of particular subjective positionalities. Schmitt's goal, therefore, is avoiding these extreme positionalities and finding a prudent balance. He aims to rectify the shortcomings of legal positivism by assigning greater importance to the concrete pole of existence in legal conceptualization. Simultaneously, the German jurist is cautious not to overly skew the balance towards the concrete. He also advocates for legal decisions to be rational and impersonal, reflecting attributes associated with the ideal pole of existence.

If viewed from this perspective, Schmitt's criteria for the correctness of legal decisions can be seen as an effort to establish a theoretical framework that provides sufficient openness for considering the dynamism of the concrete pole, while simultaneously setting boundaries to ensure rationality in decision-making. In this chapter, we will explore whether and how Schmitt achieves this formidable task, and how he ensures that in the process of humanizing law, it does not succumb to reductionist extremes. We will structure this section as follows: initially, we will elucidate the problem Schmitt addresses in *Statute and Judgment* and the solution he proposes (§ 2). Subsequently, we will scrutinize his response, highlighting the risk of interpretations that could suggest Schmitt advocates for judicial decisionism (§ 3). Then, we will argue that interpreting *Statute and Judgment* through Korsgaard's concept of "reflective endorsement" is fitting and sheds light on why Schmitt emphasizes the practical nature of his proposal(§ 4). Finally, we will draw some conclusions (§ ;5).

§ 2. Legality vs. Indeterminacy: Schmitt's description of law

The challenges confronted in Schmitt's *Statute and Judgment* faces are twofold: the legitimation of legal decisions (1), and resolving the tension between a general and abstract text, which corresponds to a past historical and legal situation, and a new, specific case presenting a contemporary problem requiring resolution (2). In other words, Schmitt's text grapples with two fundamental philosophical issues: using Kantian terminology, the *quid juris* of legal decisions, aiming "to establish the entitlement or legal claim"[361] of these decisions, and the primary challenge that philosophy of law must address, namely, that of mediating the universality of law and the singularity of particular cases (*quid facti*)[362].

Before delving into how Schmitt addresses these questions, it is important to recognize a fundamental premise guiding his analysis: legal philosophy should not seek an absolute and timeless answer to the question of the correctness of a decision[363]. Instead, his attention is firmly centered on the necessity of acknowledging the inherent dynamism of reality in order for law to be legitimate, valid, and effective. It is also crucial to remember that in this text, Schmitt's concern is not "about the relation of natural to positive law, but about the relation of positive law to the empirical facticity of the particular case"[364]. His focus lies not in the meta-positive foundation of law (which he acknowledges) but in the most concrete aspect of legal practice: judicial decisions. That being said, let's now examine Schmitt's analysis of legal decisions.

Statute and Judgment can be read as a response to ideological legal positivism (as Bobbio terms it[365]). The fact that Schmitt explicitly lashes against legalism as a theory that pretends to explain the whole legal phenomenon in terms of legal statutes seems to support this thesis. In this sense, Schmitt affirms that "the formal validity of a positive statute does not have the significance for the evaluation of legal practice that is usually attributed to it. That a decision conforms to statute does not, by

361 Kant, CPR A 84/ B 116.
362 Herrero, "Estudio preliminar," XIX.
363 See chapters one and two of this work.
364 Rasch, "Judgment: The Emergence of Legal Norms," 98.
365 Bobbio elucidates that as an ideology, positivism asserts that positive law is the sole element to which a judge must give consideration when adjudicating a case. Bobbio, *Giusnaturalismo e positivismo giuridico.*

itself, offer a sufficient answer to the question whether it is correct"[366]. That is, formal validity may allow us to distinguish between moral and legal rules[367], but it does not provide a criterion for distinguishing right and wrong legal decisions. To be more precise, ideologic positivism does provide such a criterion, but it is one that fails to accomplish its mission. This line of thought usually operates under the notion that a legal decision is correct when the deciding judge is able to subsume the case under the legal description properly[368]. That is, as long as he is able to "fit" the particular cases under the general description contained in positive law. The equation, so to speak, is already given, and the only task to be performed by the judge is replacing the variables. In that sense, the legal decision will be correct as long as the judge has followed this procedure thoroughly.

As discussed in the second chapter of this work, Schmitt identifies a two-fold problem with this type of thinking. Firstly, he argues that while subsumptivist logic offers a hermeneutical procedure for judges, it fails to provide a criterion for verifying the correctness of their decisions. Secondly, he contends that the "survival" of a law is not dependent on its "legality". Regarding the first point, Schmitt asserts that subsumptivism does not suggest a method to check if the subsumption was performed correctly. Moreover, even if it did propose such a rule, it would lead to an infinite regress. This is because that rule would then require another rule to verify if the rule for ensuring the correct application of subsumption under positive law was itself correctly applied, and so on.

Regarding the second point, Schmitt contends that the factors enabling a law to survive and retain its legitimacy are not merely rooted in legality (although this is necessary), but rather

366 Schmitt, "Statute and Judgment: An Investigation into the Problem of Legal Praxis," 49.

367 In this sense, Kelsen Kelsen, *Pure Theory of Law*.

368 Bobbio is referring specifically to positivism considered as a "formal theory of interpretation".

> the voluminous revisions of the words of a statute, their modifying penetration with a thousand scientific concepts, their reshaping into a system, the mountains of books that often weigh on one single word in the statute, the libraries of precedents: elements of all of these are effective in a decision that is to be gathered from the "statute". If one still sees in this a "conformity to statute"—if one still regards the postulate of the subjection to statute as fulfilled, in the face of the "unavoidable departures from statutory law on the part of the law that comes to the fore in adjudication"—then one has the scientific obligation to explain what one understands by the content of statute and by the claim that a judge is bound to this content[369].

Put simply, the mere legality of a statute is not sufficient for it to produce its intended effects. There are many other elements at play, which are not accounted for in subsumptivist logic.

This "insufficiency" of statutes and logical procedures in fully accounting the legal phenomenon led Schmitt to conclude that in every legal decision, there exists an inevitable moment of indeterminacy. In his words, "apart from very rare exceptions, every statute contains such a moment of indifference, which a civil lawyer might refer to as aleatory. Up to a certain degree, it is always more necessary that there be a statute at all than that the statute have a particular content"[370]. Now, this "indeterminacy" must be resolved for justice (or something akin to it) to materialize. The pertinent question then becomes how to transition from this indeterminate or aleatory state to one of legal certainty. To address this, Schmitt introduces what he terms the "principle of determination of law". According to this principle, the transition of a statute from an abstract and indeterminate state to a state of determination is facilitated by the judge. It is the judge who resolves this tension through their decision, within the context of a trial. In essence, the judge bears the responsibility of defining the meaning and scope of legal statutes for a particular case.

However, the issue with this solution is that it appears to veer towards a form of legal decisionism, where the content of statutes is

369 Schmitt, "The Value of the State and the Significance of the Individual," 53.

370 Schmitt, "Statute and Judgment: An Investigation into the Problem of Legal Praxis," 84.

subject to the judge's unrestricted discretion (and this interpretation aligns with those readings that categorize Schmitt as a proponent of decisionism[371]). If the judge is tasked with determining the meaning and scope of statutes in legal decisions, it may seem that they possess the power to rule arbitrarily, shaping legality according to their own will. However, this interpretation does not align with Schmitt's argument. In *Statute and Judgment* he explicitly states the opposite, asserting that "the criterion of correction of a judicial sentence does not rest on the subjectivity of the judge; rather, it is totally independent of him as an individual. On whether a sentence is correct or not, the praxis itself decides. The praxis has a specific criterion to declare its correction"[372]. Thus, the fact that positive law is not the only factor judges consider when resolving a case does not imply they have *carte blanche* in their decisions. Schmitt's key point is that positive law does not encapsulate the entirety of what law is; instead, other elements, albeit more abstract, must also be considered as part of this phenomenon. Herrero provides a lucid explanation supporting our thesis, stating that for Schmitt,

> the judge's task is to "search" for the decision. That decision is "next to the law", but is not derived from it. The foundation of the decision is obtained through a **reflective synthesis** of many aspects [. . .]. The formula does not define in advance which of these factors is most decisive: whether the content of the law, the valuations of the people, the weighing of the interests, the precedent, the materials of the law, the custom[373].

---

371 Such as Heinz Laufer, Karl Löwith, Helmut Kuhn and Leo Strauss. Laufer, "Das Kriterium Politischen Handelns. Versuch Einer Analyse Und Konstruktiven Kritik Der Freund Feind-Unterscheidung Auf Der Grundlage Der Aristotelischen Theorie Der Politik; Zugleich Ein Beitrag Zur Methodologie Der Politischen Wissenschaften." Löwith, "Der Okkasionelle Dezisionismus von Carl Schmitt." Strauss, "Anmerkungen Zu Carl Schmitt, Der Begriff Des Politischen."

372 Schmitt, "Statute and Judgment: An Investigation into the Problem of Legal Praxis," 125–26.

373 Herrero, "Estudio preliminar," LXI–LXII. The highlight is ours.

In other words, a judge does not decide based on his own unrestricted will but rather is bound to certain limits, such as law, the community's tradition, libraries of precedents, etc. That is why Schmitt firmly states that "the judge does not create law but appeals to il. He remains subject to the principle of legal determinacy"[374], and why he stresses the importance of having mechanisms like the right to appeal and collegial courts to correct decisions that deviate from established judicial practice.

Nonetheless, it must be acknowledged that since judges are responsible for determining the meaning and scope of law in relation to specific cases, they do, in a certain sense, "create" legality[375]. This aspect becomes more apparent when Schmitt suggests that in some instances, judges are permitted to rule even against positive law:

> [T]he formula contains a consistent solution for the complications that result from the fact that, on the one hand, the authority of statute must be safeguarded, even while, on the other hand, decisions *praeter* or sometimes even *contra legem* [decisions that "go beyond" or "against the law"]—which are regarded to be correct even though they can hardly be called "source-based", whether they are backed up by constant practice or by precedents set by the highest courts or not—may, at times, have to be issued[376].

Now, given that Schmitt argues that judges can rule even in opposition to statutes, how can we maintain that he is not advocating for judicial decisionism? The answer lies in the fact that he never suggests judges should decide *ex nihilo*, based solely on their intuition and will. Instead, as we have already mentioned, he emphasizes that their decisions are constrained by legal sources and, more significantly, by the endorsement of the judicial community (a point to which we will return).

---

374 Schmitt, "Statute and Judgment: An Investigation into the Problem of Legal Praxis," 129.

375 In this sense, Rasch affirms: "Thus, under certain circumstances, the reasons for making a decision can have, practically speaking, a creative meaning". Rasch, "Judgment: The Emergence of Legal Norms," 101–2.

376 Schmitt, "Statute and Judgment: An Investigation into the Problem of Legal Praxis," 103.

The question, then, is how does a judge determine if his decision is correct? How does he transition from that aleatory moment to a concrete legal decision without falling into arbitrariness? As we have seen, Schmitt suggests that his formula leaves open the question of which elements take precedence in legal decisions. The relevance of these elements depends on the specificities of each case. For instance, some cases may warrant direct and exclusive reference to positive law, like in criminal law, while others might require a greater emphasis on custom, as in trade law. However, this approach does not fully resolve our initial question; in fact, it complicates it further. Fortunately, Schmitt offers a solution, stating, as previously mentioned that "a judicial decision is correct, today, if it is to be assumed that another judge would have decided in the same way. 'Another judge', in this context, refers to the empirical type of the modern, legally trained jurist"[377]. This solution, however, raises several questions that need addressing: What is meant by the concept of 'another judge'? How does a judge gain the endorsement of their peers? Does this imply that the correctness or justice of a decision hinges on convention? In what follows, we will explore Schmitt's responses to these queries and argue, following Herrero, that his intention with this formulation is to establish an instance for normative reflection.[378].

§ 3. Endorsement of the community of judges: understanding Schmitt's criterion

Although we have previously touched upon this topic[379], let's delve deeper into what Schmitt means by "the other judge". It's crucial to clarify that this term does not refer to a literal, flesh-and-bone judge,

377 Schmitt, 103.
378 Schmitt, 79–80.
379 See chapter one of this work.

but is rather employed in a normative sense. The "other judge" denotes the "normal" juridically educated judge. As Schmitt clarifies, "the word 'normal' is used here in a quantitative sense that refers to the average, not as the designation of an ideal type and not in a qualitative-teleological sense"[380]. This concept is deemed normative because, as Crowell explains, "the normative is found wherever we can speak of rules, measures, standards, exemplars, ideals, concepts, and so on; wherever distinctions between better and worse, success and failure, can be made"[381]. Hence, it is normative in its function as a standard of measure for legal decisions. However, the remaining question is how the content of this normativity is determined in Schmitt's view. Considering the figure of "the other judge", we identify three possible responses: descriptive regularism (1), social regularism (2), and reflective endorsement (3)[382]. In the subsequent sections, we will examine these options to ascertain their adequacy for understanding Schmitt's criterion.

Following Brandom's perspective, descriptive regularism (1) posits that "rules are relevant only as describing regularities, and not as being followed in achieving them"[383]. In other words, rules are derived from observing patterns and behaviors in reality. Implicit norms govern these patterns, and rules serve as tools to describe these regularities. For example, one could argue that a rule against stealing is rooted in the general disapproval of such behavior within society. In Schmitt's context, descriptive regularism would argue that a judge makes decisions in a certain way because it aligns with the practices of other judges, thus resonating with the concept of the "other judge". This approach could be instrumental in elucidating the implicit norms governing judicial practice. It functions as a method to verify whether a particular

380 Schmitt, "Statute and Judgment: An Investigation into the Problem of Legal Praxis," 109.

381 Crowell, *Normativity and Phenomenology in Husserl and Heidegger*, 2.

382 The first two concepts are derived from Brandom's *Making It Explicit*, while the third is taken from Christine M. Korsgaard's, *The Sources of Normativity* (Cambridge: Cambridge University Press, 1996).

383 Brandom, *Making It Explicit*, 26.

judge's decision is consistent with the prevailing norms within the legal community. Under this model, the correctness or incorrectness of a legal decision would hinge on its conformity to the decisions made by other judges in similar cases. Here, the "measuring rod" is located at the factual pole of existence, relating to the common rulings in specific types of cases[384].

The problem with this approach to *Statute and Judgment* is what Brandom criticizes about all forms of regularisms, namely, that if you un-draw the lines between *what happens* and *what ought to* happen, the normative (and practical) character of decision fades[385], a standpoint Schmitt opposes. In the same text, the German jurist affirms that

> from what happens, one certainly cannot infer what ought to happen. [...] This means to say: what is correct cannot be derived from what actually happens in modern practice. Neither, however, can one choose any postulate whatsoever as the point of departure, in answering the question of what is to be regarded as correct in modern practice, but only one that is empirically valid within it[386].

If that were so, Schmitt contends, such a criterion would prove futile, as it is a well-known fact that judges do not always decide in the same way when confronted with similar cases[387]. In summary, he explicitly states that his formula should not be interpreted in terms of descriptive regularism.

Alternatively, the concept of "the other judge" could be interpreted as a mean of introducing a type of social regularism within a legal community (2). Brandom explains that, according to this perspective, the content of normativity arises from the implicit norms that regulate

384 Brandom, 27–28.

385 This is because, then there would "be no regress or circularity in appealing to them as part of an account of knowing-that, of expressing norms explicitly in rules and principles. For the only one who needs to understand how to apply correctly the rule conforming to which makes performances count as regular is the theorist who describes the regularity in terms of that rule". Brandom, 26–27.

386 Schmitt, "Statute and Judgment: An Investigation into the Problem of Legal Praxis," 48–49.

387 Schmitt, 48–49.

the social conduct of a specific community at a particular time. He says that "on this approach, the key to the importance of the social is taken to lie in the possibility that the performances individual community members produce are assessed, responded to, or treated in practice as appropriate or inappropriate by the community to which the individual belongs"[388]. That is, the content and binding force of a rule do not reside in the rule itself, but rather in the fact that a particular community has reached an agreement (implicitly or explicitly) on it. In this view, the statute that prohibits killing an innocent person is underpinned by a consensus within that specific community that it is preferable not to freely kill fellow citizens. However, this could conceivably be otherwise in a different context (e.g., if a community did not condemn murder and instead regarded it as a virtuous act)[389]. The issue with this approach to justifying normativity is twofold. On the one hand, "assenting, endorsing, accepting, and regarding as right are in the first instance things done by *individuals*"[390] and not by communities. Even if we accept that these actions could be performed by a community, the challenge of defining what constitutes a communal attitude still persists[391]. On the other hand, achieving truly universal agreement, even within a small community, is an excessively stringent requirement[392]. If real universal agreement is impractical, then only a subset of community members would be relevant for making decisions on these matters. But then, which members should be considered? Would communal consensus be required to establish this criterion as well? This perspective thus leads to an infinite regress that is unsolvable. Schmitt would also oppose this interpretation of his criterion, as it veers into areas of inquiry that he deems irrelevant to the legitimation of legal decisions.

388 Brandom, *Making It Explicit*, 37.

389 In his paper on Schmitt and Derrida, MCormick proposes that Schmitt's criterion should be read from this perspective. See: John P. McCormick, "Schmittian Positions on Law and Politics: CLS and Derrida," *Cardozo Law Review* 21, no. 5–6 (2000): 1693–1722.

390 Brandom, *Making It Explicit*, 38.

391 Korsgaard, *The Sources of Normativity*, 22.

392 Brandom, *Making It Explicit*, 39–40.

In fact, he explicitly states that he does not intend to "offer collective- and social-psychological observations of the judges as a social group, or of this group's relations to the members of the bar, or of a statute's effects on the people, or of the processes in the soul of the judge"[393].

To summarize, when Schmitt proposes the concept of the "other judge" as a benchmark against which every judge should hypothetically assess their rulings in specific cases, he is not referring to the actual decisions made by judges nor to a community's general consensus on particular issues. This leaves the question open: what exactly does Schmitt mean by the "other judge"? In the next section, we will propose that a satisfactory answer can be found by interpreting Schmitt's *Statute and Judgment* in the light of what Korsgaard refers to as "reflective endorsement" (3).

§ 4. The "other judge" as a methodology for judicial reflection

In her book *The Sources of Normativity* Korsgaard explains that what she terms "reflective endorsement" is a method for establishing normativity[394]. She says that "if we find upon reflecting on the true moral theory that we still are inclined to endorse the claims that morality makes on us, then morality will be normative. I call this way of establishing normativity the 'reflective endorsement' method"[395]. Normative inquiry, which interrogates the justifications of moral claims made upon us, is unique to human beings, setting us apart from animals (and, as Aristotle notes, also from children[396]). This uniqueness stems from our

393 Schmitt, "Statute and Judgment: An Investigation into the Problem of Legal Praxis," 49–50.

394 Korsgaard, *The Sources of Normativity*, 47.

395 Korsgaard, 49.

396 *Nicomachean Ethics* III, 1, 1111a22-1111b3. Aristotle, "Nicomachean Ethics."

ability to step back from our impulses and desires (such as inclinations) and critically analyze our courses of action. In Koorsgard's words,

> a lower animal's attention is fixed on the world. Its perceptions are its beliefs and its desires are its will. It is engaged in conscious activities, but it is not conscious *of* them. That is, they are not the objects of its attention. But we human animals turn our attention on to our perceptions and desires themselves, and we are conscious *of* them. That is why we can think *about* them [. . .]. And this sets us a problem no other animal has. It is the problem of the normative. For our capacity to turn our attention onto our own mental activities is also a capacity to distance ourselves from them and to call them into question[397].

In other words, as human beings we are able to distance ourselves from our "acting self"[398] and rationally examine possible courses of action, without being overwhelmed by the impulses that, in Kantian terms, affect us pathologically. Consider a simple example: if someone who is hungry is on a bus going home after work and sees another passenger eating a delicious-smelling burger, they would not impulsively snatch and eat it from the other person's hands. Instead, they might think, "That burger looks great, maybe I should get one for myself", or "I'd love to eat that burger, but I'm on a diet, so I'll probably make a salad when I get home". This restraint is typical in normal situations where we, unlike animals and small children, are not governed solely by our impulses.

According to Korsgaard, the process of reflective endorsement unfolds as follows: I experience a certain impulse; then I distance myself from my "acting self"[399] and consider whether it's appropriate to

397 Korsgaard, *The Sources of Normativity*, 48–49.

398 Korsgaard elucidates the dual interpretation of the term *self.* She differentiates between the self as the individual poised to act, and the self as the narrative construct a person formulates about themselves. Korsgaard, 84.

399 This formulation prompts several intriguing questions: Who is this "self" that observes the other self? Are there indeed two distinct selves within a single individual? How can these selves be differentiated? Which of them constitutes the authentic "me"? Who am I? Insightful responses to these profound inquiries can be found in the works of David R. Hawkins. See: David R Hawkins, *I: Reality and Subjectivity* (California: Hay House, 2014).

act on that impulse or better to refrain from action. Essentially, I assess whether there is a valid reason to follow that instinct. If, upon reflection, I find a justifiable reason to act in accordance with the impulse, it has successfully passed the test of reflective endorsement[400]. In Korsgaard's terms, "'reason' then means reflective success"[401]. Applying this to the earlier example, the option of forcibly taking food from a stranger fails the reflective endorsement test; however, the decision to buy the same food based on its appearance and aroma passes. The remaining question, though, is why this is the case (a point we will revisit).

We believe that the criterion Schmitt proposes in *Statute and Judgment* can be interpreted through the framework of Korsgaard's reflective endorsement. By urging judges to suspend their immediate sense of justice for a particular case (whatever this may be) and to hypothetically analyze the decision they are about to make from the viewpoint of other judges within the legal community, Schmitt is essentially asking them to evaluate the reasonableness of their decisions. The fact that Schmitt suggests judges should undertake this evaluative exercise even in cases where no appeal is possible reinforces our argument. To elucidate this point Schmitt indicates that in scenarios where an appeal is feasible, a judge, while applying his formulation, might typically envision seeking the endorsement of the higher tribunal that would eventually review his ruling (where there is a vested interest). However, he asserts that even in situations where an appeal is not possible, the ruling judge should still envision themselves justifying and arguing the correctness of their decision, not to a specific individual, but to "something impersonal that exists only in thought: an average phenomenon, or a circle of human beings, perhaps of jurists or educated laypersons"[402]. In other words, his formulation is not intended as a pragmatic means to, for example, spare judges the effort involved in having their rulings overturned by an appeals court. Instead, it is conceptualized as

400 Korsgaard, *The Sources of Normativity*, 79.

401 Korsgaard, 79.

402 Schmitt, "Statute and Judgment: An Investigation into the Problem of Legal Praxis," 113.

a methodology for ensuring (within the limits of what is possible) the reasonableness of a ruling. Furthermore, emphasis on the significance of substantiating a legal decision according to his criterion also appears to support our thesis[403]. This emphasis underscores the necessity of justifying the rationality of the judge's interpretation of the legal text in relation to the specific case at hand. In essence, the substantiation of the decision serves as a test of its reasonableness.

Also, Schmitt's choice of the term *praxis* in the context of his criterion for assessing the correctness of legal decisions is not arbitrary. The concept *praxis*, Vigo points out, should not be interpreted in terms of causal efficacy[404], but as referring to the dimension of normativity. This is due to the "fact that praxis, through the reason that guides it, is always, in one way or another, subject to certain demands that are imposed in the form of 'rules' or 'norms' "[405]. He further explains this by stating that "all practical demands keep a relationship, in one way or another, with the will and action of rational agents. Therefore, it is referred, to put it in Kantian terms, not to what actually happens, but, rather to what *ought* to happen, although sometimes or even very often it does not happen"[406]. In that sense, the term *praxis* always refers to a certain universality, that is, "as holding for the will of every rational being"[407]. It should also be noted, as Vigo explains, that the reference to universality encompasses not just an abstract concept of humanity,

---

403 Schmitt says, "There is no judgment without justification; the justification belongs to the decision [...] The decision must be justified – that is, it must explain why it is correct – given the specific legal situation in which it is issued. Considerations of this sort are, naturally, beside the point in case of a statute". Schmitt, 101.

404 Cf. Alejandro Vigo, "Identidad Práctica e Individualidad Según Aristóteles," *Hypnos. Revista Do Centro de Estudos Da Antiguidade* 25 (2010): 134.

405 Vigo, "Autorreferencia Práctica y Normatividad," 198.

406 Vigo, 198.

407 Kant, *Critique of Practical Reason* 5:19. Immanuel Kant, "Critique of Practical Reason," in *Practical Philosophy*, trans. Mary J. Gregor, The Cambridge Edition of the Works of Immanuel Kant (Cambridge: Cambridge University Press, 1996), 138–258.

as in Kantian practical philosophy, but also the comprehensive self-perception that the practical agent holds of himself[408]. This means that when a practical agent faces a decision about which course of action to take in a specific situation, he reflects on the various options available, rejects those that do not align with his global representation of himself (his practical identity, as Korsgaard terms it)[409], and chooses a course of action that is congruent with, and endorsed by, his practical identity. This leads us to conclude that while the term *praxis* is oriented towards a certain universality, it is also, in quite a radical way, always related to the individuality of the practical agent[410, 411]. To put it simply, when confronted to a practical situation, the agent reflects on the courses of action that his practical identity endorses and makes available to him. This identity, while unique to the individual, is simultaneously connected to a universal standard of action expected from every human being. In Kantian terms, this process of reflection ultimately performs a "reflective test" in terms of the categorical imperative.[412]

Now, how does this relate to Schmitt's criterion? It appears that his search for a legitimizing criterion for legal decisions, grounded in judicial practice, aims to mediate between the universal and the particular within the legal realm—a challenge commonly encountered in the realm of *praxis*. Essentially, Schmitt's criterion introduces an element of practical reason into the decision-making process of juridical thought. In other words, the procedure judges are to follow according to Schmitt resembles a type of reflective test, where something akin

408 Vigo, "Identidad Práctica e Individualidad Según Aristóteles," 140.

409 Korsgaard illustrates this procedure stating that the practical agent rejects the courses of action that would lead him to conclude "I couldn't live with myself if I did that". Korsgaard, *The Sources of Normativity*, 84.

410 Vigo, "Identidad Práctica e Individualidad Según Aristóteles," 99.

411 Vigo criticizes Korsgaard on this matter. He argues that she does not pay enough attention to the concrete and contingent aspect of the concept *praxis*. Cf. Vigo, "Autorreferencia Práctica y Normatividad," 208.

412 "So act that the maxim of your will could always hold at the same time as a principle in a giving of universal law". Kant, "Critique of Practical Reason," 5:30.

to Korsgaard's "practical identity" is represented by this hypothetical "other judge".

If we consider how Vigo illustrates the manner in which a practical agent carries out a practical action, the legitimacy of our assertion becomes evident. Vigo notes that when a practical agent undertakes the "reflective test", he

> can no longer understand himself as a mere individual that does not fall under a certain more or less general description. On the contrary, he will necessarily have to understand himself, at the same time, under some description that allows him to see himself as a case of application of a certain rule or norm, which will have validity also for other cases of the same type. In other words, he will necessarily understand himself as a case among others[413].

This description aligns closely with what Schmitt outlines in *Statute and Judgment.* Schmitt requires judges, when making rulings, to do exactly as Vigo describes: pause their immediate sense of fairness when confronted with a specific case and verify, through the hypothetical exercise of considering the "other judge", whether their impending decision could be regarded as an application of a rule or norm applicable to similar cases. "Reflective success" in this context is achieved if the judge, after engaging in the hypothetical exercise, concludes that another judge would find his decision reasonable and would be inclined to make a similar ruling in a similar case[414] (aligning with the same standard of reasonableness that Korsgaard attributes to reflective success). The entire situation in which a judge finds himself when presented with a case to decide must be compared with the hypothetical position in which another judge would find himself if faced to a similar case. This comparison enables the judge to derive a form of universality from the particular situation, applicable to the case at hand.

There is, however, a notable difference between the reflective endorsement method that the aforementioned authors suggest is applicable to any activity that deserves to be considered as *praxis,* and the

---

413 Vigo, "Autorreferencia Práctica y Normatividad," 201.

414 Schmitt, "Statute and Judgment: An Investigation into the Problem of Legal Praxis," 115–16.

approach Schmitt proposes for judicial *praxis*, namely, particularly concerning what is at stake in making a (practical) decision. As Vigo[415] explains, when practical agents engage with things and other people through practical decisions, they are, in a sense, putting their own being on the line. Thus, the concept *praxis* carries a creative meaning for the practical agent. As Aristotle explains it,

> men will be good or bad builders as a result of building well or badly. For if this were not so, there would have been no need of a teacher, but all men would have been born good or bad at their craft [. . .]. This, then, is the case with the excellences also; by doing the acts that we do in our transactions with other men we become just or unjust, and by doing the acts that we do in the presence of danger, and being habituated to feel fear or confidence, we become brave or cowardly[416].

The practical agent, therefore, shapes his own way of being and consistently puts his being at stake through *praxis*. Why would this differ in the context of Schmitt's proposal in *Statute and Judgment*? The reason is that Schmitt's use of the term *praxis* is more specific, referring solely to legal (or judicial) praxis. In this scenario, through the hypothetical exercise, a judge specifically risks his standing as a competent judge, rather than his entire being. In other words, by requiring himself to ensure that his decisions are reasonable and broadly endorsed by the legal community, the judge is essentially risking his "nature of judge", which, as Aristotle describes, entails being "a sort of animate justice"[417].

To summarize, Schmitt's emphasis on the fact that his criterion for the correctness of legal decisions originates *from* and is intended *for* legal *praxis* appears to be deliberate. An interpretation in light of contemporary authors' discussions of this concept, drawing on Aristotle and Kant, helps clarify Schmitt's intention. Specifically, he suggests that the individual judge must risk their standing as a competent judge through a reflective methodology. This approach involves a confrontation with the entirety of judicial practice and requires the judge to

415 Vigo, "Autorreferencia Práctica y Normatividad," 198–202.

416 *Nicomachean Ethics* II 1, 1103b7-1103b26.

417 *Nicomachean Ethics* II 4, 1131b25-1132b18

substantiate their decision in a manner that would be deemed reasonable by any other judge.

§ 5. Conclusions to the fourth chapter

We began this chapter by explaining Schmitt's view that a judicial decision is correct if it could reasonably be expected that another judge would have made the same decision. Subsequently, we sought to address several questions arising from this criterion, specifically: What is meant by "the other judge"? How does a judge obtain the endorsement of his colleagues? Does the correctness or justice of a decision depend on convention? We answered the latter two questions by indicating, through textual references, that Schmitt's criterion does not seem to advocate for either descriptive or social regularism in legal practice. Regarding the first question, we proposed an interpretation based on Korsgaard's concept of "reflective endorsement". In other words, we argued that the hypothetical exercise Schmitt suggests in *Statute and Judgment* could be viewed as a methodology for judges to suspend their immediate sense of justice in a particular case and consider whether their impending decision would be deemed reasonable by another judge. This led us to contend that Schmitt's consistent reference to his criterion as deriving from and being intended for legal praxis is not coincidental. Rather, it is indicative of his effort to address the fundamental challenge inherent in the concept of praxis, in its broadest sense: the mediation of the tension between the universal and the particular.

The recognition of the limitations of a mechanistic approach to understanding the judicial phenomenon leads Schmitt to conclude that reliance on the human element is essential for the synthesis of diverse aspects to manifest in a regulated manner within legal matters. This concept mirrors Gadamer's hermeneutics. Recognizing the tension between two poles, along with the existential *openness* it implies, is not aimed at eliminating one of the poles or providing a definitive solution to the issue. Its purpose is more modest: recognizing this existential aspect of humanity allows for the development of mechanisms that facilitate the orderly emergence of knowledge. As Gadamer articulates, acknowledging the hermeneutical nature of human understanding involves realizing that

> understanding is always the fusion of these horizons supposedly existing by themselves. [. . .] The hermeneutic task consists not in covering up this tension by attempting a naïve assimilation of the two but in consciously bringing it out. [. . .] To bring about this fusion in a **regulated way** is the task of what we called historically effected consciousness[418] .

Similarly, Schmitt's criterion functions as a mechanism that offers a moderately regulated pathway facilitating the emergence of rational, rather than capricious or unjust, legal decisions.

We are now positioned to understand the meaning or intention behind Schmitt's criterion for the correctness of legal decisions. Recognizing the absence of mechanistic logic capable of providing certainty in judicial decision-making, Schmitt turns to the human aspect: the humanity of the judge tasked with administering justice. It is within this dimension, not in the written statutes, where any semblance of certainty is attainable. Consequently, we argue that the rationale behind Schmitt's criterion directs us not towards decisionism, but into the domain of ethics. The judge should make decisions *as if* another judge, envisioned as a prudent and rational individual tirelessly striving for justice, would review and assess the decision's correctness. The sought endorsement, therefore, is not from the majority of contemporary judges, but from an idealized judge—an intellectual construct embodying all the qualities of an exemplary judge in the context of justice administration. The mechanics of Schmitt's criterion, then, are similar to that of Kant's categorical imperative, which reads that one should "*act only in accordance with that maxim through which you can*

418 Gadamer, *Truth and Method*, 317. The highlight is ours.

at the same time will that it becomes a universal law"[419]. Schmitt seems to be formulating a specific categorical imperative for juridical thought, one where the judge should decide in such a way that his decision could have been made by any average, well-educated, and prudent judge[420]. The other judge, therefore, should not be considered as a means of conformity (which would be very perilous in a totalitarian context) but as an institution. That is, as representing an ideal image or archetype to which every judge should guide his actions as a public official.

Therefore, Schmitt's reasoning aligns with a key principle of Kantian practical philosophy, which asserts a natural communicability among rational beings, laying the groundwork for morality. Schmitt seems to endorse a common criterion of justice shared among all judges, echoing Kantian practical philosophy. He interprets this communal sense of justice as a "factum of reason"—a fundamental law that asserts itself as inherently law-giving.[421]. Also, in this matter the influence of Vaihinger's post-Kantian thought is evident in Schmitt's work. As noted in earlier sections, during Schmitt's time there was a strong resistance to accepting moral premises in law (normativism)—such as the existence of a universal moral law inherent in all human beings as an indisputable fact, or *factum* of reason. Therefore, rather than asserting this as an incontrovertible fact, Schmitt draws on the philosophy of *as if* (*Als Ob*) articulated by Kant in his third critique and later expanded upon by neo-Kantians like Vaihinger[422].

Now, if we depend on the human element as a defense against dogmatic and extreme positions, then the standards of right and wrong held by those entrusted with the duty of judging must be exceptionally

419 Immanuel Kant, "Groundwork of The Metaphysics of Morals," in *Practical Philosophy*, trans. Mary J. Gregor, The Cambridge Edition of the Works of Immanuel Kant (Cambridge: Cambridge University Press, 1996), 4:434.

420 In this sense, Kay Waechter, *Studien Zum Gedanken Der Einheit Des Staates: Uber Die Rechtsphilosophische Auflosung Der Einheit Des Subjektes* (Berlin: Duncker & Humblot, 1994).

421 Cf. Kant, "Critique of Practical Reason," 5:31.

422 Cf. Vaihinger, *The Philosophy of "as If". A System of the Theoretical, Practical and Religious Fictions of Mankind.*

high. Only with such elevated standards can an individual accurately mediate between poles as disparate and antinomically opposed as the real and the concrete. As the German jurist expresses it,

> although one should not fail to recognize the practical usefulness, for matters that arise in the administration of the state and in empirical legislation, of the formula that the statutory law exists for the sake of human beings, and not human beings for the sake of statutory law, it still remains decisive that a norm that holds because it is good and right cannot hold for the sake of the interests of the sum of individual human beings. What is more important than that there are humans is that there are good and just humans[423].

That is, Schmitt himself acknowledges that a comprehensive examination of the conditions under which a judicial decision is correct inevitably extends into the realm of ethics. It is not sufficient to have good and prudent statutory laws; we also require good, prudent, and just individuals to apply these statutes. Without this crucial human element, written rules alone cannot ensure the realization of justice in specific cases.

However, as we previously discussed while reviewing *The Value of the State and the Significance of the Individual*, Schmitt is not advocating a return to the logic of substantialist natural law. Therefore, the ethical foundation we suggest underpins Schmitt's criterion should not be interpreted in this light, but rather from a rational perspective. We believe that Herrera's argument concerning Schmitt's reference to divinity clearly illustrates our argument:

> Insofar as there is no autonomous, reflective, and eventually critical thought regarding religious beliefs, but one subordinated to them, the logos plays no determining, but only a determined, role. [. . .] When the thought of the divine distances itself from faith's conditioning, it can, as is the case with any other discipline, regard its object of study (or its nonobject, in case one holds the impossibility of objectifying transcendence) by means of observation, analysis, and critique[424].

423 Schmitt, "The Value of the State and the Significance of the Individual," 226.
424 Herrera, *Carl Schmitt. Between Technological Rationality and Theology*, 48.

This context is crucial for understanding the ethical implications inherent in Schmitt's criterion for the correctness of legal decisions. When viewed as an instance of reflective endorsement within the realm of juridical thought, we can deduce that it is reason itself, rather than any particular belief system, that lends legitimacy to legal decisions.

How, then, should we interpret the "other judge" in Schmitt's criterion? It can be seen as an intellectual representation or practical identity against which judges must measure the decision they are about to make. Essentially, it is an envisioned projection of a prudent judge, one who is concerned with equity and thus considers not only the letter of the statute but also all the contingencies surrounding the specific case. Once again, we find Schmitt's reasoning closely aligning with Aristotle's philosophy, who posits that

> there are matter in which it is impossible for the lawgiver to enter into exact details in defining, and where he has to content himself with a general statement. When, then, a man gives way in these matters, and chooses those things which the lawgiver would have wished indeed to determine in detail, but was not able to, such a man is equitable[425].

Simply put, the *other judge* is to be understood as an instance of reflective endorsement through which equity, which considers all elements that come into play in the context of judgments and not only written rules, can emerge in the context of decision-making in the juridical arena.

In sum, the concept of the "other judge" as a criterion for the correctness of legal decisions facilitates openness to a variety of elements beyond statutory law in the process of judicial decision-making. Simultaneously, it demands prudence, rationality, and thoroughness in this process of synthesis. Therefore, this criterion positions Schmitt at a middle ground between legal mysticism and juridical pragmatism, effectively navigating away from both scientism and relativism.

---

425 Aristotle, "Magna Moralia," in *Complete Works of Aristotle*, ed. Jonathan Barnes, vol. 2, The Revised Oxford Translation (Oxford: Princeton University Press, 1991), 1198b25–33.

Conclusions

The primary focus discussed in these pages has been the deconstruction of the objective and "pure" model established by modernity, and on its reformulation by integrating human and, therefore, concrete and contingent elements into the juridical equation. While law was selected for this analysis, it's important to acknowledge that other phenomena such as economics, sociology, or ecology, among many others, could have served as equally suitable subjects. Our choice of law was influenced by our prior knowledge and inclinations. Fortunately, this choice proved fruitful, enabling us to reintegrate elements that had been alienated by scientism in modernity. The method by which we accomplished this was as follows:

1. Unraveling the meaning of the concept "theory of understanding"

We began by examining how Martin Heidegger's ideas influenced his intellectual disciple, Hans-Georg Gadamer, to reinterpret juridical thinking from a hermeneutical perspective. The hermeneutical-phenomenological lineage of these authors unfolded as follows: we first reviewed Heidegger's thematization of the ideal (mental articulations) and real poles (facticity) of existence, along with the ontological particularities of the subject that unifies them. We emphasized that his exploration of the nature and characteristics of human understanding was conducted on an ontological level, meaning his focus was not on the contingencies of the "ontic realm", except where necessary to illuminate the ontological nature of existence. Since our main concern was the legal phenomenon and its role in elucidating general human understanding, Heidegger's analysis was somewhat limited for this specific purpose. While it provided a valuable framework for later analyzing Schmitt's work through a theory of understanding, it did not directly address the realm of law. Fortunately, Gadamer bridged this gap, connecting the ontological understanding of human cognition with the ontically manifested phenomena that complete the ontic-ontological puzzle of human understanding. We then explored how Gadamer accomplished this formidable task.

In *Truth and Method*, Gadamer focuses on the "coming to life" of phenomena such as art, games, law, and theology. He believes, as he thoroughly justifies throughout his work, that exploring these everyday phenomena deepens our understanding of the nature and characteristics of human cognition without resorting to a reductionist, scientistic description that excludes human subjectivity from philosophical inquiry. Contrarily, Gadamer posits that these phenomena (especially art and the interpretation/application of law) reveal that human understanding is a complex, interrelated process in which every element (rules, people, and reality) has its significance. However, these elements are so intertwined that it is impossible to describe the "coming to life" of these phenomena in a purely scientific manner. Reason, while powerful in some aspects of existence, cannot fully penetrate the "game of life". Many aspects of existence are beyond our comprehension, making it unwise to assume that our limited tool of reason can fully grasp the limitless. Gadamer, like Heidegger, refers to this ontological characteristic of human understanding as "finitude". He contends that this trait is particularly evident in the legal phenomenon. According to Gadamer, every legal text requires interpretation by a concrete individual. Contrary to long-held beliefs that the meaning of a text is derived solely from the text itself, the interpreter brings their own horizon of meaning to the act of understanding. This means that the interpreter's existential characteristics, such as historicality, language, and the presence of metaphysical ideas, play a crucial role in the process. These ontological traits are projected onto the text being interpreted, which implies that the meaning with which it emerges is a fusion of the text itself and the horizon from which it is being understood.

In legal interpretation, argues Gadamer, the aforementioned dynamics are exemplified paradigmatically. The interpreter must not only articulate the actual text of the statute with the foresight and the horizon of meaning from which they are interpreting, but also mediate between the historical horizon of understanding from which the text originated and the contemporary context presented by the specific case requiring a legal solution. Thus, the solution reached is a synthesis of the past, the present, and the existential characteristics of the agent engaged in the act of interpretation. Gadamer concludes that a legal decision is the outcome of a kind of interplay among all these elements.

Gadamer, then, facilitated our journey from the elucidation of the nature and characteristics of human understanding to the realm law. This transition, however, was not entirely peaceful and reassuring. The "de-scientificization" of law as well as the inclusion of the existential characteristics of the human being in the legal decision resulted in uncertainty regarding the specific conditions under which a legal decision can be deemed correct. This uncertainty led us to the next philosopher whose thought was central to this work: Carl Schmitt.

2. Deconstruction of legal positivism: Carl Schmitt "the soldier"

The second chapter was dedicated to elucidating how Schmitt, in his early legal writings, exposes the shortcomings of the foundation upon which legal positivism is built. Legal positivism represents the dominant interpretation of the legal phenomenon in modernity. In this context, we depicted Schmitt as a soldier endeavoring to reclaim territory overrun by philosophical adversaries.

Schmitt "the soldier", through the arguments he poses in *Statute and Judgment* (1912) and *The Value of the State and the Significance of the Individual* (1914), challenges two foundational premises of normativistic legal positivism. First, he disputes the notion that existence is static and can be fully predicted by human reason alone. Second, he contests the idea that eliminating human subjectivity is necessary to raise our understanding of existence to the status of "science". Schmitt argues that these premises are not only false but also easily refutable. He points out that existence consistently demonstrates the regular occurrence of the exceptional—events not accounted for by the available rational categories of the mind. No matter how many variables are considered, there will always be unexpected elements disrupting the normative framework constructed by human reason (the COVID-19 pandemic, which is ongoing as this document is being written, strikingly corroborates Schmitt's argument).

This chapter aimed to demonstrate that, in his first two significant legal academic works, Schmitt reveals that legal positivism constructs its theory based on a worldview that does not align with the actual behavior of existence. With his legal background, Schmitt employs law as the target of his critique. However, his objectives are much broader and more ambitious. Through his critique of legal positivism, the German jurist seeks to dismantle the static, self-sufficient, and excessively rationalistic worldview that was crafted in modernity. In essence, Schmitt uses law instrumentally, as an entry point to the metaphysical battleground.

Schmitt employs a notable tactic to dismantle the positivist interpretation of the legal phenomenon. In both *Statute and Judgment* (1914) and *The Value of the State and the Significance of the Individual* (1914), he contends that the human element is essential for the actualization of law. His argument unfolds as follows: legal statutes, by their nature, are abstract, meaning they are not permeated by the concrete aspects of human life. Although legal texts refer to everyday situations, their reference is purely normative, addressing these situations hypothetically. In contrast, concrete human life is characterized by sheer facticity, devoid of normative abstraction. The challenge arises from the interaction between these two realms, the normative and the concrete. Facticity calls for the intervention of a normative element to prevent political chaos. Conversely, legal normativity, designed to impact concrete reality practically, cannot remain solely in the realm of abstraction. Its purpose is to transition into the realm of facticity, aiding in the realization of justice.

The core issue, then, lies in the insurmountable divide between the two poles of existence: the abstract and the concrete. These realms are inherently unable to connect with each other on their own; they require assistance to build a bridge between them. This is where Schmitt's proposition becomes particularly intriguing. He asserts that only a concrete human being can facilitate the connection between these realms. This concept forms the crux of his argument in these two early legal works. In *Statute and Judgment* (1912), he elucidates how this articulation should function in the realm of judicial decision-making. Meanwhile, in *The Value of the State and the Significance of the Individual* (1914), he delves into its operation within political law, especially concerning the interplay of power, law, and the individual. Schmitt's argument in these texts extends beyond the idea that only a concrete human being, whether a judge or a public servant, can reconcile the tension between these dichotomous poles of existence. He further explains that this assertion leads to a philosophical conundrum. For law to effectively impact concrete reality, it must relinquish some of its abstraction. Since it is through a human being that abstract normativity crosses over to facticity, the only way for the abstract pole to shed part of its abstraction is by adopting some characteristics of the human agent facilitating this articulation. In other words, its only viable option is to "humanize itself".

To adequately thematize the legal phenomenon, then, it is necessary to elucidate the nature of human understanding. The third chapter was dedicated to elucidating how Schmitt accomplishes this task, specifically by exploring how his thematization of the legal phenomenon leads him to a broader inquiry into human understanding in general.

3. Reconstructing the legal phenomenon: Carl Schmitt "the artist"

After dismantling the theoretical and practical foundations upon which legal positivism is built, Schmitt focused his efforts on understanding law in the most scientifically unbiased way possible. This entailed attempting to rid his thought process of the scientistic biases that were predominant from an intellectual standpoint in modernity, aiming to present the legal phenomenon as it truly is, rather than how we might wish it to be. This approach led Schmitt down a perilous path, one where, as Herrera discusses in his latest work[426], he encountered various extreme (and dogmatical) ways of understanding the world.

426 See: Herrera, *Carl Schmitt. Between Technological Rationality and Theology*.

Herrera's thematization allows us to understand how Schmitt, throughout his work, is faced with the dilemma of articulating a horizon of meaning which avoids extremes (such as the theological, technical, or romantic). In contrast, our approach provides a roadmap aimed at identifying how fundamental structures of human understanding emerge within juridical thought. The content presented in the third chapter can be seen as a modest contribution to the interpretation of Schmitt's legal work. To accomplish this, we selectively reviewed Schmitt's early legal writings (spanning from 1912 to 1922), but from a very specific viewpoint. Our focus was solely on whether Schmitt's treatment of the legal phenomenon reveals broader insights into the general operation of human understanding. This necessitated referencing the themes he discusses in each work, but only as a means to uncover the existential implications of his arguments.

The first ontological structure that Schmitt identifies in the realm of law is historicality. Specifically, he acknowledges that abstract law must relinquish its timeless nature to effectively influence human reality. This necessity arises from the fundamental impact of history on human existence, as we elaborated in the first chapter. Schmitt's insights regarding historicality can be summarized as follows:

a. In *Statute and Judgment* Schmitt contends that while law is inherently an abstract manifestation of normativity, it necessitates historical concretion for justice to materialize. He argues that the modern endeavor to find a timeless and absolute solution to the problem of justice was bound to fail. This is because it overlooked the fact that justice is not just an abstract concept but a quality that can only be ascribed to judicial decisions which consider the specific factual and historical characteristics of each case.
b. The fact that both the juridical realm and human understanding are influenced by historicality implies that the rules set forth by the political system or tradition (concepts) should not be mechanically applied to cases. Instead, applying legal statutes involves a reflective process. This means that the

interpretation and application of a rule or concept depends, to some extent, on the specifics of the case at hand. In this way, every legal decision becomes an act of creation, which Schmitt later likens to a miracle. For example, the meaning and scope of the concept "sanitary prudence" evolve based on specific circumstances. Before 2019, it generally meant staying home when afflicted with a mildly infectious disease. After the onset of the pandemic, it expanded to include practices such as consistently wearing masks in public and limiting outings (and then it reverted to its original meaning again). This dynamic applies to legal regulations as well; the specific situation to which a rule is applied can alter its original meaning.

c. Law and human understanding are affected by historicality in a more fundamental manner. As Schmitt seems to argue in *The Value of the State and the Significance of the Individual,* as well as in *Political Romanticism* and *Political Theology*, there exists a metaphysical aspect of historicality manifested in law. It's not just that "times change" and we, as human beings, must adapt to existence's inherent dynamism. Echoing Heidegger and Gadamer's later assertions, Schmitt posits that human beings are embodiments of time and history; they flow through us. This implies, at least according to Schmitt, that the concepts underpinning our horizon of meaning are dynamic, subject to transformation. When such a conceptual shift occurs, the perceived meaning of reality also changes. For instance, a tree would not be interpreted the same way by a medieval monk as by a 19th-century businessman. The former, seeing God as the binding metaphysical concept, might view the tree as a manifestation of divinity (with specifics varying according to his faith). The latter, however, might see the tree as a resource for economic gain, envisioning it as a potential product like a table for sale. While the tree itself remains unchanged, the core concepts shaping our interpretation of it differ, altering the "meaning" with which it emerges in our understanding.

Owing to its inherent historicality and temporality, law must also be recognized as finite. Schmitt, echoing Aristotle[427], contends that positive law is incapable of foreseeing the trajectory of existence. Inevitably, exceptional situations arise, whether natural, political, or other, which were not anticipated by existing norms but nevertheless require legal resolution. A similar limitation is present in human understanding. Our inability to predict the future inevitably leads to encountering the limitations of our rational conceptualizations of existence. For instance, advancements in quantum physics are challenging the fundamental assumption that the world is made of tangible "stuff", suggesting the need to shift or expand our conceptual paradigm for understanding reality. This doesn't necessarily mean a complete overhaul of our existing knowledge but likely entails an expansion or reformulation of our current conceptual categories[428]. In the realm of law, Schmitt argues, we encounter a parallel, if not identical, scenario. His articulation of this argument unfolds as follows:

a. From a legal standpoint, Schmitt posits that each case requiring a legal solution is, in a sense, its own unique universe. Although the same statute may be applied to numerous cases, the specific meaning the text assumes will vary depending on the unique characteristics of each case. Consequently, the correctness of legal decisions should not rely solely on subsumption, as verifying the adequacy of subsuming a case under the law is impractical (this would necessitate another rule for verification, leading to an infinite regress). Instead, the correctness of a judicial decision hinges on the specific features of the case and its historical context. Judges, therefore, should provide thorough substantiation for their decisions and ensure, at least through a hypothetical exercise, that their rulings align with how other judges would have likely decided. We will

427 This argument is extensively elaborated upon in the following paper: García-Huidobro and Pérez-Lasserre, "Acoger la excepción. La prudencia del juez como punto de conexión entre las ideas schmittianas y aristotélicas."

428 Although in this process there is always something that is bound to be lost.

revisit this topic in the section of these conclusions dedicated to our fourth chapter, but for now, it is crucial to recognize that it is the acknowledgment of the finitude of legal texts that led Schmitt to advocate for the complementation of these texts with well-considered decisions to facilitate the emergence of justice.

b. In *Dictatorship*, Schmitt contends that the political phenomenon, where law plays a pivotal role, exemplifies the finitude inherent in human nature. He argues that due to the finitude imparted by humans onto their creations, legal statutes eventually demonstrate their inability to handle the unfolding political contingencies. This logic mirrors his earlier arguments: lawmakers, unable to foresee the course of history, will invariably face situations where political institutions, especially constitutions, fail to address extraordinary circumstances. Essentially, the legality that binds political communities is designed for relatively normal situations with a certain level of predictability. Nonetheless, exceptional situations, those that fall outside the conceptual and factual scope of legal norms, will inevitably arise, potentially destabilizing both the political system and its regulatory framework. In such scenarios, Schmitt suggests, we must acknowledge the limitations of legal texts and entrust the resolution of these exceptional situations to the sovereign. Thus, it is through recognizing the finitude of legal texts that Schmitt concludes that only a human being is capable of *recalibrating* the misalignment between the normative and factual poles in the political realm.

In sum, Schmitt's argument is that a thorough analysis of the legal phenomenon inevitably leads to the acknowledgment of its finitude and the limitations of human understanding.

We also posited that Schmitt's early legal writings hint at an understanding of language as an ontologically determined vehicle for human cognition. Schmitt seems to suggest, similar to Alan Watts' arguments in later years, that language is a limited construct we use to explain reality. This implies that our primary tool for defining words is, paradoxically, words themselves, leading inevitably to a kind of circular reasoning (as demonstrated in certain linguistic games)[429]. Moreover, Schmitt implies that there are aspects of reality beyond our comprehension yet still influential in our daily lives, which is where his concept of *abstraktes Recht* becomes relevant.

Another aspect of language that we discerned in Schmitt's examination of law, is the notion that "the word is not the thing". In essence, language functions as a medium to describe the world, but its descriptions do not necessarily capture the world as it truly is. The concept of an object is distinct from the object itself, thus caution is needed when claiming that language enables us to understand the world "objectively". This is because another entity with its own linguistic framework[430] would understand existence otherwise. Differently put, we must become aware of the fact that the language through which we understand existence is relative not only to the context that gave rise to the horizon of meaning from which we interpret reality, but also to our ontological constitution as human beings[431].

Finally, we observed that Schmitt contends the recognition of the inevitable influence of these human ontological structures on the legal phenomenon necessitates the intervention of a being subject to the same existential conditions—a human. This argument, discernible "between the lines" in the German jurist's work, unfolds as follows: both human beings and law are finite, historical, and linguistically determined. Humans have an openness to the exceptional and dynamic nature of existence, allowing us to adapt to extraordinary existential situations. Law, in contrast, is characterized by its static nature. This disparity leads Schmitt to propose infusing some of the human capacity for dynamism into law. While he acknowledges the need for periodic normative changes, his broader aim is to expand the concept of legality,

429 Alan Watts, *Limits of Language*, CD, Essential Lectures - Tao of Philosophy (California, 1971).

430 Schmitt uses an alien as an example.

431 For instance, an entity experiencing time in a non-linear fashion would likely struggle to comprehend many of our concepts. This is because human language is fundamentally rooted in a key aspect of human existence: temporality.

enabling it to accommodate exceptional cases in practical reality without necessitating constant legislative amendments.

In summary, Schmitt's exploration of legal and human understanding aims to conceptually reframe legality. His objective is to transform it into a phenomenon that is genuinely beneficial for political communities, rather than just an abstract construct of great conceptual finesse but little practical use for legal praxis.

4. Coming back to legal certainty. Carl Schmitt "the prudent"

Having argued that Schmitt infuses the dynamism of human existence into legal matters, we found ourselves revisiting the challenge of determining a criterion for the correctness of legal decisions. This prompted us to return to Schmitt's first academic work, *Statute and Judgment* (1912). However, our focus shifted this time. Instead of concentrating on the weaknesses of legal positivism identified by the German jurist, we examined the specific way in which the criterion he proposes for the correctness of legal decisions protects the legal phenomenon from becoming a realm of unrestricted decisionism.

Our primary argument is that while Schmitt emphatically states that the modern aspiration for an absolute criterion to verify the rectitude of legal decisions—one that disregards time, space, and human finitude—must be abandoned, this does not mean the search for a valid criterion for legal decision-making should be forsaken. Instead, the German jurist underscores the importance of this quest but insists that it must incorporate the existential characteristics of human beings and the specific details of cases requiring legal resolution. Thus, it's essential to recognize that Schmitt's expansion of the concept of legality was not an endeavor to forcibly impose a particular viewpoint by relativizing legal and political institutions. Rather, it was an attempt to more robustly establish the foundations of the legal phenomenon by acknowledging and integrating the various elements involved in it.

The primary question we endeavored to answer in this final chapter was: How does Schmitt's criterion for the correctness of legal decisions, which invokes the hypothetical agreement of a community of judges, offer any form of legal certainty? To provide a coherent response, we drew upon contemporary literature addressing the issue of normativity (referencing authors such as Brandom, Korsgaard, and Vigo[432]). Our argument can summarized as follows:

a. As discussed in Chapter 2, Schmitt proposes a criterion for determining the correctness of legal decisions, which can be described as follows: A judge can deem his decision regarding a specific case as correct if, after engaging in a hypothetical exercise, he concludes that the decision would be considered reasonable by any other judge. While this exercise is hypothetical in nature, it necessitates a tangible action: judges must provide thorough justifications for their decisions, thereby publicly demonstrating their reasonableness.
b. Schmitt does not support any form of regularism, whether descriptive or social. In other words, he opposes the idea of establishing a criterion for determining the correctness of legal decisions based on "what actually happens" or "the usual manner in which judges decide". Therefore, Schmitt's acknowledgment of the complexity and dynamism inherent in the legal phenomenon does not imply an endorsement of a relativistic approach.
c. Schmitt's criterion is aimed at providing legal certainty within the confines of human nature's inherent limitations. Recognizing our intrinsic finitude naturally precludes the possibility of achieving an absolute and eternal standard for determining the correctness of legal decisions. As such, while Schmitt's proposal might appear to be limited, it represents the extent to which we can realistically aspire, given our own finitude and the consequent inability to completely transcend human ignorance. Therefore, Schmitt's criterion should be viewed as an effort to offer the greatest degree of legal certainty achievable by finite human beings.

432 Who primarily anchor their argument in the Aristotelian and Kantian exploration of the normative problem.

d. The specific way Schmitt seeks to ensure legal certainty is by incorporating into legal practice a method that compels judges to step beyond their own horizon of meaning. This approach requires them to evaluate the reasonableness of their decisions from an external perspective. Similar to Korsgaard's concept of reflective endorsement, Schmitt's method necessitates that judges distance themselves from their immediate viewpoints. They are encouraged to consider their rulings in light of a broader horizon, engaging in this reflective process before making a final decision.
e. In essence, Schmitt acknowledges that judges are an integral part of the legal system. Their ontological characteristics and personal horizons of meaning significantly influence how law is interpreted and applied in specific cases. This understanding carries a significant risk: overlooking the active role judges play in the realization of justice and treating legality as an external, rigid framework to be mechanically applied to cases could lead to a relativistic and decisionistic approach to law. However, by acknowledging the inevitability of the legal practitioner's ontological traits influencing legal interpretation, we can create mechanisms to manage these influences in a controlled manner. Schmitt's proposal of a hypothetical criterion aims to bridge this gap, offering such a regulatory mechanism.

In summary, our legal and philosophical journey began with an exploration of the anatomy and nature of human understanding, progressed to an examination of legal hermeneutics, and then led us to deconstruct the positivist understanding of the legal phenomenon. This process illuminated how fundamental structures of human understanding are revealed through law. Our exploration concluded with an attempt to practically interpret this expanded legal horizon. Specifically, our endeavor culminated in a reevaluation of Schmitt's first academic work, seen through a lens that recognizes Schmitt's aim was not to advocate decisionism in jurisprudence. Rather, his efforts were focused on "rationally calibrating" the inherent human characteristics that legal normativity embodies as it transitions from the abstract to the concrete realm of facticity.

Epilogue

§. Carl Schmitt and philosophy of life

Carl Schmitt seems to be an admirer of the extraordinary. By this we mean that through his philosophy one can recognize a constant amazement at the mysterious manner in which existence unveils. Consequently, his philosophy of finitude is one where the precarious nature of the human being is not seen as tragic. On the contrary, there appears to be admiration. It impresses him that an entity which is subject to space, time, and historicality, and the limitations of language is able to elevate itself from *its self* and grapple with matters which seem to far exceed its finite entitative characteristics.

Schmitt's juridical thought can be read as an attempt to make explicit the way through which transcendence, that which is extraordinary and not subject to human limits, manifests itself immanently in our daily lives. The meaning of the "exceptional" represents the realization of this idea. As Herrera puts it,

> the law operates once the question of transcendence is in place. The law's contribution consists in explicitly thematizing the relation and tension between the concept and "the intangible (*das Ungreifbare*)"; the rule and the case; the abstract and the concrete; the norm and the exception. Insofar as the exceptional is brought to the fore as a condition for existence, that effort can be considered as theology, but only in the sense that it is a thought that thematizes transcendence and the exceptional and its relation with normality and immanence. The exception, the other, God, the meaning of existence, escape conceptual determinations. And it is through the recognition of such overabundance of the real, and

> of the contrast between it and the concept, that juridical thought emerges, in the broad sense in which Schmitt considers it, as "a philosophy of concrete life"[433].

Thus, juridical thought not only reveals the limitations inherent in our nature and understanding of the world as human beings but also acknowledges that existence at large arises from a background that is exceptional, extraordinary, and transcendent.

If we understand Schmittian work from this perspective, it seems that his thought is fairly close to what is known as *philosophy of life*. Though the determination of the specific conditions that a line of thought must comply with in order for it to be considered a philosophy of life is not settled, in general terms, it is usually understood that "authors whose work was supposedly characterized by a metaphysical conception of life conceived as an original transformative force, and by their reliance on a method or a faculty irreducible to the ones used by science"[434] are considered *Lebensphilosophen*[435]. This movement can be better understood not by examining the positive content of their proposals, but rather by considering their common adversary: excessive and reductionist rationalism. In the words of Bianco,

> these authors, who were describing a non-deterministic universe animated by spiritual forces, were influenced by Romanticism's reaction against a narrow Enlightenment rationalism and the Industrial Revolution, namely by its emphasis on feeling and immediacy, by its insistence on affective and intuited experience as opposed to the narrowness of rationality, and, finally, by its search for a unifying principle prior to the "abstractions" of scientific reason[436].

---

433 Herrera, *Carl Schmitt. Between Technological Rationality and Theology*, 57.

434 Giuseppe Bianco, "Philosophies of Life," in *The Cambridge History of Modern European Thought.*, ed. Warren Breckman and Peter Eli Gordon, vol. 2 (Cambridge New York Port Melbourne New Delhi Singapore: Cambridge University Press, 2019), 154.

435 Authors such as Scheler, Bergson, Hadot, Dilthey, and Plessner, among many others, are considered to be philosophers of life. See: Karl Albert, *Lebensphilosophie: Von den Anfängen bei Nietzsche bis zu ihrer Kritik bei Lukács.* (Freiburg: Verlag Karl Alber, 2018). Robert Josef Kozljanič, *Lebensphilosophie: eine Einführung* (Stuttgart: Kohlhammer, 2004). Jürgen Große, *Lebensphilosophie* (Stuttgart: Reclam, 2010).

436 Bianco, "Philosophies of Life," 156.

That is, the philosophers of life share a common goal of challenging the mechanistic worldview put forth by rationalism in modernity. They also hold a non-reductionist perspective on existence, suggesting that it can be better understood through inner experiences rather than solely through rational conceptualizations[437].

Schmitt could be regarded as a philosopher of life, given his efforts to dismantle the rationalist and reductionist worldview in the domain of law. From this perspective, one might interpret his work as a challenge to legal positivism's refusal to acknowledge a vital force or an exceptional and extraordinary foundation underpinning the legal phenomenon. This interpretation finds resonance in Schmitt's famous statement from *Political Theology* where he declares that "the exception in jurisprudence is analogous to the miracle in theology"[438].

Clearly, adequately justifying a statement like the one previously made necessitates extensive research[439]. However, interpreting Schmitt as a philosopher of life reveals an interesting aspect of his thought. While authors such as Krug distinguish between *Schulphilosophie* (academic philosophy) and *Philosophie für die Welt* (philosophy for everyone), suggesting the latter is more suited for delving into the mysteries of the vital force from which existence emerges[440], we contend that Schmitt advocates for a prudent balance between intellectuality and factuality. In other words, Schmitt does not dismiss the value of science in understanding existence. He views reason as part of the living force animating the cosmos, capable of partially unraveling its mysteries. However, he also acknowledges that reason alone cannot fully

437 Cf. Bianco, 168. Cf. Max Scheler, *Die Stellung des Menschen im Kosmos* (Hamburg: Felix Meiner Verlag, 2018).

438 Schmitt, *Political Theology*, 36.

439 It is important to note that Schmitt frequently references Helmuth Plessner, a thinker regarded as a philosopher of life within the social sciences. This consistent citation lends some plausibility to the argument that Schmitt's perspectives may align with the philosophy of life.

440 Bianco, "Philosophies of Life," 159. See: Wilhelm Traugott Krug, *Allgemeines Handwörterbuch der philosophischen Wissenschaften nebst ihrer Literatur und Geschichte* (Leipzig: Brockhaus, 1828).

comprehend existence and that relying solely on reason for understanding reality results in a severely limited worldview. Thus, he proposes that the ideal pole of reason must be harmonized with the concrete and real aspects of existence. This interpretation of Schmitt recognizes the value of reason while understanding, as Hawkins suggests, that reason "does not in and of itself provide a guide to truth. It produces massive amounts of information and documentation, but lacks the capability to resolve discrepancies in data and conclusions"[441]. A more thorough justification of this interpretation, however, must be reserved for future research.

441 Hawkins, *The Map of Consciousness Explained*, 77.

Bibliography

Albert, Karl. *Lebensphilosophie: Von den Anfängen bei Nietzsche bis zu ihrer Kritik bei Lukács*. Freiburg: Verlag Karl Alber, 2018.

Aristotle. "Magna Moralia." In *Complete Works of Aristotle*, edited by Jonathan Barnes, Vol. 2. The Revised Oxford Translation. Oxford: Princeton University Press, 1991.

Aristotle. "Metaphysics." In *Complete Works of Aristotle*, edited by Jonathan Barnes, Vol. 2. The Revised Oxford Translation. Oxford: Princeton University Press, 1991.

Aristotle. "Nicomachean Ethics." In *Complete Works of Aristotle*, edited by Jonathan Barnes, Vol. 2. The Revised Oxford Translation. Oxford: Princeton University Press, 1991.

Belgrano, Mateo. "'El Origen de La Obra de Arte': ¿un 'Oasis' En El Pensamiento Heideggeriano?" *Areté* 32, no. 1 (2020): 7–29.

Bendersky, Joseph J. *Carl Schmitt*. Princeton: Princeton University Press, 1983.

Bendersky, Joseph J. *Carl Schmitt. Theorist for the Reich*. Princeton: Princeton University Press, 2016.

Bendersky, Joseph W. "Introduction: The Three Types of Juristic Thought in German Historical and Intellectual Context." In *On the Three Types of Juristic Thought*, edited by Carl Schmitt, 1–42. Westport, Conn.: Praeger Publishers, 2005.

Bianco, Giuseppe. "Philosophies of Life." In *The Cambridge History of Modern European Thought*, edited by Warren Breckman and Peter Eli Gordon, 2:153–75. Cambridge New York Port Melbourne New Delhi Singapore: Cambridge University Press, 2019.

Bielefeldt, Heiner. *Kampf und Entscheidung: Politischer Existentialismus bei Carl Schmitt, Helmuth Plessner und Karl Jaspers*. Würzburg: Königshausen & Neumann, 1994.

Blattner, William. "Authenticity and Resolutness." In *The Cambridge Companion to Heidegger's "Being and Time,"* edited by Mark A.

Wrathall, 320–37. Cambridge Companions to Philosophy. Cambridge: Cambridge University Press, 2013.
Bobbio, Norberto. *Giusnaturalismo e positivismo giuridico.* Madrid: Editorial Trotta, 2015.
Böckenförde, Ernst-Wolfgang. "Konkretes Ordnungsdenken." In *Historisches Wörterbuch Der Philosophie*, edited by Joachim Ritter and Karlfried Gründer, 6:1312–13. Basel: Schwabe Verlag, 1984.
Brandom, Robert. *Making It Explicit: Reasoning, Representing, and Discursive Commitment.* Cambridge: Harvard University Press, 2001.
Burnham, Douglas. *An Introduction to Kant's Critique of Judgement.* Edinburgh: Edinburgh University Press, 2000.
Calvo García, Manuel. "La voluntad del legislador: genealogía de una ficción hermenéutica." *Doxa*, no. 3 (1986): 113–27.
Croce, Mariano, and Andrea Salvatore. *The Legal Theory of Carl Schmitt.* New York: Routledge, 2013.
Crowell, Steven Galt. *Husserl, Heidegger, and the Space of Meaning: Paths toward Transcendental Phenomenology.* Northwestern University Studies in Phenomenology and Existential Philosophy. Evanston: Northwestern University Press, 2001.
Crowell, Steven Galt. *Normativity and Phenomenology in Husserl and Heidegger.* New York: Cambridge University Press, 2013.
Dahlstrom, Daniel O. *Interpreting Heidegger: New Essays.* New York: Cambridge University Press, 2011.
Davey, Nicholas. "Dialogue, Dialectic and Conversation." In *The Gadamerian Mind*, edited by Theodore D George and Gert-Jan van der Heiden, 61–77. New York & London: Routledge, 2021.
Derrida, Jacques. "Force of Law: The 'Mystical Foundation of Authority.'" In *Deconstruction and the Possibility of Justice*, edited by Drucilla Cornell, Michel Rosenfeld, David Carlson, and Benjamin N. Cardozo School of Law, 3–67. New York: Routledge, 1992.

Dilthey, Wilhelm. *The Formation of the Historical World in the Human Sciences*. Edited by Rudolf A Makkreel and Frithjof Rodi. Vol. III. Princeton & Oxford: Princeton University Press, 2002.

Emad, Parvis. *On the Way to Heidegger's Contributions to Philosophy*. Madison: University of Wisconsin Press, 2007.

Figal, Günter. *Der Sinn Des Verstehens: Beiträge Zur Hermeneutischen Philosophie*. Stuttgart: P. Reclam, 1996.

Figal, Günter. *Objectivity: The Hermeneutical and Philosophy*. Albany: State University of New York Press, 2011.

Figal, Günter. "The Doing of the Thing Itself: Gadamer's Hermeneutic Ontology of Language." In *The Cambridge Companion to Gadamer*, edited by Robert J Dostal, 102–25. Cambridge: Cambridge University Press, 2006.

Gabriel, Markus. "The Ontology of the Work of Art and the Universality of Hermeneutics Reconsidered: Gadamer and New Realism." In *The Gadamerian Mind*, edited by Theodore D George and Gert-Jan van der Heiden, 532–45. New York & London: Routledge, 2021.

Gadamer, Hans Georg. *Heideggers Wege: Studien zum Spätwerk*. Tübingen: Mohr, 1983.

Gadamer, Hans-Georg. *Hermeneutik II: Wahrheit und Methode*. 2nd ed. Gesammelte Werke. Tübingen: J. C. B. Mohr, 1993.

Gadamer, Hans-Georg. *Truth and Method*. London & New York: Bloomsbury, 2013.

García-Huidobro, Joaquín, and Diego Pérez-Lasserre. "Acoger la excepción. La prudencia del juez como punto de conexión entre las ideas schmittianas y aristotélicas." *Daimon*, no. 83 (2021): 185–99.

George, Theodore D, and Gert-Jan van der Heiden. "Introduction." In *The Gadamerian Mind*, edited by Theodore D George and Gert-Jan van der Heiden, 1–6. New York & London: Routledge, 2021.

Gethmann, Carl Friedrich. "Philosophie Als Vollzug Und Als Begriff Heideggers Identitätsphilosophie Des Lebens in Der Vorlesung Vom Wintersemester 1921/22 Und Ihr Verhältnis Zu Sein Und Zeit." *Dilthey-Jahrbuch Für Philosophie Und Geschichte Der Geisteswissenschaften* 4 (1986): 27–53.

Golob, Sacha. *Heidegger on Concepts, Freedom and Normativity*. Cambridge: Cambridge University Press, 2014.

Gragl, Paul. "The Pure Theory of Law and Legal Monism – Epistemological Truth and Empirical Plausibility." *Zeitschrift Für Öffentliches Recht*, no. 70 (2015): 665–736.

Grondin, Jean. *Hans-Georg Gadamer: A Biography*. New Haven: Yale University Press, 2011.

Grondin, Jean. *Introduction to Philosophical Hermeneutics*. New Haven: Yale University Press, 1997.

Grondin, Jean. "The Metaphysical Dimension of Hermeneutics." In *Hermeneutics and Phenomenology Figures and Themes*, edited by Saulius Geniusas and Paul Fairfield, 125–37. London: Bloomsbury, 2020.

Grondin, Jean. *The Philosophy of Gadamer*. Translated by Kathryn Plant. Hoboken: Taylor and Francis, 2014.

Grondin, Jean. "The Universality of Hermeneutic Understanding. The Strong, Somewhat Metaphysical Conclusion of Truth and Method." In *The Gadamerian Mind*, edited by Theodore D George and Gert-Jan van der Heiden, 24–36. New York & London: Routledge, 2022.

Große, Jürgen. *Lebensphilosophie*. Stuttgart: Reclam, 2010.

Guyer, Paul. *Kant and the Claims of Taste*. 2. ed. Cambridge: Cambridge Univ. Press, 1997.

Habermas, Jürgen. "The Hermeneutic Claim to Universality." In *Contemporary Hermeneutics: Hermeneutics as Method, Philosophy and Critique*, edited by Joseph Bleicher, 181–211. London: Routledge & Kegan, 1980.

Hawkins, David R. *I: Reality and Subjectivity*. California: Hay House, 2014.

Hawkins, David R. *The Map of Consciousness Explained*. California: Hay House, 2020.

Hawkins, David R. *Transcending the Levels of Consciousness*. California: Hay House, 2015.

Heidegger, Martin. *Being and Time*. Translated by John Macquarrie and Edward Robinson. HarperPerennial, 2008.

Heidegger, Martin. *Nietzsche.* Edited by David Farrell. Translated by Joan Stambaugh, David Farrell, and Frank A. Capuzzi. Vol. III. IV vols. New York: HarperCollins, 1991.

Heidegger, Martin. *Sein Und Zeit.* Tübingen: Max Niemeyer Verlag, 1967.

Heidegger, Martin. "The Age of the World Picture." In *Science and the Quest for Reality*, edited by Alfred I. Tauber, translated by William Lovitt, 70–88. Main Trends of the Modern World. London: Palgrave Macmillan UK, 1997.

Heidegger, Martin. *The Essence of Human Freedom: An Introduction to Philosophy.* Translated by Ted Sadler. London & New York: Continuum, 2002.

Heidegger, Martin. *The Fundamental Concepts of Metaphysics: World, Finitude, Solitude.* Bloomington, Ind: Indiana University Press, 2012.

Heidegger, Martin. *What Is Metaphysics?*, 2018.

Henrich, Dieter. *Hans Georg Gadamer: Splitter eines Gedenkens.* Warmbronn: U. Keicher, 2008.

Herrera, Hugo. "Análisis de Los Aspectos Fundamentales de La Comprensión Jurídica En Carl Schmitt y Exposición de Sus Alcances Filosófico-Generales Para La Comprensión." *Kriterion: Revista de Filosofia* 60, no. 142 (2019): 85–102.

Herrera, Hugo. "Aristóteles y Carl Schmitt Sobre El Derecho Natural." *Kriterion: Revista de Filosofia* 55, no. 129 (2014): 205–22.

Herrera, Hugo. *Carl Schmitt. Between Technological Rationality and Theology.* New York: State University of New York Press, 2020.

Herrera, Hugo. "Carl Schmitt como jurista." *Derecho y Humanidades*, no. 28 (2016): 55–63.

Herrero, Montserrat. "Estudio preliminar." In *Posiciones ante el derecho*, by Carl Schmitt. Madrid: Editorial Tecnos, 2012.

Herrmann, Friedrich-Wilhelm von. "Die 'Beiträge Zur Philosophie' Als Hermeneutische Schlüssel Zum Spätwerk Heideggers." In *Heidegger Neu Gelesen*, edited by Markus Happel. Würzburg: Königshausen und Neumann, 1997.

Hobbes, Thomas. *Leviathan*. Translated by Richard Tuck. Cambridge: Cambridge University Press, 1996.

Hoelzl, Michael, and Graham Ward. “Translators’ Introduction.” In *Dictatorship: From the Origin of the Modern Concept of Sovereignty to Proletarian Class Struggle*, by Carl Schmitt, x–xxxvii. Cambridge: Polity, 2014.

Hofmann, Hasso. *Legitimität gegen Legalität: der Weg der politischen Philosophie Carl Schmitts*. Berlin: Duncker & Humblot, 2010.

Husserl, Gerhart. *Recht und Zeit*. Frankfurt: V. Klostermann, 1955.

Kant, Immanuel. “Critique of Practical Reason.” In *Practical Philosophy*, translated by Mary J. Gregor, 138–258. The Cambridge Edition of the Works of Immanuel Kant. Cambridge: Cambridge University Press, 1996.

Kant, Immanuel. *Critique of Pure Reason*. Translated by Paul Guyer and Allen W. Wood. The Cambridge Edition of the Works of Immanuel Kant. Cambridge: Cambridge University Press, 2009.

Kant, Immanuel. “Groundwork of The Metaphysics of Morals.” In *Practical Philosophy*, translated by Mary J. Gregor, 37–108. The Cambridge Edition of the Works of Immanuel Kant. Cambridge: Cambridge University Press, 1996.

Kant, Immanuel. “On the Common Saying: That May Be Correct in Theory, but Is of No Use in Practice.” In *Practical Philosophy*, translated by Mary J. Gregor, 274–309. The Cambridge Edition of the Works of Immanuel Kant. Cambridge & New York: Cambridge University Press, 1996.

Kaufmann, Arthur. *Rechtsphilosophie*. München: C. H. Beck Verlag, 1997.

Kaufmann, Matthias. *Recht Ohne Regel?: Die Philosopische Prinzipien in Carl Schmitts Staats- Und Rechtslehre*. Freiburg: Alber, 1988.

Kelsen, Hans. *General Theory of Law and State*. Cambridge: Harvard University Press, 1949.

Kelsen, Hans. *Hauptprobleme Der Staatsrechtslehre*. Tübingen: J. C. B. Mohr, 1923.

Kelsen, Hans. *Pure Theory of Law*. Translated by Max Knight. New Jersey: Lawbook Exchange, 2005.

Kelsen, Hans. *The Essence and Value of Democracy*. Edited by Nadia Urbinati and Carlo Invernizzi Accetti. Translated by Brian Graf. Lanham: Rowman & Littlefield, 2013.

Kisiel, Theodore J. *The Genesis of Heidegger's Being and Time*. Berkeley, Calif.; London: University of California Press, 2003.

Kögler, Hans-Herbert. "Dialogue on Dialogue: Gadamer and Habermas." In *The Gadamerian Mind*, edited by Theodore D George and Gert-Jan van der Heiden, 288–303. New York & London: Routledge, 2021.

Korsgaard, Christine M. *The Sources of Normativity*. Cambridge: Cambridge University Press, 1996.

Kozljanič, Robert Josef. *Lebensphilosophie: eine Einführung*. Stuttgart: Kohlhammer, 2004.

Krämer, Hans. *Kritik der Hermeneutik Interpretationsphilosophie und Realismus*. München: Beck, 2007.

Krug, Wilhelm Traugott. *Allgemeines Handwörterbuch der philosophischen Wissenschaften nebst ihrer Literatur und Geschichte*. Leipzig: Brockhaus, 1828.

Lafont, Cristina. *Lenguaje y Apertura Del Mundo: El Giro Lingüístico de La Hermenéutica de Heidegger*. Madrid: Alianza, 1997.

Laufer, Heinz. "Das Kriterium Politischen Handelns. Versuch Einer Analyse Und Konstruktiven Kritik Der Freund Feind-Unterscheidung Auf Der Grundlage Der Aristotelischen Theorie Der Politik; Zugleich Ein Beitrag Zur Methodologie Der Politischen Wissenschaften." Thesis doctoral, Würzburg, 1961.

Löwith, Karl. "Der Okkasionelle Dezisionismus von Carl Schmitt." In *Sämtliche Schriften*, VIII: 32–71. Stuttgart: Metzler, 1984.

Mannies, Whitney. *Inheriting Gadamer: New Directions in Philosophical Hermeneutics*. Edited by Georgia Warnke. Edinburgh: Edinburgh University Press, 2016.

Marder, Michael. *Groundless Existence: The Political Ontology of Carl Schmitt*. London: Bloomsbury Publishing, 2014.

McCormick, John P. *Carl Schmitt's Critique of Liberalism: Against Politics as Technology*. Modern European Philosophy. Cambridge ; New York: Cambridge University Press, 1997.

McCormick, John P. "Schmittian Positions on Law and Politics: CLS and Derrida." *Cardozo Law Review* 21, no. 5–6 (2000): 1693–1722.

Neumann, Volker. *Carl Schmitt Als Jurist.* Tübingen: Mohr Siebeck, 2015.

Oakes, Guy. "Translator's Introduction." In *Political Romanticism*, by Carl Schmitt. Massachusetts & London: MIT Press, 1986.

Ojakangas, Mika. *A Philosophy of Concrete Life: Carl Schmitt and the Political Thought of Late Modernity.* 2nd ed. Bern: Peter Lang, 2006.

Olafson, Frederick A. "The Unity of Heidegger's Thought." In *The Cambridge Companion to Heidegger*, edited by Charles Guignon, 97–121. New York: Cambridge University Press, 1993.

Palmer, Richard E. *Hermeneutics: Interpretation Theory in Schleiermacher, Dilthey, Heidegger, and Gadamer.* Studies in Phenomenology & Existential Philosophy. Evanston: Northwestern Univ. Pr, 1972.

Pardo, Celestino. "Estudio Preliminar." In *El Valor Del Estado y El Significado Del Individuo*, by Carl Schmitt, XIII–CCXL. translated by Celestino Pardo. Clásicos Políticos. Madrid: Centro de Estudios Politicos y Constitucionales, 2014.

Pérez-Lasserre, Diego. "El 'Otro Juez' y La Hermenéutica: El Ficcionalismo Como Criterio Legitimador de La Decisión Jurídica." *Revista Chilena de Derecho* 45, no. 2 (2018): 363–80.

Pérez-Lasserre, Diego. "Gadamer y la hermenéutica jurídica: ¿un insumo útil?" *Vniversitas* 68, no. 138 (2019).

Pérez-Lasserre, Diego. "Humanidad y derecho: una lectura de la obra temprana de Schmitt" Díkaion 31, no. 2 (20): e3123.

Philipse, Herman. *Heidegger's Philosophy of Being a Critical Interpretation.* Princeton: Princeton University Press, 1999.

Polt, Richard. *The Emergency of Being. On Heidegger's Contributions to Philosophy.* London: Cornell University Press, 2006.

Rasch, William. "Judgment: The Emergence of Legal Norms." *Cultural Critique* 57, no. 1 (August 12, 2004): 93–103.

Ratcliffe, Matthew. "Why Mood Matters." In *The Cambridge Companion to Heidegger's "Being and Time,"* edited by Mark A. Wrathall,

157–76. Cambridge Companions to Philosophy. Cambridge: Cambridge University Press, 2013.
Richardson, William J. *Heidegger: Through Phenomenology to Thought.* Dordrecht: Springer Netherlands, 2013.
Rodríguez García, Ramón. *Heidegger y La Crisis de La Época Moderna*. Madrid: Ediciones Pedagógicas, 1994.
Rorty, Richard. *Gadamer's Repercussions: Reconsidering Philosophical Hermeneutics*. Edited by Bruce Krajewski. Berkeley: University of California Press, 2004.
Saralegui Benito, Miguel. *The Politics of Time: Introduction to Carl Schmitt's Political Thought.* Santander: Cantabria University Press, 2021.
Schear, Joseph K. "Historical Finitude." In *The Cambridge Companion to Heidegger's "Being and Time,"* edited by Mark A. Wrathall, 157–76. Cambridge Companions to Philosophy. Cambridge: Cambridge University Press, 2013.
Scheler, Max. *Die Stellung des Menschen im Kosmos*. Hamburg: Felix Meiner Verlag, 2018.
Schmidt, Denis J. "Gadamer. Humanism, and the Humanities." In *The Gadamerian Mind*, edited by Theodore D George and Gert-Jan van der Heiden, 105–16. Routledge, 2021.
Schmidt, Lawrence K. "Experience." In *The Gadamerian Mind*, edited by Theodore D George and Gert-Jan van der Heiden, 105–16. Routledge, 2021.
Schmitt, Carl. "Appendix: Weimar Constitution, Article 48." In *Dictatorship: From the Origin of the Modern Concept of Sovereignty to Proletarian Class Struggle*, translated by Michael Hoelzl and Graham Ward, 180–302. Cambridge: Polity, 2014.
Schmitt, Carl. *Der Wert des Staates und die Bedeutung des Einzelnen.* Berlin: Duncker und Humblot, 2004.
Schmitt, Carl. *Dictatorship: From the Origin of the Modern Concept of Sovereignty to Proletarian Class Struggle.* Translated by Michael Hoelzl and Graham Ward. Cambridge: Polity, 2014.

Schmitt, Carl. *Die Diktatur: von den Anfängen des modernen Souveränitätsgedankens bis zum proletarischen Klassenkampf.* Berlin: Duncker et Humblot, 2015.

Schmitt, Carl. "Die Sichtbarkeit Der Kirche: Eine Scholastische Erwägung." *Summa*, no. 1 (1918 1917): 71–80.

Schmitt, Carl. *Gesetz Und Urteil.* Berlin: Verlag von Otto Liebmann, 1912.

Schmitt, Carl. *On the Three Types of Juristic Thought.* Translated by Joseph W Bendersky. Westport: Praeger Publishers, 2004.

Schmitt, Carl. *Political Romanticism.* Translated by Guy Oakes. Massachusetts & London: MIT Press, 1986.

Schmitt, Carl. *Political Theology: Four Chapters on the Concept of Sovereignty.* Translated by George Schwab. University of Chicago Press ed. Chicago: University of Chicago Press, 2005.

Schmitt, Carl. *Politische Romantik.* Berlin: Duncker & Humblot, 2012.

Schmitt, Carl. *Politische Theologie.* Berlin: Duncker & Humblot, 2015.

Schmitt, Carl. *State, Movement, People: The Triadic Structure of the Political Unity.* Translated by Simona Draghici. Corvallis: Plutarch Press, 2001.

Schmitt, Carl. "Statute and Judgment: An Investigation into the Problem of Legal Praxis." In *Carl Schmitt's Early Legal-Theoretical Writings: Statute and Judgment and the Value of the State and the Significance of the Individual*, translated by Lars Vinx and Samuel Garrett Zeitlin, 39–157. New York: Cambridge University Press, 2021.

Schmitt, Carl. "The Value of the State and the Significance of the Individual." In *Carl Schmitt's Early Legal-Theoretical Writings: Statute and Judgment and the Value of the State and the Significance of the Individual*, translated by Lars Vinx and Samuel Garrett Zeitlin, 159–243. New York: Cambridge University Press, 2021.

Schmitt, Carl. *Über die drei Arten des rechtswissenschaftlichen Denkens.* Berlin: Duncker & Humblot, 2006.

Strauss, Leo. "Anmerkungen Zu Carl Schmitt, Der Begriff Des Politischen." In: *Carl Schmitt, Leo Strauss Und «Der Begriff Des*

Politischen». Zu Einem Dialog Unter Abwesenden, edited by Heinrich Meier. Stuttgart & Weimar: Metzler, 1998.
Thaning, Morton. *The Problem of Objectivity in Gadamer's Hermeneutics in Light of McDowell's Empiricism*. Cham: Springer, 2015.
Thomson, Iain. "Death and Demise in Being and Time." In *The Cambridge Companion to Heidegger's "Being and Time,"* edited by Mark A. Wrathall, 260–90. Cambridge Companions to Philosophy. Cambridge: Cambridge University Press, 2013.
Vaihinger, Hans. *The Philosophy of "as If". A System of the Theoretical, Practical and Religious Fictions of Mankind*. Translated by C.K. Ogden. London: Routledge & Kegan Paul, 1935.
Vigo, Alejandro. "Autorreferencia Práctica y Normatividad." In *Practical Rationality. Scope and Structures of Human Agency*, edited by A. Vigo and A. González, Vol. 1. Reason and Normativity. Hildesheiml, Zurich, New York: Olms Verlag, 2010.
Vigo, Alejandro. "Identidad Práctica e Individualidad Según Aristóteles." *Hypnos. Revista Do Centro de Estudos Da Antiguidade* 25 (2010): 129–64.
Vigo, Alejandro G. *Arqueología y aleteiología: estudios heideggerianos*. Berlin: Logos Verlag, 2014.
Vydrová, Jaroslava. "Spirituality from the Perspective of Philosophical Anthropology: Against the Background of Helmuth Plessner's Conception." *Spirituality Studies* 8, no. 1 (2022): 42–49.
Wachterhauser, Brice. "Getting It Right: Relativism, Realism and Truth." In *The Cambridge Companion to Gadamer*, edited by Robert J. Dostal. Cambridge: Cambridge University Press, 2002.
Waechter, Kay. *Studien Zum Gedanken Der Einheit Des Staates: Uber Die Rechtsphilosophische Auflosung Der Einheit Des Subjektes*. Berlin: Duncker & Humblot, 1994.
Walhof, Darren. *The Democratic Theory of Hans-Georg Gadamer*. Cham: Springer, 2018.
Watts, Alan. *Limits of Language*. CD. Essential Lectures - Tao of Philosophy. California, 1971.
Wieland, Wolfgang. "Kants Rechtsphilosophie Der Urteilskraft." *Zeitschrift Für Philosophische Forschung* 52, no. 1 (1998): 1–22.

Wolin, Richard. "Carl Schmitt, Political Existentialism, and the Total State." *Theory and Society* 19, no. 4 (1990): 389–416.

Wrathall, Mark. A. "Heidegger on Human Understanding." In *The Cambridge Companion to Heidegger's "Being and Time,"* edited by Mark A. Wrathall, 177–200. Cambridge Companions to Philosophy. Cambridge: Cambridge University Press, 2013.

Wrathall, Mark. A, and Max Murphey. "An Overview of Being and Time." In *The Cambridge Companion to Heidegger's "Being and Time,"* edited by Mark A. Wrathall, 177–200. Cambridge Companions to Philosophy. Cambridge: Cambridge University Press, 2013.

Zimmermann, Jens. "Gadamer's Century: Life, Times and Works." In *The Gadamerian Mind*, edited by Theodore D George and Gert-Jan van der Heiden, 9–23. New York & London: Routledge, 2021.

Disclaimer

This book, which is the published version of my doctoral thesis, was developed during a joint PhD program in Philosophy at Universidad Diego Portales (Chile) and FernUniversität in Hagen (Germany). This dissertation, now published, was written under the mentorship of Prof. Dr. Thomas Sören Hoffmann and Prof. Dr. Hugo Herrera Arellano.

I hereby certify under oath that I have composed the present dissertation independently and without the improper use of third parties. In doing so, I have only used the sources and aids specified and have appropriately acknowledged in accordance with academic requirements any content directly, contextually, or conceptually derived from these sources. This declaration of independent work also applies to drawings, sketches, or graphic representations. This work has neither been submitted in the same or a similar form to the same or any other examination authority, nor has it been published previously.

This book was supported by Vicerrectoría de Investigación y Doctorados de la Universidad San Sebastián—Project VRID_FAPPE22/03 and VRID Fund_APC23/10.

Berner Reihe philosophischer Studien

Band 1: Gerhard Heinzmann
Schematisierte Strukturen. Eine Untersuchung über den Idoneismus Ferdinand Gonseths auf dem Hintergrund eines konstruktivistischen Ansatzes. 185 S., 1982.

Band 2: Vincent F. Brunner
Probleme der Kausalerklärung menschlichen Handelns. 112 S., 1983.

Band 3: Jean-Claude Wolf
Sprachanalyse und Ethik. Eine Kritik der Methode und einiger Folgeprobleme sowie der Anwendung des universalen Präskriptivismus von Richard Mervyn Hare. 142 S., 1983.

Band 4: Duen Jau Marti-Huang
Die Gegenstandstheorie von Alexius Meinong als Ansatz zu einer ontologisch neutralen Logik. 136 S., 1984.

Band 5: Claudia Risch
Die Identität des Kunstwerks. VIII, 189 S., 1986.

Band 6: Andreas Graeser (ed.)
Mathematics and Metaphysics in Aristotle/Mathematik und Metaphysik bei Aristoteles. 333 S., 1987.

Band 7: Stephan Hottinger
Nelson Goodmans Nominalismus und Methodologie. 94 S., 1988.

Band 8: Michael Schrijvers
Spinozas Affektenlehre. 233 S., 1989.

Band 9: Andreas Gunkel
Spontaneität und moralische Autonomie. Kants Philosophie der Freiheit. IX, 238 S., 1989.

Band 10: Andreas Bächli
Untersuchungen zur pyrrhonischen Skepsis. XI, 90 S., 1990.

Band 11: Hansueli Flückiger
Sextus Empiricus. Grundriss der pyrrhonischen Skepsis. Buch I – Selektiver Kommentar. 126 S., 1990.

Band 12: Gérard Bornet
Naive Semantik und Realismus. Sprachphilosophische Untersuchung der Frühphilosophie von Bertrand Russell (1903–04). 315 S., 1991.

Band 13: Herbert Schweizer
Bedeutung. Grundzüge einer internalistischen Semantik. 201 S., 1991.

Band 14: Jürg Freudiger
Kants Begründung der praktischen Philosophie: systematische Stellung, Methode und Argumentationsstruktur der „Grundlegung zur Metaphysik der Sitten". 123 S., 1993.

Band 15: Erwin Sonderegger
Aristoteles, Metaphysik Z 1-12: philosophische und philologische Erwägungen zum Text. VIII, 369 S., 1993

Band 16: Lutz Danneberg / Andreas Graeser / Klaus Petrus (Hg.)
Metapher und Innovation: die Rolle der Metapher im Wandel von Sprache und Wissenschaft. 324 S., 1995.

Band 17: Gérard Bornet
Die Bedeutung von „Sinn" und der Sinn von „Bedeutung": auf dem Weg zu einem gemeinsprachlichen Wörterbuch für formale Philosophie.
XVI, 246 S., 1996.

Band 18: Cinzia Ferrini
Guida al „De orbitis planetarum" di Hegel ed alle sue edizioni e traduzioni.
259 S., 1995

Band 19: Urs Bruderer
Verstehen ohne Sprache. Zu Donald Davidsons Szenario der radikalen Interpretation. 80 S., 1997.

Band 20: Peter Zimmermann
Soziologie als Erkenntniskritik. Die Wissenssoziologie Karl Mannheims.
64 S., 1998.

Band 21: Thomas Gfeller
Was ist wichtig: Beschreibung, Wertung und ethische Theorie. 112 S., 1998.

Band 22: Gerald Bechtle
The Anonymous Commentary on Plato's „Parmenides". 285 S., 1999.

Band 23: Ursula Thomet
Kunstwerk, Kunstwelt, Weltsicht. Arthur C. Dantos Philosophie der Kunst und Kunstgeschichte. 112 S., 1999.

Band 24: Pierfrancesco Basile
Experience and Relations. An Examination of F.H. Bradley's Conception of Reality. 197 S., 1999.

Band 25: Andreas Graeser
Prolegomena zu einer Interpretation des zweiten Teils des Platonischen Parmenides. 60 S., 1999

Band 26: Martin Flügel / Thomas Gfeller / Charlotte Walser
Werte und Fakten. Eine Dichotomie im Spiegel philosophischer Kontroversen.
268 S., 1999.

Band 27: Rebecca Iseli
Kants Philosophie der Mathematik. Rekonstruktion – Kritik – Verteidigung.
110 S., 2001.

Band 28: Helen Plüss
Bedeutungstheorie und philosophische Psychologie bei Paul Grice.
76 S., 2001.

Band 29: Alain Metry
Speusippos. Zahl – Erkenntnis – Sein. 198 S., 2002.

Band 30: Heiko Holweg
Methodologie der qualitativen Sozialforschung. Eine Kritik. 176 S., 2005.

Band 31: Thomas Ruprecht
Die Unbestimmtheit der Verursachung. Ein philosophischer Essay über Kausalität. 138 S., 2003.

Band 32: Evangelos Zoidis
Notes on a Metaphysics of Presence. 113 S., 2003.

Band 33: Philipp Keller
Ein Dritter Blick auf Descartes' Erste Philosophie. Eine analytische Interpretation der cartesianischen Metaphysik.
In Vorbereitung.

Band 34: Marcel van Ackeren
Heraklit. Vielfalt und Einheit seiner Philosophie. 167 S., 2006.
ISBN 978-3-03910-815-2.

Band 35: Mika Ojakangas
A Philosophy of Concrete Life. Carl Schmitt and the Political Thought of Late Modernity. 2nd revised edition, 225 S., 2006.
ISBN 978-3-03910-963-0 / US-ISBN 978-0-8204-8362-7.

Band 36: Erwin Sonderegger
Aristoteles' Metaphysik Λ: Ein spekulativer Entwurf. Einführung, Übersetzung, Kommentar. XXXII, 514 S., 2008. ISBN 978-3-03911-477-1.

Band 37: Thomas Schindler-Wunderlich
Kritik der neuzeitlichen Wunderkritik. Eine religionsphilosophische Studie.
217 S., 2008. ISBN 978-3-03911-510-5.

Band 38: Gianluigi Segalerba: Semantik und Ontologie. Drei Studien zu Aristoteles. 547 S., 2013. ISBN 978-3-0351-0544-5

Band 39: Franiois Grandjean: Aristoteles' Theorie der praktischen Rationalität. 346 S., 2009. ISBN 978-3-03911-674-4

Band 40: Charlotte Walser: Personen – Inwiefern wir sind, wofür wir uns halten. 235 S., 2009. ISBN 978-3-0343-0080-3

Band 41: Paul Taborsky: The Logic of Cultures. Three Structures of Philosophical Thought. 266 S., 2010. ISBN 978-3-0343-0378-1

Band 42: Alba Papa-Grimaldi: Orphans of the One or the Deception of the Immanence. Essays on the Roots of Secularization. 239 S., 2010. ISBN 978-3-0343-0410-8

Band 43: Stefano Marino: Gadamer and the Limits of the Modern Techno-Scientific Civilization.
295 S., 2011. ISBN 978-3-0343-0663-8

Band 44: Stephan Millett: Aristotle's Powers and Responsibility for Nature. 303 S., 2011. ISBN 978-3-0343-0679-9

Band 45: Fabrizio Moser: Subjekt-Objekt-Intersubjektivität. Eine Untersuchung zur erkenntnis- theoretischen Subjekt – Objekt – Dialektik Hegels und Adornos mit einem Ausblick auf das Intersubjektivitätsparadigma Habermas. 181 S., 2012. ISBN 978-3-0343-0575-4

Band 46: Christian Michael Schenkel: Moralische Verpflichtung in der Politik. Grundlegung zu einem pragmatischen Modell deliberativer Demokratie. 251 S., 2012.
ISBN 978-3-0343-0585-3

Band 47: K. Noack: Platon und der Immoralismus. Die Prototypen des extremen Naturrechts, Kallikles und Thrasymachos, in der Darstellung Platons. 221 S., 2012.
ISBN 978-3-0343-1201-1

Band 48: Carlo L. Calanchini: Ueber Gemütsregungen. Emotionen zwischen philosophischer Theorie und psychotherapeutischer Praxis. 157 S., 2012. ISBN 978-3-0343-1017-8

Band 49: Louis Caruana: Nature: Its Conceptual Architecture. 332 S., 2014. ISBN 978-3-0343-1577-7

Band 50: Morgan Gaulin: Figures de l'infini. Du panthéisme de Schelling à Mallarmé. 318 S., 2017.
ISBN 978-3-0343-2925-5

Band 51: Martin Walter: Der Schmerz des andern. Eine Lösung des Problems des Fremdseeli- schen. 262 S., 2018.
ISBN 978-3-0343-3490-7

Band 52: Diego Pérez-Lasserre: Existential Openness in Law. A hermeneutical approach to Carl Schmitt's early legal thought. 258 S., 2024.
ISBN 978-3-0343-4779-2

Bände 1–32 erschienen im Paul Haupt Verlag, Bern

www.peterlang.com

www.ingramcontent.com/pod-product-compliance
Ingram Content Group UK Ltd.
Pitfield, Milton Keynes, MK11 3LW, UK
UKHW020153290926
15471UKWH00005B/846

9 783034 347792